THE CRUEL WAY

Other Volumes in the Virago/Beacon Traveler Series

Isabella Bird/*Unbeaten Tracks in Japan*

Isabella Bird/*The Yangtze Valley and Beyond*

Dora Birtles/*North-West by North*

Susanna Moodie/*Roughing It in the Bush*
With a New Introduction by Margaret Atwood

Kate O'Brien/*Farewell Spain*

Flora Tristan/*Peregrinations of a Pariah*

THE
CRUEL WAY

ELLA K. MAILLART

With a New Introduction by
MARY RUSSELL

Beacon Press   Boston

Beacon Press
25 Beacon Street
Boston, Massachusetts 02108

Beacon Press books
are published under the auspices of
the Unitarian Universalist Association of Congregations.

Introduction ©1986 by Mary Russell
First published by William Heinemann Ltd in 1947
First published as a Beacon paperback in 1987
by arrangement with Virago Press Limited
Printed in the United States of America

94 93 92 91 90 89 88 87   8 7 6 5 4 3 2 1

The cover shows shore of the Black Sea.
Reproduced by kind permission of the Royal Geographical Society.
Author's photograph by J. Mayerat.

LC number: 86-47870

To
Christina
In Memoriam

I would like to express my gratitude to the late Lewis Thompson who not only corrected my mistakes in English, but also with selfless patience gave me his advice, literary as well as spiritual. In his life-time he did not allow me to mention his name. But nearly forty years after his untimely death, I take advantage of this new edition to express my respect for his memory as a man of amazing intuition.

Ella Maillart

"You are seeking a 'New World'. I know one that is always new because it is eternal. O adventurers, conquerors of Americas, mine is an adventure more difficult and more heroic than all yours. At the cost of a thousand sufferings worse than yours, at the cost of a long death before the fact, I shall conquer this world that is ever young. Dare to follow me and *you will see!*"

SAINT TERESA
(1515–1582)

"Nay, be a Columbus to whole new continents and worlds within you, opening new channels, not of trade but of thought. Every man is the lord of a realm beside which the earthly empire of the Czar is but a petty state, a hummock left by the ice. Yet some can be patriotic who have no SELF-respect, and sacrifice the greater to the less. They love the soil which makes their graves but have no sympathy with the spirit which may still animate their clay."

HENRY DAVID THOREAU
(1817–1862)

". . . the healers of the soul have found to be true: that to make manifest to the mind what is in the heart is to ease suffering. This itself I think is part of a cosmic process, serving the purposes of soul for which the universe exists, a process by which we are ever becoming more self-conscious, drawing nigher to the depths in ourselves and the true in being. Every step, even if painful, by which we gain a profounder self-consciousness brings with it a wisdom which is compensation for our grief and whose dawning indicates, as I truly believe, the absolution of our sin."

Æ.
(Foreword to *MORS et VITA*)

CONTENTS

ILLUSTRATIONS

INTRODUCTION

PARIS in June 1939 was sparkling. The chestnut trees were in blossom and the air was warm. Ella Maillart, who, at thirty-six, had already found considerable fulfilment in her independent way of life, suddenly found tears streaming down her cheeks. "It was as if the flesh and the spirit of Paris were maimed, martyred, torn apart and as if I had become a mass of compassion large enough to envelope the whole witty capital I knew so well." It is not in Ella Maillart's way of thinking to consider the future, which to her is nothing more than a concept and a most uncertain one at that. So why, on that park bench in sunny Paris, did she weep? Had she, perhaps, a foreboding that the journey she was about to embark upon might equally tear her apart?

Traveller, writer, philosopher – Ella Maillart is all these but to her friend, the ill-fated Christina, she was that most precious of people, a steadfast companion. During those uneasy months preceding the declaration of war, the two women travelled across Turkey, Iran and Afganistan, and while Christina fought a hopeless battle against her addiction to drugs, Ella did everything in her power to uplift and sustain her. Just as her beloved Paris seemed about to disintegrate under the heel of the invader so too did it seem to her that the young and talented writer Christina, with her infinite capacity for suffering, might be destroyed at the very moment when she was searching so desperately for reality.

It was not an easy journey for either of them and *The Cruel Way* tells not only of Christina's struggle but of Ella's also. For, devoted though she was to her friend, at heart she was – and still is – a solo traveller.

Born in 1903, into a middle-class family in Geneva – her father was a fur-dealer – Ella Maillart decided, at an early age, to shape her own future. Refusing to be drawn any further into the educational sausage machine which she suspected would lead to nothing more than a job as a bilingual secretary, and stung by her father's comment that since she would be unable to earn a living for herself marriage was the only remaining option, she set out to prove him wrong by leaving home at the age of twenty-one and taking up a post as French teacher in a boys' prep school in Wales. There, the small boys looked in wonder at this blonde, tanned young woman who had not only captained Switzerland's Ladies Hockey Team but had represented her country in the Olympic Games as a single-handed sailor – the sole woman competitor among sixteen men. And not just the small boys. A fellow teacher, the writer Monk Gibbon, enchanted by – if not actually in love with – the intriguing woman devoted a third of his book, *Mount Ida*, to eulogising her: "Slim, lithe, active rather than graceful – she seemed to show in every movement she made that her body was the trained servant of her mind."

After teaching in Wales, she managed to earn a living as a sailor and in 1925, she sailed for Crete with an all-woman crew. It was while she was working on an archaeological dig in Crete – a lonely place in those days – that she began to appreciate both the benefits of open air living and of getting close to what she calls "the real life in nature". Communing with nature, however, is one thing; finding the wherewithal to do it another. A chance gift of 50 dollars – a lot of money in 1930 – enabled her to set off for Moscow where she hoped to study film-making with a view to writing a book on the subject. There, she supported herself with odd bits of writing and found friends among the old hands in the press corps who knew their way round the black market better than she. From Moscow, she trekked through the Caucasus with a group of Russian students and then continued on alone through Georgia to the Black Sea. Later, travelling through Russian Turkestan, so recently devastated by famine, she discovered the great generosity of those who, with little to give, give all.

These nomads were forced into collective farms run by Russians who were new to high-mountain pastures.

Having reached the Celestial Mountains on the eastern edge of Russian Turkestan, the twenty-nine year old Ella – known as Kini to her friends – stood and gazed across at the forbidden land of China and vowed she would reach it one day. Three years later, she did, in the company of another traveller – the clever, charming, ex-public schoolboy, Peter Fleming.

They made an odd couple – he dreaming sometimes about the familiar comforts of home and England – grouse shooting, the Fourth of July and the London scene while she, wanting to leave behind the trappings of Europe, preferred to stop and stare, to listen to and talk to the nomads whose way of life was taking an increasing hold upon her psyche. "They were," she said many years later, "at their right place." It is a familiar theme throughout her life – the search for equanimity, balance, equilibrium.

To Fleming she was something of an enigma – dashing and a good trooper though not entirely his cup of tea. She rode a horse well – and a camel – and smoked the odd pipe. "Maillart is tough, thirty-one and slightly wolf-like in appearance," he wrote. "She is a very good traveller, and we get on fairly well." In fact, considering they had both previously made highly adventurous journeys on their own, it was a wonder they managed to endure each other's company at all along the 3,500 difficult miles which they had to cover to get from Peking to Kashgar.

The presence of a travelling companion, Ella found, had its disadvantages, the most irksome one being the manner in which it prevented her getting closer to her beloved nomads: "When a girl is on her own, she can travel easily. She gets taken in by people and looked after, for nomads have good hearts. If there's a couple, however, they form a unity and people leave you alone. You are two Europeans, isolated."

It was her need to get away from a Europe that was moving inexorably towards war that led her towards Christina and the journey to Kabul.

Christina, a fugitive from marriage, from herself, from life, lacked the will to live and Ella sought to give it to her. It was a task of unimaginable proportions and only a woman such as Ella Maillart, who carries the banner of freedom within her own soul, could have undertaken it.

Once you embark upon *The Cruel Way* you will find there is no going back – you travel at Maillart's speed and at her bidding. The sand will burn your feet and the whistling wind will sting your face. Ahead of you, disappearing into time, you will catch a glimpse of the shadowy caravans of Genghis Khan, Marco Polo and Ibn Batuta for you follow in their footsteps. And all the time you will hear Ella talking, bullying, cajoling – never ceasing in her efforts to awaken in Christina a perception of Now, the Eternal Present.

Had Christina not been so obsessed with her own problems she might well have found Ella a demanding companion, for everything had to be remarked upon, savoured, enjoyed. We hear of the grapes that tasted "like drops of dew from Paradise" and of the pleasure of drinking cool buttermilk, flavoured with mint. We are told of the "shout" of a bright red flower and of the dazzle of blue glazed tiles on the mosque.

But these are the ups. There are the downs as well, for this is a supremely honest story of two people trying to live together and having to cope with the irritations which inevitably dog the footsteps of incurable travellers such as they.

Ella is ecstatic about life and Christina, to whom living is such a burden, becomes sullen. There is panic when a terrible smell of burning pervades the little Ford roadster. They have to take on board an unmentionable guide whose unwholesome socks are the nicest things about him and Ella finds a novel way of silencing another escort who dares to tell them where they can and cannot go. However, none of these things deter them and despite arrests, intractable officials and Christina's attacks of despair, they managed to reach Kabul – their arrival coinciding with an announcement which was to change the course of all our lives – the outbreak of the Second World War.

When I first met Ella Maillart in Geneva, she had temporarily come to rest. Now aged eighty-two, she gets around the city on a bike and bemoans the fact that she can no longer ski – although she did up to four years ago. Her time is now spent guiding interested parties round South India and Asia for she is as enthusiastic a traveller now as she was when a young girl. Set in a face tanned and weathered by sun and wind, her blue eyes were intense as she concentrated on what we were talking about and I noticed nervously that her energy was far greater than mine. I also had the suspicion that in a world turned upside down she seems to have found an answer to her quest. "It is simple," she said. "The only real thing is the here and now. The past is dead, the future doesn't exist and the present now is at once the past."

To the untutored, like myself, this is all far from simple and there seemed nothing else to do but concentrate instead on the delicious soup which she had made in her tiny kitchen, neat as a ship's galley. But she was kind. "Though now I am certain, I was a long time looking for the truth. I was searching for twenty years, but along the wrong path."

She had thought that by living among the nomads she would achieve their natural balance; but then, after parting from Christina, and appalled by the impending carnage in Europe, she went to South India where she spent five years living near the sage Sri Ramana. He it was who led her to the realisation that Reality lies within. "If you are a traveller, this is very important because if you travel intelligently, you become what you are, you forget your European roots. You become yourself."

And so the enigma remains, for Ella Maillart has not become someone else. What she has done is find the depth of her real being (the Changeless I, she calls it) and it is this knowledge that lends a brightness to her eyes so that you want to stay close to her in the hope that some of the light will settle on you also.

Mary Russell, Brill 1986

I

THE IDEA

"If it's not warmer to-morrow when I take you to the station, the car might easily break down: it can no longer cope with such frosts." Christina made that remark by the way and I hardly heard it, for my thoughts were still in Prague: she had just described the soul of that city, the life of her Czech friends, their utter helplessness and despair as the might of Hitler approached them with steady relentlessness.

We were both looking through the small window-panes of her peasant's house in the Engadine. Winter ruled. Across the valley, clouds hid the slope of the Fextal where we had skied that morning between luminous red-brown larches. A dark, low sky oppressed the valley—shadowless, dead. Though high in the Alps, the land looked flat and broad, for the house stood by a lake now frozen hard under many layers of snow. Nothing but that desolate expanse barred us from the southern horizon where the Maloja pass leads into Italy.

Christina must have added: "The car is worn out and Father has promised me a Ford"; I only heard that last name and it seems to have been responsible for all.

That one word was enough; flocking ideas arranged themselves in the right order, vague tendencies crystallised into a solid plan. As if it were a kind of long-drawn echo, I heard a voice like mine begin to say:

"A Ford! That's the car to climb the new Hazarejat road in Afghanistan! In Iran too, one should travel in one's own car. Two years ago I went lorry-hopping from India to Turkey: I am not likely to forget that dusty journey with its many breakdowns, the fervour of the pilgrims, the sleeping on the road or in overcrowded caravanserais, the police inspections at each village and—more difficult to laugh away—the necessity of staying by the lorry instead of roaming at will."

In the clouds above the Maloja a diffused light seemed to show the way: after a drop of five thousand feet into the warmth of Lombardy it would wind through the Balkans and take us to the Bosphorus, gate to the immensities of Asia. My mind was already in Persia.

"East of the Caspian we shall drive to the ancient tower of the Gumbad-i-Kabus and camp among Persian Turkomans: they may still follow the customs I sought in vain among their kinsmen modernised by the Soviets. We shall see the golden dome of the Imam Reza shrine—smooth, compact, and precious shell aimed at the sky. Then we shall reach the giant Buddhas in the pure valley of Bamian, the incredibly blue lakes of the Band-i-Amir. Further still, down the northern side of the Hindu Kush, up the valley of the mighty Oxus, we shall vanish into the mountains before any prohibition from Kabul can stop us. There live the men I want to study in a country where I feel happy: mountaineers not enslaved by artificial needs, free men not forced to increase their daily production. If access to Kafiristan is barred, we can traverse India, take the Burma Road and live with the Lolos of Eastern Tibet. When I have collected new facts about these tribes, I shall at last be admitted into the brotherhood of ethnologists. Then all will be well: I shall belong to an organisation, it will be my job to rove, I shall no longer be tempted to write books to make a living." A power dormant in my talk had given birth to a plan already so mature that it at once imposed itself: it was like the mango trick.

At last Christina had a chance to speak: "When I was in Teheran I longed to go further East where traditional ways of living had not been abolished."

Her voice brought me back to the present. I looked at her coldly: though she was still convalescing after months of an exhausting cure, the look in her eye was sound and determined. Trying to dam the new current with the nearest bricks I could lay hands on, I said:

"My dear, I am a fool to talk like this. Unless you put on twenty pounds of flesh you cannot possibly tackle such hardships. Besides, who would finance us? And anyway war will soon break out . . . And if it doesn't I shall probably lecture in the States." I didn't mention my main objection: provided she were soon normal, how long could we bear each other?

Though she probably guessed my thought she said nothing,

nothing. Her thin hand held a cigarette, the yellow knuckles sharp under a skin as thin as tissue-paper. She was sitting on the bench—with hollowed chest, hugging her knees, her adolescent body leaning against the great stove built in the corner of the room. But for her tense presence it would have been restful in the quiet old house while the squalls whistled abroad, in that peasant house of bare larch (the oblong lozenges of its red grain are like watered silk). Table and walls were clean, smooth and friendly under the palm eager to feel them.

Though apparently impassive, Christina did not know how to be at rest.

Calm as usual, her colourless face was a symbol I was trying to read: devoid of all pretence, it was a "simple" face in the sense of true, artless, not concerned with itself. Under the mass of close-cropped hair the head seemed too big, too full of thoughts for so frail a neck. The forehead was not high but arresting by its broadness, its density, its determination—nearing stubbornness sometimes.

I knew that behind it thoughts could take to high flights once they had surmounted an obsession I could not yet define. The eyes set wide apart, showed changing shades of dark-blue grey under eye-brows much darker than her hair. Those eyes belonged to a soul in love with beauty that would often wince away from a discordant world; they could shine with enthusiasm, with affection, they could smile back at you, but I never saw them laugh. Unexpectedly fleshy when you studied it, the nose suggested that her constitution was perhaps not so weak as it seemed. Melancholy in the modelling of the pale, irregular mouth—lips that were inhaling smoke with silent voracity. (The dark shades of her teeth increased, she had told me, whenever her vitality was ebbing.) The small chin was particularly youthful, making one think of a puzzled child ready to ask for protection. Her hands were those of a patient craftsman who knows how to chisel a pure line: I have seen her turn seven sheets one after the other into the type-writer before that paragraph had attained the perfectly flowing curve which alone could satisfy her. Writing was the only ritual of her life: she subordinated everything to it.

Impassivity was quite natural to her concern for perfect

form: she could never have displayed an untidy face like mine.
It was partly because of this strange tense serenity that a friend
of ours used to call her the "Fallen Angel". Her subtle body,
her pensive face lighted by the pale brow, put forth a charm
that acted powerfully on those who are attracted by the tragic
greatness of androgyny.

She spoke, determined to allay my fears:

"Kini: I must go away. I am finished if I stay in this country
where I no longer find any help, where I made too many
mistakes and where the past weighs on me too heavily . . . I
had thought of going to Lapland but I would much rather
come with you to Afghanistan. You see . . . I have not yet
learned to live alone! As for exploring, I needn't go with you
into the mountains: you are a friend of the Hackins and I might
perhaps help them if they are excavating there. You know
I have already worked with archæologists in Syria and in
Persia."

After a short pause she continued: "You are concerned for
my health and I admit I am weak. But you don't know my
constitution. You must ask the doctors. They can never
explain my recoveries. I promise you to ski every day instead
of smoking too much; then I shall have more appetite, eat
more and put on weight. As for money, our publishers ought
to help us. I have just finished my last book and I can get an
advance on a story about Afghanistan. The Geographical
Magazine will also support us." Then, in a more subdued
voice, she added: "I am thirty. It is the last chance to mend
my ways, to take myself in hand. This journey is not going to
be a sky-larking escapade as if we were twenty—and that is
impossible, with the European crisis increasing day by day. This
journey must be a means towards our end. We can help each
other to become conscious, responsible persons. My blind way of
life has grown unbearable. What is the reason, the meaning of
the chaos that undermines people and nations? And there must
be something that I am to do with my life, there must be some
purpose for which I could gladly die or live! Kini . . . how do you
live?"

"Now, listen. Let's be practical. We agreed long ago that
we shall have to know ourselves better before we can know
anything else; we also inferred that the chaos around us is

linked with the chaos within. But first of all you must gain
strength, cease to be at the mercy of your health. Are you
willing during the coming months, to devote your marvellous
energy to building a new body for your renovated nerves?
Will you stop worrying about questions you can't yet solve?
Don't say 'Yes' just to quiet me but, please, see what you
owe yourself. For instance, you often said you would fight
Hitler with all your might when war breaks out; but what will
you do then if you are still a mere shadow?"

Thus my voice, with as much authority as I could. But I
knew the torment that lay behind Christina's simple words.
And deep down, where life is secret and smooth in its flowing,
I uttered a silent prayer: May it be in my power to help you,
impatient Christina so irked by the limitations of the human
condition, so oppressed by the falsity of life, by the parody of
love around us. If we travel together, may it be given me
not to fail you, may my shoulder be firm enough for you to
lean on. Along the surface of the earth I shall find our way
where I have journeyed before; and inwardly, where I have
long ago begun to ask myself questions so like yours, may
the little that I have found help you to find what each of us
has to find by himself.

2

THE START

SILVAPLANA in the Engadine was the spring-board of our imagination in its soaring East by South to the great water-sheds of Asia. But the actual take-off was the rocky pass of the Simplon whence, wheeling, swooping, banking down the mountain road and the dark gorge opening into Italy, we went abroad.

Patches of snow invisibly thawing under the soft wind dotted the grey sides of the bovine mountain near us; no traffic, no noise disturbed us on that road still walled in between the banks of hardened slush. Thousands of feet beneath us a train was probably worming its way along the twelve-mile tunnel: we were happier here, poised between lowlands and high ranges, between southern and central Europe, between the charm of Latin warmth and the heaviness of Germanic reserve, admiring a natural border that no politics can alter.

Let us linger there a moment before we look at Switzerland for the last time; let us evoke a little of what we left behind us then, in 1939. Our good-bye went also to Paris, London and Berlin, the monstrous towns that were still booming as usual; they built the background of our world, a world we knew condemned. Until "it" happened we must pursue our strife because we felt it less futile than any other activity.

Paris. Rushing from consulate to publisher, from dress-maker to museum, from bank to tip-giving journalist, from car-specialist to editor, from anthropologist to camera-man, from doctor to librarian, one day I found myself walking down the Champs-Elysées. The pollen of the blossoming chestnut-trees seemed to sparkle in the morning air, the sky was light blue, warm and gay. I turned into the Avenue Montaigne on my way to my stylish guestroom by the river. I was happy. But aware of the beautiful moment, my throat contracted suddenly. Tears were soon streaming down my cheeks, gushing out continuously. Deeply moved, half blind, I had to find a bench where I could gather myself together.

Very slowly that overwhelming impersonal emotion became a thought—that something was keenly suffering for Paris. It was as if the flesh and the spirit of Paris were maimed, martyred, torn apart and as if I had become a mass of compassion large enough to envelope the whole witty capital I knew so well. What else could be done about such misery but cry—cry with an intensity of feeling at which I soon began to marvel.

After a while more normal thoughts began to shape themselves: "it" had not happened yet and even if it did it might not be so terrible as all that . . . Here and now I only knew that I was taking leave of Paris. I was right to look at it with intensity for I felt I should never again see it as it used to be.

There was nothing to explain this shattering experience. Only last evening, Blaise Cendrars had invited me to spend the summer in the Forêt des Ardennes: he asserted there would be no war. Since he spent much time in the office of *Paris-Soir* and ought to know more than ordinary mortals, I had felt cheered. Charming but wavering Robert was calmly becoming a bourgeois, pretending he was not worried by the future. Hackin had just left the Musée Guimet for Afghanistan as if life in Europe were quite normal. We had arranged to join him at Begram where he would dig in July: he had agreed to take Christina in his group.

But because he was an active socialist my friend Professor Rivet was no longer received in certain houses—a small sign that an ominous gap was widening, that ways of thinking had at last some bearing upon practical life. Political refugees had been expelled. Jean's "left" paper had been confiscated and some of his friends arrested. "Fascism will reign for a long time," he said. And as we parted he warned me: "This time, I assure you, war is quite near." But he had said the same thing on the eve of Hitler's march to Vienna.

As for Paul Valéry and Lucien Fabre, I was convinced that whatever might happen they would not be upset. Fabre seemed to understand my vague gropings. "The rational explanation of the world doesn't work," he said. "We throw a network of meridians and parallels over it but they don't contain everything and they explain nothing. Go and see more of the East, since you are so inclined. Perhaps in India, where many believe in a spiritual life, there is a climate favourable to revelations."

In London the atmosphere was quite different—more unanimous, more youthful than when I was last there. It looked as if the English had taken to eating lion at breakfast. But I could not help remembering how in September 1938, Hilary St. George Saunders as well as Denison Ross had lost their heads as soon as it seemed that the country might be bombed. In the rage and despair of their surprise, they had clamoured for the lives of sixty million Germans. Now each of them admitted that, caught unprepared, he had been in a bad mess but that he and his country were prepared to fight once more to the death.

Steve King-Hall had a clear vision of what was happening and I liked his way of proving that modern wars are cataclysms that only postpone a lasting settlement. Many peoples' problems may be simplified when they know they must fight for their country. But the suffering war involves is useless until the survivors know what to live for.

Frere had time to lunch me at the Savoy though he was now working at the Labour Ministry as well as for the firm that publishes my books. He had become detached and wise: chatting or joking was a thing of the past. He went as far as to say that spiritual problems were at the root of the European crisis.

The Royal Geographical Society had ceased to be august and imperial: in a busy atmosphere, precious books and documents were being packed off to safe places in the country. Choosing the maps we needed for our journey, I met Eric Shipton and Campbell Secord who were leaving next day for the Karakoram. Should the Afghans object to my plans, I was to join Shipton in his remote valley and there spend the winter among the Shimshalis, studying the women while he would deal with the men. (The only thing that happened at the time of our supposed meeting was that their expedition came back because of the war; but one of Shipton's companions disguised himself into me and "my" arrival was enacted at Gilgit where the Political Agent was deceived for a while.)

During these London days I was staying with Irene who had met Christina at Teheran in 1935. She thought I was unwise to start with such a companion—predicted that we would reach neither Kabul nor Iran. Assuring her she was wrong, I tried to convince her that I knew the "Fallen Angel" better than she. Deep in my heart was an unshakable confidence in Christina and that my double aim—Kabul and helping her—would be attained.

But frolicking through London with Audrey in search of a hold-all that would keep me warm if I got benighted among the snows of the Pamirs, I saw what fun it would be to rove with a witty companion, sparkling with *joie de vivre*. Then I knew I was not quite easy about our enterprise.

From London I flew to Germany to meet Dr. Herrlich whose book on Kafiristan (now called Nuristan) had just been published. The Afghan Government had forced upon his expedition an escort of twenty-one soldiers: they wanted to be sure that no German would enter a native house. The soldiers were to forestall any incident that might show the world at large that "progress" had not yet reached the steepest and most hidden valleys. But every time a pass lay ahead, the Germans, good mountaineers, put on a spurt, out-distanced the soldiers and gained half an hour to study the Kafirs! These fair-haired men still worshipped the god Imra and his spouse Nurmelli. One of the initiation rites was to sacrifice a goat to Gish the god of war. Boys and girls dance arm in arm around the fire and sing in harmony. Women give birth in the "Nurmelli-house" where they stay twenty days. Until the effigy of the dead man has been erected, the high-priest cannot enter the house of the deceased. In Kafiristan, too, cocks are sacred animals and men milk the cows. And the people use stools—the only Asiatics, except the far-away Chinese, who do not live on the ground.

I gathered that the Dr. Herrlich's permission to explore Kafiristan had been obtained at a time when the Afghan Government had wanted machinery from Germany at an advantageous price. Deprived of such bargaining powers, I had little chance of being officially allowed in these valleys; nevertheless, in a defiant gesture, I bought calipers to measure the heads of those mountaineers!

I was intrigued and charmed by the wooden objects the expedition had brought back—heroes on horseback which, in the cemeteries, keep guard over the thick coffins of cedar wood; carved figures with stiff faces under pointed helmets; bowls with geometrical patterns that recalled the art of the South Seas.

On my way back to Geneva I stopped at Zürich where Christina had obtained the help of a museum.

I called on C. G. Jung, hoping (very foolishly) that he could give me a key to the mentality of the so-called primitives. I offered him one of my books. He looked at it and asked: "Why do you travel?" "To meet those who know how to live peacefully" was the first answer that came to my lips. But the great man had looked at me with suspicion; did I look like a lunatic traveller who wants to be cured?

I felt giddy at the science he displayed in analysing the recesses of what he called "the Old Man's mind" or in describing the supra-conscious heights he was going to study systematically. I asked if such research were not dangerous. Years later, when I met spiritual masters in India, I was to remember his answer, and the glance of those small piercing eyes: "Yes, it is dangerous. But he who wants to know must take into account the possibility of going mad."

Bathed in the light reflected from the lake, Zürich was in a festive mood; a streaming multitude was delighted with the clever "Swiss Exhibition", which, on the eve of another world war, reminded the Confederates what Switzerland stood for, toning up the fibres of their disparate characters. In a flash of memory I remembered a similar atmosphere during the *Fête de Juin*, the pageant that took place in Geneva in 1914. I saw the wide theatre whose vast stage opened on to the natural background of Lake Léman; the choir chanting the life of our free people; the heart-moving scene when the huge barques sailed up to the stage full of Swiss soldiers of the past coming to liberate Geneva from Napoleon.

Has it perhaps a meaning that these two magnificent shows quickened the spirit of the Swiss before two world tragedies? Why, for what purpose should Switzerland be spared twice? But has life a purpose? and if it has, how can we know it? Every line of thought led me back to this same question that I asked for the first time in 1918 when I saw how many lives were foolishly wasted!

In Geneva while I said to friends "I leave to-morrow for Kabul", I was as calm as if I had said "I am going to Paris". Could it mean that from then on I was to feel at home in the

East? It was casually, too, that I kissed mother good-bye on the landing by the lift while she asked once more: "Have you got everything?"

From the height of our fourth storey, motionless on the dark road between two white cliffs of modern flats, our roadster looked small, compact and powerful: narrow at the radiator and broad in the stern, it was a ship that would smoothly open Europe or Asia in a sliding bow-wave during many months.

We were under way—rolling on the silky tarred roads I know so well, crossing the Pont du Mont-Blanc, following the quays where red tulip-beds danced in the blue breeze from the lake.

It was the sixth of June, 1939.

Though our inner gaze was fixed on a goal impatiently desired, we left home slowly. Though we longed for the desolate expanse of the Persian desert and the sharp winds of the Hindu Kush, our eyes were sensitive to the Pays Romand. How moved I was by a country endowed with such variety, a country where nothing is in excess; so proud the hills of rocks, so radiant the snowfields caressed by passing clouds, so odorant the long hay mixed with daisies, so pure the waters, so deep the murmuring foliage of the parks, so classical the pediments of the old grey houses. How unbelievable all this would seem evoked in the monotonous plains of Iran! Lizard-like little towns under the brown scales of their tiles, inns where the shaded tables rest against a wall lapped by transparent wavelets, golden tiers of vineyards worshipping the sun! All that coast, a curved amphitheatre facing the Alps enthroned beyond the liquid arena of the Léman—what abundance, what perfection, what calm it breathed, as if there were no frantic men under the German skies!

But like a satiated cat with closed eyes seemingly lost in bliss, the country was yet alert, its burrowed mountains hiding weapons, its telegraph antennæ ready to catch the least omen.

Good-bye clean country, great Rhône valley lined with vibrant poplars, where every bounding torrent we pass evokes a place of beauty—Arolla, Zermatt or Saas-Fee! I linger by a water-fall pretending to take trial shots with the ciné, but I only want to break the trance woven by so many miles of tarmac gliding underneath our singing wheels. I want to touch your earth once more.

3

ITALY

THE first camp was pleasant.

As we stepped out of our sleeping-bags our blue-grey tent shone under the diamond powder of the dew. Supple like yellow satin, new leaves trembled, thrilled to be noticed by the young sun. Even the waters of our stream were new, snow-born in the mountains above Domodossola.

Neither a carabinero nor the owner of the field had arrested us—as a pretentious youth had threatened last evening, showing off before peasant-women all in black. Timidly they had watched the lighting of our petrol stove. The rich aroma of our "Nescafé" provoked the remark that there was no coffee to be had in their country—and coffee the favourite drink of Italy! Out of her folded apron a girl took a handful of roasted wheat: "We replace it with this!"

At midday we lunched by the lake of Garda. My thoughts crossed the waters to the "Villa delle Rupi" where Cecil Lewis had invited me for the summer. I compared the uncertain enterprise on which we had started with the months of peaceful work I might have accomplished in that idyllic spot. Could it be that I was fond of difficulty?

I don't like motoring and on an "autostrade" I loathe it: it makes me a dull automaton that can only listen to the purr of the machine. Milan ought to have been near but from our billiard-table road we could see nothing, not even the fields. The few cars about were all German, the women in them with kerchiefs round fat faces reddened by too much wind.

We stopped at a filling station which I recognised: arriving here from Turkey two years ago, at night, we had run short of petrol and of money. No "liras" could be cashed because of the maddening money regulations. In a depressed voice I had asked: "What angel will help us?" At midnight there was hardly any traffic so when a car stopped at the pump I boldly addressed the owner. I proposed to repay him by money-order from Geneva. He trusted us and bought our petrol. When he gave me his visiting card, I saw that his Christian name was Angelo!

Christina was at the wheel most of the time; either her trained "road-sense" suffered from my clumsiness or she did not trust me while the valves of our new Ford were still not ground. Since all that concerned the car was her domain, I did not argue.

We had to halt to let a long procession go by: the men in black, the girl-communicants in white, the clergy in bright red, the holy emblems gilded on their palanquin and all the shy women at the rear. Trampled flowers lay dying on the road. The scene struck me as very oriental with its tired people walking in a dream: it reminded me of similar ceremonies that I had seen in India or in China.

The approaches to charming Trieste were still defaced by huge DUCE painted on every wall of the corniche road.

We sipped ice-creams on the quay where brown trawlers' nets hung by the green Adriatic. That flagged piazza will always be linked in my memory with Christina's words. It was from Trieste that she had sailed for the Near East where she was to marry Francis. "I felt that I was heading for a prison. I don't know why," she said in a detached voice, "but I was too weak-minded to free myself while it was still possible." I thought I could guess how difficult it must have been for these two to become a couple. As long as one is single it does not matter if one is extremely self-centred, but in marriage it is almost inevitable that one of the pair will have to live for the other. Christina lived solely for her writing. While Francis had learned to compromise between his private life and his life as a diplomat, Christina could never attempt such a tour-de-force: she knew that legations are but the glass-cases of life, pleasant only for a moment. Francis, therefore, had assured her that she needn't change her ways at all.

They had first met at Teheran where he was working as Secretary; she was helping archæologists at Rey not far from the capital. They enjoyed talking together and often their discussions lasted late into the night. People gossiped. The wife of the Minister whom Christina stayed with when she was in town advised either marriage or restraint. It seemed foolish to hamper a friendship: the first solution seemed easier though they were determined to go on living in every way as independently as before.

But by the time they were married, Francis had become Chargé d'Affaires: as the wife of Number One she had to appear at receptions. Awkwardly, with an immense effort, she tried, or thought she tried her utmost to deal with that hated new life. She put her work aside: when cook blunders, the country you represent loses face for a long time! She assumed that Francis did not notice her increasing misery, that he showed no compassion, encouragement or understanding while she gasped in her glass-case.

Life dragged on in an atmosphere of latent crisis. A way out might have been to laugh at herself: but for those who live with great intensity the business of living is so urgent that there is no leisure for the palliative of humour. She rebelled, fell prey to a nervous breakdown. According to what she told me, she began to think that in marrying Francis her main aim had been to free herself from her mother. I imagine that part of this latent antagonism was due to the love that Christina felt during her childhood for that great amazon, her mother. With the years this feeling had become more complex. And it seemed that neither mother nor daughter could ever get used to a different state of affairs.

"Mother foretold disaster if I married. And it was happening. There was no way out, for Francis' people were strict Catholics. It was very foolish of me to be always acting against mother—the person who knows me better than anyone else. I had no hope of freeing myself from her, no hope of ever being simply myself."

From then on, Christina had begun to live a new instalment of the particular hell she used to carve out for herself. Some hints about it were enough to teach me that hunger or poverty are less to be dreaded than an illness of the mind. A bad wound in her leg and a tormented friendship with a beautiful Turkish girl were added to her troubles. But one day she reacted, seized an opportunity to run away from doctors and drugs; she joined Marjorie at her summer camp high up on the slopes of the Demavend, where horses are left free to roam, where the torrent is like leaping crystal, the air as sparkling as the snowfields where it was born. There the silence whispered to her anguished pride that all was still not lost. But if she were to live again she would have to strive alone.

Three years later she freed herself at last from her Teheran nightmare by writing a long poem in prose. I had seen her at it at Neuchâtel during her convalescence, a prey to her inspiration, cigarettes and coffee hidden from the doctors. That beautiful, feverish poem exhausted while renewing her. "One sheds one's sicknesses in books—repeats and presents again one's emotions to be master of them" wrote D. H. Lawrence. It was true of Christina.

Now, having exorcised the past and feeling virginal once more, she was ready to be preyed upon by life again. But could she not adopt a less violent rhythm? Was there a remote chance that my normality might become ever so slightly contagious?

Before leaving Trieste we went to buy hats—in case of breakdowns in the roasting desert. Coming out of a department-store wearing that latest sixpenny-worth, I remarked that it might even serve if we had to appear at a garden-party! But Christina did not smile back: she had lost the flat little key of the car. Our Ford had suddenly become as inaccessible as the nearby Lancia. We remained calm under this blow, the first one borne in common. With beating hearts we retraced our steps very carefully; and in the big shop we had the luck to find our key lying on the floor.

Then, lightheartedly, we sent the car darting up the great road that conquers the stony Karst, a dull grey plain honeycombed with gaping caves.

Springtime and a road wide open ahead, when you are free to drive on for thousands of miles, free to camp or eat, to stop or change itinerary at will, can give a great exhilaration. Only leaving harbour in one's own boat could one be more deeply stirred, for at sea the whole immensity is offered—no roads to force the keel along given lines. Or in the air, with a new element under control, a boon till now conceded only to the birds.

4

YUGOSLAVIA

WE had not long crossed the border into Yugoslavia when a furious rain that hid the luscious green hills forced us to spend the night in a village by the side of the swollen Save. The butcher Medven rented rooms to travellers. In spite of his Slavonic name, he called himself a German. He missed the *Kultur* of Austria where he had lived until the Anschluss forced him to return to the country where he was born. His wife told us that under the old Imperial regime the boys came back from their military service in the north transformed into gentlemen. "But nowadays" she said, "the Yugoslavs send them back just as stupid as they were. They are not even capable of rising from poverty."

Next day in the beautiful market-place of gay Zagreb, there were no signs of poverty. With baskets on their heads and voluminous skirts enhancing their waddling hips, healthy country girls wore colourful blouses. The whole square was bright with big umbrellas. In their shade rose mountains of juicy black cherries, firm red strawberries, snowy lace, leather embroidered with flowery designs. As for the vegetables, we were not to see their like for months to come.

Floods, we heard, had washed away the roads further south. At Klostar, then, we remembered to buy a spade. In the same shop we bought blue-enamelled mugs. Mine was to serve me faithfully for years; I still boil my tea in it. I remember how it hung anonymously in that old dark shop—the last object I bought in a Europe still at peace.

Along the road, people often greeted us with the Nazi salute. A schoolmaster raised his arm with great determination staunchly followed by his gaggle of kids. Were we taken for Germans? or if not, were we to be flattered all the same? Could it mean that only Germans were using the roads nowadays? Or was it that we were still in that part of the world which the Empress Maria Theresa had peopled with German colonists? There are only half a million Germans among thirteen millions of Yugoslavs. That evening beyond Vukovar where we camped by the shore of the Danube, it was again a German who spoke to us, a strong blond ferry-man. A gliding mass of grey water, the river was a broad and magnificent conveyor-belt transporting motionless freighters to a far-away sea-port.

In every country we crossed we were to learn how the German tentacles gripped—aided by a clever barter-system. Buying most of the produce of these lands (nominally at a good price), Germany was sending in exchange machines taxed to repay her amply. In the meantime competitors from other countries had been eliminated.

As soon as we entered the Yugoslav plain, we felt that we were approaching the East where the earth is not narrowly measured as in western Europe. Wideness of the fields, of the far horizon, of the triple highway—the motor-road flanked on either side by dusty tracks for market-carts. Wideness of men's blouses, of women's petticoats. Boys ride bareback on lively little horses like Mongolian ponies. Girls work barefooted in the fields. And men do nothing. Long poles hang balanced over the wells, silhouetted against the sky. Dignified white cows with lyre-shaped horns remind me of their sacred sisters in India.

At the blacksmith's in Russian-looking villages, animals to be shod are fastened with belly-girdles under a horizontal pole just as they are in Turkestan. Each courtyard has its own baking-oven, a small clay tunnel shaped like an Islamic tomb. Russia is also evoked by the Cyrillic lettering above the doors of shops, and by the double cross of the Orthodox churches. Many men wear the red fez or the black astrakhan cap. And their embroidered waistcoats are first cousins to the Afghan ones.

We passed a bride adorned with ribbons and flowers. It seemed to me that the geometrical designs of her apron could be related with those of the embroidered plastron that brightens the dresses of Brahui women in Baluchistan: the same affirmation, strong and joyful, emanates from both. The same boldness and symmetry often appears in carpets made by nomadic tribes. These patterns "speak" to me so directly I feel as if I had lived with them before.

At Belgrade, while we were drinking coffee outside a restaurant, the streets were choked with people patiently waiting for a religious procession. Dishevelled, in rags, bright-eyed and quick as squirrels, the daring boys who dodged under the elbows of the grown-ups were exactly like the Russian *bezprizornis*. Later, when hundreds of covered waggons were leaving Belgrade it might have been the migration of the Kazaks of old coming out of Alma Ata. (When I arrived here from Central Asia two years ago, my eyes were noticing another kind of new sight—cinemas, newspapers, railings, pavements, electric wires.)

At dusk we stopped near a gypsies' camp where smoke lingered above the carts. They surrounded us, their keen eyes and sharp faces not European. Soon they were asking for cigarettes: they are the only people I know who can beg with dignity. They look as if they thought within themselves: "Give or don't give, it's all the same to me."

I was asking myself why they always attract me—even in Turkestan, where it cannot be said that they evoke far-away countries. Is it that they are the symbol of what I am trying to be?—unencumbered by possessions, everywhere at home, intensely alive, without masters, without the limitations imposed by nationality. (I doubt if Russian and German gypsies would fight each other in the national armies of those countries, or if they do they must have declined from type.) The French call them bohémiens or romanichels, the Hungarians Tsiganis, but they call themselves simply *Romani*, "men".

We were to see them as Jatts in Afghanistan, as Luris further south. History-books say that in the fifth century the Sassanian King Bahram Gur attacked the White Huns on the borders of India; as a reward from the Indian ruler, he received the provinces of Sind and Makran. When he returned to Persia he brought back with him twelve thousand Luris to provide music and dancing for his people. At the beginning of the eighth century Jatts were transported from the Indus to the Tigris where they grew dangerous as highway robbers. In the end the Caliph Ojayf cut their communications and they were expelled beyond the Turkish border. They had been exhibited in boats at Baghdad wearing their costumes and playing their instruments. They can claim to have introduced the buffalo

to the Near East and to Southern Europe. To this day words
of Hindi have survived in their language.

Our camp that evening could be called "New Hay": everywhere the smell of ripe grass and the rustling of leaves high up
in the wind. Behind us at the foot of a wall, a fountain in which
we bathed as soon as darkness veiled us; before us, framed by
stately trees, a sloping meadow. Christina seemed to revive.

Though simple, our supper was international. The macaroni
we had bought in Trieste. The butter came from Trevise. (In
the cool, narrow streets of that old town, we hadn't met a single
woman; in the café too there were only men: Italian purdah
seemed as strict as any in Kabul.) Our bread was stamped
with a heart: dark, round, heavy, hardly risen, and so dense
that it squeaked when the knife forced its way through, it was a
tasty mountain bread baked once a month at Simplon-
Dorf, high up where the new grass had not yet risen from the
sopping earth. This Swiss bread was to last us till Constantinople.

Hay-makers woke us, yelling goodheartedly, shouting at
each other across the dale, then singing at the new morning.
With ease and rhythm they balanced their scythes, with ease
and rhythm downhill fell the crescent-shaped swaths of grass.
Sharp calls, birds making straight for the sun, boundless
energy in the bounding scythes, men drunk with the joy of a
new day . . . the scene could have inspired a matutinal
counterpart to the Prince Igor Ballet around its evening fire.

That day we passed through Jagodina. Outside the village
soldiers were exercising on a slope. Driving first above and
then below them, we had time to admire their officer in white,
sword trailing on the ground; his tongue was licking pink
ice-cream in a wafer. He waved at us with enthusiasm. At
last we had outrun people who click heels and project the
right arm! We were so distracted by the scene that we only
just missed running over a goose that fear had petrified one leg
in the air.

Our *vie à deux* had begun some days ago and we were still
observing one another. My companion was easy to deal with:
she did not mind washing the cooking pan or turning the

light out; nor was she prone to "just finish a sentence" when a gasping Primus needed petrol from the car. Her way of packing was tidy and her loading of the dicky systematic. And I soon learned not to interfere with her frequent coffee and cigarettes.

But she slept badly. Because she was so thin, she could not get used to the hard ground. I showed her how to lie sideways with the upper knee bent at right angles, the body leaning forward on the other thigh beneath.

"I did not want to pass for a softy. Why should I mention my sore hip when you yourself never complain?"

"But I like sleeping hard!" I answered: "At home I have a plank in my bed so as not to feel my lumbago!" She smiled at herself: all this time she had thought she was emulating me.

We decided to observe a few rules that would make our journey easier. Tent and supper were to be ready before light failed. Fatigue should be frankly acknowledged since neither of us was in good health (I had a chronic pain in the spine). Pre-arranged stages could be altered: it was important to travel intelligently, noticing all those little changes that make one country different from another.

We aimed at being able to stop on the slightest pretext: to practise this we were to hold our eighteen "horses" with a firm hand. Most car-owners drive as if it were a crime to break the spell of a continual rush at "50". They reach a state in which they lose all initiative save the one to go ahead. To get them to go back three hundred yards is as good as asking for the moon: the silence that meets your demand could not be more disapproving had you wanted them to push the car back by hand.

Nor would we allow speed to build an invisible wall between us and the life around—sound of voices, smell of new spices wafting from a farm, coolness of a shy breeze near a brook! This journey was to be ours and not the car's. I recounted my astonishment when, in Kabul, I met the Baroness Blixen-Finecke. She had just arrived, alone, from Sweden—and let me say, by the way, that even for unaccompanied women there is no danger nowadays in travelling through Afghanistan, and so my story will disappoint anyone who is looking for adventures. Cocking a snook at the Persian gendarmes who tried to stop her, she had covered the distance in record time. But she had seen little, stopped nowhere and her photographs showed

nothing but her Ford in sand, in water, in crowds, in deserts.
So when she invited me to accompany her, I refused. And felt
obliged to lecture her: what a pity that with a car superbly
fitted for Asiatic travels she did not go to remote places where
little-known tribes were on the eve of disappearing. Eva
Blixen-Finecke travelled with a letter of introduction that said
approximately this: "I, Sven Hedin, shall be grateful for any
help given to my god-daughter, the bearer of these lines, who
is on her way to China through Soviet Turkestan if possible.
And as a reward I pledge myself to send a letter of thanks
written by me."

We decided, then, not to be the slaves of our machine.
Should it fall ill, we would not worry: our attention was due to
all that could be seen and not to what we sat in. If the car
broke down altogether we were to continue by local transport.

But if I say little about the third member of our party the
reader must not imagine that, having won Fate to our viewpoint, we two girls just sat on a kind of flying carpet. Christina
was a perfect driver (I think I have already mentioned my
failings in that line) but that was not enough: at the start we
lacked the advice of an expert, my brother having fallen gravely
ill just then. A second spare-wheel, a luggage-rack, a second
tank had been loaded on at the back. Like an over-ripe melon,
the chassis began to open as soon as we reached the bad roads
of Yugoslavia: the doors would not shut any more and the
rubber joint between the tanks leaked so badly that we condemned it. When we ran short of petrol, I siphoned the spare
tank by sucking at a long rubber tube. Sometimes it would not
work. Again and again the tube filled my mouth with a foul
liquid so adulterated that my singed gums and lips felt as if
the dentist had emptied his essence of clove in my mouth.
Forced to give up the luggage-rack we had to cram bed-rolls
and tent into the dicky already chock-a-block with water tanks,
medicine chest, suitcases, typewriters, tool-box, spare springs,
negative films for our cameras, a rucksack full of food and
cooking things.

What a cargo! and covered with how thick a dust in the
evening! Every pot-hole that shook the car sent a cloud of
"Rachel-powder" straight up our miserable noses. I wonder
why car-makers think that a Ford will always remain on

5

SOFIA

THE first mistake had been our reaching Sofia too late. At the border-post I had caused an exasperating delay. Of the six visas we needed, I had forgotten the Bulgarian one. When at last that little matter was settled, we found the main road under repair and had to crawl at a snail's pace along a track in a small valley. There, against the red of the earth and the green of the great tobacco leaves, the black aprons of the women looked surprisingly severe.

When we reached the beautiful plain of Sofia the lingering snowfields of Mount Vitosha were already powdered pink by the declining sun. Tacitly we went on: with no tent or meal to think of, we could continue till we found a hotel.

Christina was so tired that she went to bed as soon as we arrived. I took the car to a garage, driving for the first time through the maze-like lanes of a capital where crowds stroll in the middle of the roads without fear or remorse. The success of my performance excited me so much that it wiped away my tiredness. Back at the hotel I found Christina dressed: she had rung up Marjorie and soon a taxi took us to Boulevard Osvoboditel.

In the wake of Marjorie, we lunched and dined out: I came across smart Silianoff, the only Bulgar I knew. Gloomily we spoke of the League of Nations at Geneva where we had last met. We chatted about our friends who had quitted the big building before it sank—cheerful Hilary St. George Saunders the gourmet, Clarence Streit the elegant Utopian carrying about the manuscript of his *Union Now* which was to cause a great stir in the States. Meanwhile, in a nearby public garden, I was watching a group of school-children gathered around their national flag: they were taught patriotism and that their country had been freed from the Turks seventy years ago. There was a general prayer at the end of which the children looked as if they were catching flies on their noses; but no:

they were hurriedly crossing themselves before the lowering of the flag at sunset.

Next day Christina was seedy. She vomited and slept throughout the afternoon. Even when she opened her eyes, looked at me from the depth of her helplessness and said she felt like death, I failed to grasp what was happening. Her words rang so true that I should have been frightened had I not decided to believe that all was due to her extreme lassitude.

But the evidence flashed when I saw on the floor of the bathroom the brittle glass of an empty ampoule. She had succumbed once more. She had disregarded our compact; she had done what she pretended to abhor. My presence, my confidence in her, the fear of displeasing me had had no effect.

What did it mean? What were we to do?

Which was the true Christina? Grey like wood-pulp, her face looked dead, the eyelids brown, the lips bluish, the stiff chin frozen by an inner contraction. That could not be the true Christina. She was lost in a world to which I had no access. I did not know what to say: my words might hurt or exasperate. And indeed I had nothing to say!

Leaving Sofia behind, we drove in silence. Having put us on the right road, Marjorie had wished us "bon voyage" with all the power of her kind heart. Last evening, delicately, she had tried to help Christina by mentioning a deep experience of her own. One day when she was utterly drowned in woe she had the revelation of how little she mattered: since then, it was impossible for her to dramatise her difficulties.

In silence we followed the "Valley of Roses": attar is made with the flowers of every crop. In the villages, the men wore small turbans and drank coffee out of tiny Turkish cups; the women were wrapped in black shawls: and old 'uns sitting on a bench held up their distaffs like so many queer weapons.

At the edge of a wide field we bought a small crate of strawberries for ninepence. We heard that German students had volunteered to help the gatherers. They told them that but for Hitler who bought their eight thousand tons of strawberries as well as their tobacco and essence of flowers, there would be all-round starvation. Some of the women pickers wore ample musulman breeches which we photographed perfunctorily.

Back in the car, an invisible heaviness seemed to rest on our shoulders.

Christina drove by my side with her usual nonchalance. Silence was tangible, a viscosity for which I had no solvent. How soon would she cease to identify herself with that living corpse, how soon begin to speak about what mattered?

She was probably suffering agonies . . . Even so I should be firm and treat her like a man, showing no emotion or tender weakness that she might use towards her ruin. I wondered if those who helped her before had not been too fond of her, too worried by her misery, too ready to let her have her own way? I hoped to succeed where they had failed because I was different from them, not loving her as they did: this was probably why I had a slight hold on her. In our ordinary life I sometimes felt so distant from her that I could not bring myself to respond to her "thou". Such reserve is most unusual with me.

Nevertheless, I think I loved her profoundly. I loved the generous courage she showed in her campaigning against injustice, the honesty with which she judged herself, the way she bore her solitariness, her conviction that love is a mystery we have to penetrate. But a jealous fatality made her strangle what she embraced: she asked too much from love.

I had been moved to see that in her distress last winter it was to me she wrote from Neuchâtel: "This nursing-home drives me crazy. I should like to talk with you if you could spare the time." I felt strong, coming down from the mountains where I had "managed" our ski-ing team. We met at the station where she came in her car. She was harassed by her fight with the doctors: they would not understand that writing was life and food to her, that the regenerative cure of enforced rest applied to dyspeptics and hysterics could not suit her. Around us, all was white, covered by new snow. It was exhilarating to walk near the lake through the crisp, frosty, sparkling air. A mass of thick long bristles, Palazi, my Eskimo dog, was playing at dragging Christina along the deserted road. The strong animal had crossed Greenland as the leader of Robert's pack. One look at the sincerity of that kingly creature was enough to cheer you, gave the proof that goodness and nobility exist. In the presence of Christina also, narrow or mean thoughts were banished. The gist of our dialogue had been that if she was mad I was mad too: I was unwilling to let myself be strangled by that prudent life that everybody advocated. I also was convinced that—whether we succeed or not—it is our job to search for the significance of life.

That night outside Sofia, by a small stream under a big elm, she spoke at last, sullenly:

"If you decide to keep me with you I suppose I shall have to submit to a constant control. You won't trust me any more?"

"I will do it if you want. I have not ceased to hope: I am sure that when you know yourself better this misery of your own making will vanish like a harmless mist." I wanted to say much more but I knew she was not willing to listen.

Next day she looked like an ordinary convalescent.

South of Philippopoli the country turned out to be miserable: bare, with nothing but a few huts built haphazardly. Desultorily we switched on our wireless. A suggestive *czarda* submerged us in its passionate waves. And I entered my inner landscape. This was my fifth journey to the East. I knew the way as far as Herat in Afghanistan, so till then I could not be entranced by the feeling of discovery. Besides, the chief object of this journey was to rescue Christina from a negative atmosphere, to find conditions such that she would of her own accord live normally. I felt sure I could reach the Hackins if we followed the road I knew: but it barred any escapade into difficult (and really interesting!) country. Briefly stated, my main aims were to acquire self-mastery and to save my friend from herself.

The second aim depended upon the first. Only clear knowledge of myself would allow me to help Christina in the fundamental problem she was raising. Of course that mastery of myself should bring me nearer to reality, and ever since I began roughing it among sailors and nomads I was in search of a "real" life. Towards achieving my aim I could so far only visualise a whitewashed room in a Pamirian village where I might learn to think: this training was to take place in the morning before I went abroad in search of heads for my calipers!

Lucien Fabre had thought that an Islamic country could not

help to master the self. But I did not want help. Away from a shaky and feverish Europe I simply wanted to look within. My search for an Edenic mountain tribe was merely the excuse for breaking away from the helplessness prevalent in Europe. I knew that self-knowledge can be acquired wherever one is but I was too weak or too silly to insulate myself from the revolt, panic, militarism and febrile planning that was sweeping Europe off her feet. Distance would help, I felt sure. In the West, anyway, everyone seemed as lost as I was: why not try the East?

As for my second aim, if at the start there was an elan of unselfishness in my desire to help Christina, it was mixed by now with pride and vanity: I, Kini, could not bear to be beaten—could not, therefore, fail. But my doubts of success were as sincere, now, as the confidence I had felt in London when I picked up the gauntlet thrown by Irene.

I repeated to Christina the sombre predictions I had listened to then. But to counterbalance them I added that Blaise Cendrars had felt her sterling quality and was impatient to meet her again. On her side, Christina had been advised not to travel with me because I was an immoral cynic: had I not written in a book that I started for Central Asia with salvarsan in my luggage?—proof that I had made up my mind to live licentiously. Christina had calmly answered: "Kini had a great desire to live with nomads. They are known to be plagued with venereal diseases. Therefore she bought a remedy in case she should be contaminated through drinking from their filthy vessels."

A pungent smell of burning alarmed us. The car was stopped and we searched for the causes. Approaching Christina I found it was due to her first Bulgarian cigarette, just lighted!

We were advancing through the plain of the Maritza, wide, treeless, dotted with storks patiently standing in the high grass. With their oppressed skulls, flattened horns, tired and swollen eyes, shiny skins, wallowing for protection in the mud under the culverts, buffaloes were typical of hot mosquito-lands.

The car reached the barrier at the Turkish border. In spite of our explanations, the clerk in the office got muddled. He had taken down that Madame Silvaplana *née* Francis, was Legation Secretary. "No, that is her husband's profession."

"Then what shall I call her? Professor?" At that moment, discovering that he was handling a diplomatic passport, the man became afraid: rubber stamps one after another thudded on our documents. Hurrying as he did, the Turk probably forgot to warn us that we were entering a military zone.

The map told us we were nearing Edirne (Adrianople) and soon we reached its vegetable gardens. But we were not prepared for what we saw when we rounded a small hill. Lit by the horizontal rays of the evening sun, a vision from the *Thousand and One Nights* floated above the lilac mist. Many minarets arose, slender and precious in the level golden light; incredibly tall beside huge round domes powdered with purple shadows, they looked like the masts of a marmoreal ship anchored in iridescent skies. Fading out, the glorious vision left only a few outlines, livid after that shining splendour.

Curious to see how the morning sun would play on such a setting, we pitched camp on the spot. But so many children pestered us that we packed up again, all the time answering that we were not German: "*Aleman iok*—no, no!"—a denial we were to repeat day after day from then on.

Having traversed the town and gained the country, we looked for a by-lane where we might spend the night. But the east side of Adrianople was deserted: abandoned steles showed that it was a huge cemetery, sure sign that the town had once been a Muslim capital. Giving up our search, we rigged the tent in the waste-land. (That night, the ground as hard as rock, Christina decided to buy a circular air-cushion for her hip!)

Daylight showed the town far behind. We wanted to reach Istanbul that Saturday evening before closing-time. So from our camp, we took leave of its monuments. One of them, built by the great Sinan in the sixteenth century, is said to be his masterpiece—the mosque of Sultan Selim II, as big as Santa Sophia.

We were right to have started early: the foundations of the "international road" were being laid and in three atrocious hours we covered only eighteen miles. In deep ruts made by high-bodied lorries, the Ford was either stuck or grating against stones. On reaching the good road at Chorlu, in the enthusiasm of relief we filmed our first stork's nest topping a minaret.

Handling a camera is a risky business in Turkey and the

danger increases as you approach Persia, Russia or Japan. I knew this very well but had never expected that our first arrest would be so early. Our storks were unluckily within twenty yards of a Poste de Gendarmerie. We very soon found ourselves sitting inside: it was one of those old wooden houses I was so keen to visit!

I could not think how to propitiate the Inspector who sat behind our five cameras. Their number looked most suspicious, they were not sealed and we had used them in military territory. "Why were we feigning ignorance? Would we give an account of every hour we had spent in Turkey? Where had we slept last night? Why did not our passports bear the obligatory stamp of the hotel? Slept on the road outside Adrianople! You want me to believe that? I shall release you only when your films have been developed."

It took a long time to grasp that: the Inspector spoke nothing but Turkish and in that tongue we could only say *Aleman iok*. Unhappily the country swarmed with German spies saying all the same thing. The village photographer was sent for and a schoolmistress who spoke French. In the presence of authority, they shook with fear. Christina's patience was exhausted: she was thinking what kind of threat would work on the Inspector. She made me tremble; I used all my power of persuasion to explain to her that in newly reformed countries it pays to pretend one is much impressed by officials.

With thick fingers tanned by acids the photographer was in vain trying to open our small-film cameras. At last he said he could not handle or develop such material. To our immense surprise, we were at once released. The Inspector, no doubt being human, was hungry: we had spent more than four hours in his office.

Fields of yellow wheat waved as we speeded onward, while the motionless dark-blue line of the Sea of Marmora barred the south.

At sunset we approached another capital. Dark foliage covered an undulating strip of land. Above it, plunging and rising in noble style, looking like a Wall of China astray among clusters of trees, towered the grand walls of Constantinople. In 1453 the last emperor of Byzantium fought and died on this wall, defeated by Muhammad II. Powerful enough to bring a world to its end, the world of the Roman Empire whose magnificence had endured for a thousand years, this terrible Turk was only twenty-one when he led his one hundred and sixty thousand men into battle. Before the final attack he said to them: "There are three conditions for winning a war—to want victory, to be ashamed of defeat and to obey your chief."

By the Gate of Adrianople that Saturday evening there were only a few men wearing worker's caps, bored, taking an airing.

Somewhere in the huge town spread at our feet there would have to be an explanation between Christina and myself.

6

ISTANBUL

THERE was no need for us to do the sights, we both knew Istanbul. I only went to Sultan Ahmed, the great mosque with polished wooden floor from whose silent bay-windows the view over the Bosphorus is the one I like best. When you are used to the pull forward in our cathedrals, it is a great experience to enter domed buildings where you feel drawn up from above.

North of Istanbul, Therapia is a hamlet where the well-to-do have their villas. We reached what used to be the Sumer Palace-Hotel: there lived in great simplicity the architect Holzmeister who built Ankara for Kemal Ataturk. On the first floor were the desks, drawing-tables and rooms of our host and his staff (composed of Austrian and Czech refugees). The whole atmosphere was pleasant—the concern for proportion and detail, the cleanliness, the eight or ten rooms artfully commanding each other.

Holzmeister took us to the little harbour where he knew that country girls were selling raspberries. Rowing-boats and yachts swung leisurely at anchor; some lads were diving noisily. Moved by the etesian breeze, the water showed its blue-green depths and lapped a marble quay. Slow fishermen rowed caiques with perfectly curved bows. Its coast turning purple in the later afternoon, here was my *rieuse Méditerranée*, the caressing sea where trees bend over the water, that Middle Sea whose culture and atmosphere are made to the measure of man. How could I be foolish enough to turn my back on the world that I belonged to?

On a terrace under the great sky, we sat to a supper of vegetable pottage, cold meat, salad, cheese and fruit. Christina's neighbour was a doctor who had once treated her at Ankara.

Our host—I could see his white hair shining in the night— was a respected leader. His intense vitality kept melancholy from creeping in when we spoke about their homes. My handsome and athletic neighbour touched his guitar and sang in our honour a few Swiss melodies. Then a choir took shape and all the songs evoked the far-away Alps. Andreas Hofer's *Lied*, the last and the most beautiful, ended movingly: *Gott sei mit euch, Und mit dem Land Tirol! Ade, mein Land Tirol!* Full of calm determination, the grave words became heart-rending from having passed through the chests of these exiles. They had little in common with other émigrés I know, Russians who wait for the miraculous reappearance of a Tsar, unwilling to see that Stalin is the greatest tsar they can ever have.

We drove back to our "London Oteli". Christina was silent: no doubt she was deeply moved.

Christina was on the ground, curled up, bloodless, more like a dying dog than any human being. Standing over her, I kicked and shouted in a frenzy: "Will you speak? Why don't you answer me?" I felt that if I could hurt her enough she would speak again, then all would be put right. Trying to do as much damage as possible I hacked at her lifeless head. Useless. But I must make her speak! Enraged, I landed such a kick in the yielding softness of the stomach that I hurt my ankle . . . and awoke. My actual bones still shook from the rage that had lived in my dream-body.

Daylight. Christina's bed is empty. Where is she? Has something happened? I must act. But how? I open the door, walk in the passage, hesitate. The house is built about a square well that lights the doors of all the rooms. I advance like an automaton. I hear Christina's voice. Monosyllables. Then I see her by the telephone at the far end of the landing. She wears her sullen face. She sees me. My expression is probably still affected by my nightmare. She seems to shorten her conversation. A few minutes ago I was ashamed to be a brutal executioner; now I feel a spy and hate my job.

We are back in our room. She says: "It was my neighbour of last night. He told me he had some leucodal in case I needed it." "Did he ring you up?" "Anyhow, I told him I could do without it." "Christina, do you know why I woke up? I hadn't heard your bare feet but . . ." and I relate my dream, omitting none of its shocking details.

We are moved. This nightmare shows that we are linked more deeply than we thought. I am very upset to see myself capable of such ferocity. Not far from our hotel stands the famous Pera Palace where, before I knew her, I had imagined Christina the first time I heard of her: Miette's husband had met her there to discuss archæology. Some three years ago he told me how well she had received him—*avec toute l'aisance que donne la fortune*. In my turn I am now in Constantinople with Christina, but what a contrast between these two scenes: just now in this faded room I was kicking that same smart person to death.

"I think I would kill you rather than see you become the human rag of my dream."

"Kini, for some time I've been wanting to ask you why do you bother about me?"

"Why do I bother about you? . . . I don't know. I can't say it is because I love you because I detest you when I see such gifts as yours spoilt as they are. I said gifts. You are not their author: they came from an intelligence greater than your present foolishness. Can't you see you've been entrusted with them to make them fructify? But to answer your question: I am travelling with you . . . because I am travelling with you! It is only afterwards that one finds explanations." There was silence before I added: "To think that all the time you know you can do without that poison: you've lived without it for months. What shall I do now? I cannot help you against yourself! Should I lock you up at night, search your suitcase, keep watch all the time? Good God, on what grounds could I dare to limit your independence?"

"I give you complete power over me, day and night. Don't leave me alone. If it happens again, I leave the car with you and go back. Let's go away quickly. I have to be far from towns. Then I know I can't get it and I live more easily. In towns I can't help thinking: the temptation may come next moment, I shall yield, lured by the few minutes of forgetfulness it gives me—though I pay for them by hours of sickness. It does not even give pleasure; it is more like a pause in nothingness . . . the only relaxation that I know. The rest of the time, even during the endless nights, I live fearing that my fear will overpower me . . . that this gimlet-like temptation will pierce the wall of my resolution. I live in a half-paralysed state, terrorised by what might happen."

"Nonsense! You are the plaything of your imagination. I feel that in order to live intensely you lend yourself too readily to excesses of all sorts—feelings, drink, work, social revolt. Do you choose this way of annihilating yourself as quickly as possible? You must be forced to live duⁱly for some time. Then you will learn how intense and rich a so-called ordinary minute can be."

"But see how fate is against me: again and again when I have been off it, circumstances put it under my hand . . . And it is supposed to be impossible for ordinary people to obtain it!"

"This happens because a part of you still wants it; but you try to delude yourself. You are like the 'peace-loving' nations that stage a disarmament conference well knowing that they are not prepared to make war an impossibility. If you had no desire for it, you could let it be by your side even. But look, when you enjoy our Adrianople evening, when you are absorbed in your writing, what have you in common with that person full of fear that you describe?"

"That's why writing means so much to me. . . ."

"When you investigate working conditions in the States or piece together facts to write your last biography, that despicable being of yours is nowhere. It is a question of finding what will absorb you, then you are saved."

"The more I study different problems, the more I see reason to despair of justice in this world. . . ."

"But who can say what is just?" I interrupted her, "anyhow, we agreed not to complain about the world until we know more. We thought that if there is a 'Kingdom of Heaven within' there is no reason why we should not reach some certainty about it. We also agreed that this would be more absorbing than the daring things we have been doing in order to feel our lives more keenly. Let's look ahead; and for God's sake, be more patient."

7

BLACK SEA

To steam away from the bridge of Galata on board the *Ankara* was like starting life anew; with our continent, our past and our failures faded away.

I had been lucky that day: at the last moment the post brought me my "choga" forgotten at Sofia. Not only had I no other overcoat but it was a lovely white-wool garment made by the mountaineers in a valley of the Pamirs; though worn like a cape it had long sleeves that dangled down as far as the knees; you only used them in winter and then they made an accordion-like muff. I wore that "choga" as a ship hoists the Blue Peter— as an emblem of departure for a great country that was calling me back.

The Ford too, one could almost have thought, must have been pleased to leave Pera and its narrow streets, cobbled, dark, sinuous, malodorous, sisters of similar alleys in Malta and Marseilles—where old men sit on the thresholds, where baskets are lowered from upper storeys, where the washing hangs across the street, where one cat or another is always watching the traffic. At night our car must have heard a good story from its neighbour in the garage, the long red Mercedes which had just snatched away King Zog of Albania from his Italian enemies. Its radiator-cap was a helmet with chamois horns topped by a silver eagle! A plaque screwed to the switch-board, showed that the car was a present from Adolf Hitler. On it was engraved: "With luck for now and ever!"

Of all the towns I know Constantinople is the most inter-national: nothing can compare with the variety of its people, religions, alphabets, fashions, styles of architecture. Seen from the sea, Pera even offers a sky-scraper's silhouette. I suggest that Constantinople, more central than Geneva, should harbour the next League of Nations. There the daughters of Stalin, King George and Nehru could easily meet Madame Chiang to decide if Eurasia is to fight the two Americas ruled by the sons of Roosevelt!

Christina was also in a gay mood: the paymaster had addressed her as Monsieur! The further we moved eastward, the more often was she taken for a boy. And this not only by Asiatics: in Delhi smart Major Gastrell spoke to her for fifteen minutes before suspecting that she was a woman.

Once more it was forbidden to photograph—good incentive to snap unobtrusively the medieval fortifications of Rumeli Hissar; and, later, queer fishing-boats that showed the unexpected outlines of men standing half-way up truncated masts, each of them keeping watch upon a solitary stilt.

Amid the umbrella-pines of Therapia the Austrians waved napkins as we sailed past.

Our Swiss Consul had told us that three Swiss boys were also on their way to Kabul by car but he was betting that we girls would get there first. It seemed quite likely, for our competitors had taken to the long bad roads of Anatolia. Besides, they evidently knew very little of the jealous gods who delight in wrecking plans: they announced their goal with a big KABUL painted on their car and they were letting the sticky black fingers of Her Majesty the Press rummage among their long-cherished plans. Needless to say, we committed no such blunders.

Rich in coal but not in oil, the Turks have so far devoted their efforts to building railways: the roads were still in an appalling state. Hence our decision to avoid them by gliding as far East as possible on the smooth Pont-Euxine. Like Leon of Thurié, what we longed for was "to sail the rest of the way stretched out on our backs like Odysseus". We were to follow the whole length of Turkey, elongation of Asia thrust like a bridge towards the open hand of Greece. Landing at Trebizond, we should soon reach the high threshold of Iran—Persia as it used to be called.

At our London Oteli we had met a very intelligent engineer whose information added tang to a journey likely to be dull. Eastern Turkey was brimming with "Aryan spies", he knew it for certain. The experiences we were to go through would for ever disgust us with travelling. People were arrested, their cameras confiscated and their papers. "You will surely be sent back. Anyhow, whatever you do, don't ask questions," he ended by saying.

But travelling is questioning!

Our ship had been built in Holland: her dining-room was decorated with blue tiles showing windmills, clogs and bonnets. We could have forgotten where we were but for the Turkish music incessantly howling out of a loud-speaker—in spite of our hints and ingratiating smiles at the head-waiter who controlled it. Putting on absorbed expressions and scratching our heads now and then, we wrote the first *Lettres de Voyage* we owed our press-agency. In spite of her greater training, Christina was nearly as slow as myself in producing what was needed. Like me she was displeased with her efforts, but her prose was more fluent than mine.

After reading the poor article I had just typed, as her habit was she praised it. It moved me to make a confession:

"Christina, you seem to see nothing but qualities in me . . . and now I know why. You never criticise others, only yourself. You accept us without ever exercising your judgment. But it's time for you to know what sort of person I am. Just now I was meanly jealous of you for I know you are the better man of us two . . . Soon, as soon as you choose to give up your fear, you will be great. And in spite of that I continually bully you, I am supposed to be your mentor! The blind leading the paralytic: what a farce!"

"But Kini, you are wrong. My books don't reach so many editions as yours. And you know I haven't been translated yet!"

"Your remark is as childish as your desire for popularity. Reuter's news is everywhere translated and has more readers than the best poem of the century: your argument proves nothing. You are now writing worthless articles in order proudly to support yourself; leave that to those who have to do it. Take your father's allowance and give more time to good writing. Why be ashamed of having money? there is probably a reason for the circumstances in which you were born. However much you simplify your life there will always be someone having less than you, so where are you to draw the line? Anyhow the greatness I mentioned is in you much more than in your books."

To-day, and that is six years later while I write these lines, I think that if the purpose of being born is to live long, then, since you are no more, I win. But—and this I prefer to believe—if what we are meant to do is to manifest what we understand of our deepest nature, then you win. To achieve that victory you first had to express your anguish before the frustration of human life, before the paltriness of love.

This giving form to our innermost tendency goes beyond ethics: a time comes when, in spite of everything, we have to be as true as we can, revealing the essence of ourselves. Our death may express it as well as our daily life, the way a mother loves her child, a sudden act of heroism as well as a good poem. Thus I feel that even cowards, thieves or conceited dictators, not only patient clerks or artists, can realise a similar fulfilment once they have exhausted their innate particularity. The lily or the serpent, the nettle or the cat accomplish the miracle of being faithfully themselves. We are complicated beings tormented by our innate contradictions but we should unravel ourselves so as to free the fundamental ''note'' from our Centre. Our way of doing it may seem unmoral but I know there is good in it nonetheless, for we are more than moral beings. Morality is not the aim of life but merely one short-cut to Reality. And only by completing our own particularity can we go beyond it to our core. "The Hero is he who is immovably centred," wrote Emerson. The same applies, of course, to the Happy Man who is not, and cannot be, torn apart from his Centre. The sooner we transcend our anguish, cowardice or conceit, our patience, courage or our love towards a limited end or creature only, the sooner shall we reach our deepest ''note'', our Centre, the same in all—that silent ''note'' towards which variety was really pointing though we took it to be divergent and isolating.

Not only did you express yourself, Christina, you also experienced the deepest in you, you went beyond your self-destroying torment. I shall show, later on, how I came to that conclusion.

In search of the sun we climbed to the upper deck where we found the wireless operator alone in his world of sounds. A garden in wooden boxes grew on his roof; a bird sang in a cage; in the cabin a plush flower bent over a tin model of a ship. He was a smiling hermit. With great concern he said: "Alas, Kemal Ataturk died eight months ago, and we need fifteen more leaders like him to make something out of our miserable country!"

Off Zonguldak—a sloping green coast where a railway brings coal and iron from the interior—frames of German lorries were swung overboard into dancing lighters. Stiffened buffaloes and helpless sheep volplaned through the air, the first seized round their middle, the sheep tied by their legs. Men fought their way up the hull along hanging lines; pushing through the noisy crowds of the maindeck, they offered cherries and blackberries, bread, baskets, ribbons and flowers. Our Ford became the baker's counter: he stood on the running-board with his loaves displayed on the hood.

We also anchored for a few hours off the harbours—Inebolu, Sinope, Samsoun, Girasun.

Noisy living went on uninterruptedly among the congestion of the lower deck. Our ship offered a summary of mankind: the few bored rich of the first and second class scattered on empty decks while below swarmed a medley of humanity, each trying to win enough space to lie down without having unknown feet or elbows in his face.

We had much time to notice how privileged we were. Christina probably felt that there was too great a difference between the decks; or even imagined that, grumbling about the injustice of life, the squeezed ones down there were envying us. But having travelled steerage more than once, I remembered our feelings: none of us ever gave a thought to the "upper ones" and if some of my neighbours had been shifted up there they would have felt miserable. They needed the herd around them, they enjoyed its noise, its warmth, its struggle for life. They counted their change, deloused the hem of their wide breeches, minded the babies, fed the hens in their coops, re-wound a turban, cut their square nails with a pen-knife, stitched a carpet-slipper, scratched a viol, shared dripping slices of water-melon or went to the galley with a kettle and a meagre pinch of tea. Meanwhile, I'm pretty sure, their minds were pondering over past dealings or hatching plans for the future.

With its old roofs of rounded tiles, its cobbled streets smelling of fish and its walled gardens where pomegranates blossomed

D

red against the blue of the sea, Trebizond nestled into the coast like an Italian town—but for her white minarets where the muezzin calls Allah under his Turkish name of Tanri.*

After the car had been rowed to the shore in a barge splendidly bulging at the bows, we went to the hotel in the central square. In the afternoon a compatriot called on us, who did not conceal his surprise: he had been told that a lady and a boy of fifteen had just arrived from Switzerland! His job was to buy Turkish hazel-nuts for Swiss chocolate-factories. He dealt but with one twentieth of the crop, the rest went to Germany.

Export of dolphin oil was the other main trade of the town. But it looked as if the fishes had at last understood that some one was after them: they no more visited this part of the world and the factories stood idle. Dolphin oil was already exploited at the time of Xenophon. His men used it to replace their beloved olive oil; they made their bread of "flat-nut" flour, which must have been their name for the hazel-nut.

Trebizond seemed only half awake. Men with shoes curved up in front walked slowly in the besprinkled streets, leaving me time to be puzzled by the cut of their baggy trousers. Though unveiled, some women had a corner of their head-cloth pinched in the mouth; the further inland we went, the more noticeable was that custom.

Visiting the French consul in a villa under a vine arbour, we learned that there was not a single Frenchman in this part of the world. As for the Italian consul, he was idle too: his ships had stopped calling since Russia had closed her ports to them: all the export went to a German line.

None of the people we visited confirmed the alarming reports of our Istanbul engineer, but it was true that Germans had had their films confiscated. This decided me to send home the harvest of my previous journey—a great number of photos meant to illustrate the articles we were now writing. Rather forgo this simplification of our work than run the risk of losing all this valuable material. This borderland has probably always been very "sensitive": when he travelled by way of Erzerum in the second half of last century, E. G. Browne, the

* Emperor Babur writes in his Memoirs that *Tangri* means the deity. Current all over Asia, the word is probably of Mongolian origin.

Persian scholar, feared to see his papers confiscated. He decided to hide while writing his diary so as not to arouse the suspicions of the *zaptieh* who was continually spying on him.

We failed to meet the Governor from whom we wanted recommendations for the up-country officials. But our attempt to see him gave us a pleasant drive up the steep coast among orchards, villas and forests. Seen from such a height, the sea had become a gentian-blue immensity. It is said that by clear weather the Caucasian range is visible. I scanned the eastern sky for the chain I had crossed nine years ago but I only saw what my memory conjured from the past.

We were ready to conquer the highlands beyond a nine-thousand-foot pass in the Pontic range: a quick change of altitude rich in contrasts. Three times during our journey we were to climb from sea-level to very high passes: from the Black Sea to Armenia, from the Caspian to Khorassan, from Turkestan to Afghanistan.

8

PONTIC RANGE

TREBIZOND and the coast of Colchis were a Greek colony for a
long time. They called it Trapezus because of the shape of a
table-land in the neighbourhood. When the Ten Thousand
reached it they celebrated their successful flight over more than
two thousand miles by paying thank-offerings to Zeus and
Heracles. They organised their athletic games on one of the
slopes we saw. "This hill is superb for running wherever you
please" said Dracontius. But the men complained that they
could not wrestle on ground so hard and so overgrown.
Dracontius replied: "The one that is thrown will be hurt a
bit more!"

A few centuries later Trebizond became the end-station of
one of the oldest trade-lines whose history we know: the trans-
asiatic Silk Road. Among the host of soldiers, kings, travellers,
missionaries, merchants, ambassadors and men of letters who
followed it, I feel sure that Marco Polo at the end of his return-
journey from China must have been as joyful as the harassed
Ten Thousand to see at last the waters of his Midland Sea. He
was with his uncles, good navigators. After their long sea-
passage, they had safely delivered to the Khan of Persia the
beautiful Mongolian Princess Kogatun. Rich in presents of
every kind, they decided to avoid the risk of travelling through
Syria, then occupied by inimical Egyptians; so they came to
Trebizond where they were sure of a welcome from the ruling
house of the Christian Comneni, Byzantine emperors dislodged
by the Fourth Crusade.

Now Trebizond was behind us. Heading for Erzerum, we
followed a green valley where the moist sea-breeze was still
noticeable. The slopes were covered with hazel-nut shrubs
regularly planted like tea-bushes. Here and there, seemingly
forgotten on the hill-side, rose the sober lines of Greek chapels.
They had the simplest forms, naves and apses just a cube and a
hemisphere. At the six thousand six hundred feet of the Zihana

pass it was cold and misty: we could not be thrilled by spying the sea from where Xenophon might have stood. Gumusaneh, the nearest village of some importance, is probably the Gymnias of the Greeks. But as Grote writes: "To lay down with any certainty the line they followed from the Euphrates down to Trapizond appears altogether impossible."

The Mount Teches the Ten Thousand climbed has not been identified. Perhaps it is the hill of the Zihana pass. It was in 402 B.C. The Greeks had fought for Cyrus the Young. Cyrus being defeated at Cunaxa by his brother Artaxerxes Mnemon, the Greeks started for home and went north as far as the Black Sea. Out of the fourteen thousand, nine thousand reached the goal. The fact that they had successfully fought their way among so many mountainous kingdoms helped to convince Alexander the Great that with a good army he might accomplish much in Asia.

The Ten Thousand suffered from the icy cold winter of Armenia where they waded through thick snow. "From this city of Gymnias the ruler of the land sent the Greeks a guide in order to lead them through territory that was hostile to his own. When the guide came he said he would lead them within five days to a place from which they could see the sea and if he failed to do so he was ready to accept death. Thus taking the lead, as soon as he had brought them into hostile territory, he kept urging them to spread abroad fire and ruin thereby making it clear that it was with this end in view that he had come and not out of good will towards the Greeks. On the fifth day they did in fact reach the mountain; its name was Teches. Now as soon as the vanguard got to the top of the mountain a great shout went up. And when Xenophon and the rear-guard heard it they imagined that other enemies were attacking in front for enemies were following from behind from the district that was in flames; and the rear-guard had killed some of them and captured others by setting an ambush and had also taken some twenty wicker-shields covered with raw, shaggy oxhides. But as the shout kept getting louder and louder as the successive ranks came up, all began to run at full speed towards the rank ahead that were one after another joining in the shout; and as the shout kept growing far louder as the number of men grew steadily greater, it became quite

clear to Xenophon that here was something of unusual importance. So he mounted a horse, took with him Lycius and the
cavalry and pushed ahead to lend aid; and in a moment they
heard the soldiers shouting "the Sea! the Sea!" and passing the
word along. Then all the troops of the rear-guard likewise
broke into a run, and the pack-animals began racing ahead and
the horses. And when all had reached the summit, then indeed
they fell to embracing one another and generals and captains
as well, with tears in their eyes. And on a sudden, at the bidding
of someone or other, the soldiers began to bring stones and to
build a great cairn. Thereon they placed as offering a quantity
of raw oxhides, and walking-sticks and the captured wicker-
shields."*

It took them five more stages through the countries of the
Macronians, Scythinians and Colchians before they reached
Trebizond. On the way they halted for four days, drunk or
crazy with too much honey that they had eaten on the way.

To us, on the night of our arrival, Gymnias was merely a
dark village with lorries clustered near the inn.

Tired as we were by the many slippery bends of the clayey
road, we welcomed our glasses of raki. The strong drink washed
away the unmistakable flavour of petroleum that accompanied
the fried liver. Raki was in great demand among the drivers
and road-labourers around us. No sooner had we climbed to
our primitive room, than a *zaptieh* came to collect our passports.
Until they were returned we were at his mercy.

In the morning we bought a basketful of the juicy apples for
which Gumusaneh is famous. There was something of a
holiday-resort atmosphere about the houses of this mountain-
village (with their balconies and sloping roofs they could
almost be called chalets). They were to be the last of all
European houses we should meet: soon there would be nothing
but mud houses and flat roofs. And slopes too, bare of the
sheen of tender blades: only tufts of coarse grass in yellowish
patches on the grey earth.

We often passed by sections of the cobbled caravan-road.
I was amused to see how often, forgetting that I sat in a car,
my reactions were those of a member of slow-moving caravan:
"Now is the time to collect firewood for the treeless stages

* Xenophon : Anabasis. Transl. Brownson.

ahead," I found myself thinking in earnest. Or "Up there the animals will find some grazing to-night. And to-morrow we must start as early as possible so as to be well over the Kop pass before nightfall". Many had been the merchants thronging this way who thought of the loads they would soon bring back— silks and turquoise, carpets and lapis lazuli. Trading with the East means fortune. And in modern times even more than when Pliny wrote: ". . . the sea of Arabia sends us pearls and at the lowest computation India and Seres put together drain our empire of a hundred million sesterces (over £1,000,000) every year. That is the price our luxuries and our womankind cost us."

Our roadster needed only twelve hours to cover these three hundred and fifty mountainous kilometres, not ten or fifteen days according to the fitness of the pack-animals. But my mind still bore the impress made by two caravan-journeys along the more eastern parts of this same Silk Road, that inordinately long track through the emptiness of dead lands, along gobis, gorges and pamirs, rare oases and mosquito-plagued marshes.

I had been sufficiently shaped, too, by life on small ships to be wedded to the wind in a sailor's way: caressing breezes or threatening squalls arouse in me feelings that no landlubber could imagine. I am glad that I left home when I was young and followed the wake of the subtle Ulysses, glad to have lived the sea and the desert instead of helping father to air the silky softness of the deep sealskins, to value the bunches of ruffle-tailed silver foxes or by trying on the latest *modèles de Paris*— glad I accomplished most of what I set out to do: once and for all I know how short-lived the joys of vanity are. Now, like a spider that has spread its web to the end of the branches, my horizon has been enlarged: as if I had left everywhere something spun out of myself, I am directly stirred by what happens along the far-flung threads of my experience.

In a wide valley, Baiburt was a grand fortress of flame-coloured stone with crenellated walls, a village at its feet. We turned south over the pass of Kop. We met trucks in teams of four or six, their drivers, the caravan-chiefs of to-day, friendly disposed towards us. They probably took us to be rich idlers, and would have been surprised to learn that we felt we were not unlike them: we, also, were earning our living with our trick at the wheel day after day, week after week, month after month. Only our pay-bill was far more distant than theirs, depending not upon the length of road covered but upon the surface of paper blackened!

A wild wind ruled over the round-hilled pass. Near a lonely rest-house we walked to a cement platform where a great bell of pale metal hung; it was adorned with hieratic saints embossed on a blue enamel ground. Meant to be used in a Russian church, it tolled now for travellers lost in wintry storms when the track has vanished under many feet of snow.

From their height these saints untiringly contemplate hundreds of miles of weary country too old to rise in tumultuous pinnacles. Over the treeless undulations the metal voice can carry far. On some ridges, bulging clouds seemed to have left a bit of their whiteness—stubborn patches of surviving snow. Compact indigo shadows cut the land into a gigantic puzzle. Breathing deeply, I felt I wanted to remember that magnificent sight.

Reading Armenia's history teeming with strife corroborates one's first impression of an age-worn atmosphere—Armenia so torn between mighty neighbours that she might be called the Poland of the Middle East. Rich Copper Age settlements thrived in this valley that sheltered neolithic colonies seven or eight thousand years before Christ. Before the Persians left the place to Alexander the Great, Assyrians and even the troops of Pharaoh Thutmose III had conquered the country. The Parthians ruled over it; then the Persians fought over it—till it fell to the lot of the Roman Empire. In A.D. 415 Anatolius founded Theodosiopolis, the modern Erzerum; the Arabs disputed it with the emperors of Byzantium till the Seljuks became its undisputed masters. One after another the Mongols of Genghis Khan, the Turks of Timur and at last the Ottomans occupied Armenia.

At the foot of the hills we crossed the shining infant Euphrates gliding over pebbles. Running parallel with it, the new railway from Scutari to Erzerum was being completed: the journey was said to take two days and two nights.

We had reached the Anatolian highland within the loop built

by the Taurus and the Pontic ranges. A similar belt of northern and southern mountains encircles the plateau of Persia. A third magnificent ring formed by the Kuen Lun and the Himalayas contains the table-land of Tibet. With the mind's eye I saw that succession of plateaux inside their girdles of rocks, each of them ending eastward in a mighty knot of mountains giving birth to equally mighty rivers. What an impressive pattern of relief the earth has thrice repeated! We were near the first of these knots—Armenia topped by the seventeen-thousand-foot Mount Ararat, cold wind-swept Armenia whose rivers belong to the three wide-apart watersheds of the landlocked Caspian, the Black Sea and the warm Persian Gulf.

The Iranian loop (not quite closed at the south-eastern end of the Zagros) rises to eighteen thousand six hundred feet at the Demavend which is linked by the Khorassan range and the Hindu Kush to the grand cluster of the Pamirs. From that puissant knot, rivers tumble down to Sinkiang and Russian Turkestan in the North, to Afghanistan and India in the South. I have seen the Tarim, Syr-Darya and Oxus, the Hari Rud, Helmand and Kabul. Joyfully plunging into their waters during snowstorms or in the scorching heat of noon, I came to love them.

The third colossal arena of Tibet, is hidden behind the highest rim of mountains on the earth. Towards the East of that immense country still partly fabulous, we know of convulsions and rocky strangulations of a magnitude that defies the imagination. From this tangled skein, huge rivers gush forth towards the gulfs of Bengal and Siam and to the distant Yellow Sea saturated with Mongolian loess: for a while, before heading towards their different destinies, they flow near each other squeezed in parallel gorges of such forbidding shape that even cold-blooded geologists are astonished at them.

Anatolian, Iranian, Tibetan—three vast plateaux commanding each other, each greater and higher than the last, each plexus of hills harbouring groups of greatly differing men. Enough variety to occupy many a lifetime of travel, beauty enough to thank whatever is responsible for a diversity no human brain could have devised.

9

BAYAZIT

WE were stopped at a military post. An officer who spoke nothing but Turkish jumped on board, handing each of us a dark eglantine. He asked for our cameras: it was forbidden to photograph.

Having wound our way through the triple gates of Erzerum (the Argiron of Marco Polo), I found that the town had already altered: pavements had appeared, avenues, electric wires as well as the embryo of a public garden. But the severe low houses with their layers of grey slabs interrupted by horizontal wooden beams still lined the streets—top-heavy, the flat roof projecting forward and so thick it was a wonder it did not crash to the muddy ground.

At the leading inn, the *Republic*, a commercial traveller was made to cede us his room!

On the southern slope of the desolate valley the ramparts of the citadel rise from a mass of fallen ground. Not a tree is to be seen. Seated between a stray cow and the shining bronze of an old cannon, we listen to the silence. A child slaps his cakes of dung against the wall of the rectangular citadel. The great blocks of rusty stone show traces of having belonged to finer and older buildings. When Theodosiopolis was built it was meant to defend the easternmost province of Byzantium.

Fired by a low sun that sinks at the end of the valley, the citadel is a flaming wall that seems to defy the ages. Dark silhouetted minarets rise above the dull town. Deadly yellow in the shade, the plain stretches far away. A rainbow links one sombre side of the valley to the other.

Turning our backs, we face a sharp contrast of colours: against a raven-black cloud and struck by the sun, the blazing flutings of two minarets shoot up from a dazzling façade: they rise above a narrow arched portal where turquoise shines softly among spirals of stone. It is the Chifteh Minaré. The good proportions, the pure lines of stones deeply chiselled and turned into sculptured leaves, Arabic lettering, double-headed eagle, are strikingly beautiful.

In spite of the delicacy of its columns, the inner courtyard is pervaded by a severe atmosphere; a small closed building stands at one end of the empty space, probably a *liva* for religious studies. When years ago I entered the stern Ulugh Beg medresseh at Bokhara-the-Noble, a somewhat similar impression of puritanical religion arose from the dead and silent court; though this last building built of brick at the end of the fifteenth century cannot compare with the proud stone Chifteh of the thirteenth.

In a forlorn enclosure behind its back wall is one of these tombs I find so fascinating—round, topped by a conical roof, made of great stones, simply ornamented by round arches outlined with rope-like mouldings. Some work had been undertaken to free the sunken base of the monument.

As we step into the uneven street, low clouds thunder threateningly; but my young friend is still sitting on his wall. A while ago, glad to see the bright face of a boy in this forlorn suburb, I had tentatively thrown at him: *Parlez-vous français?* and he had shyly answered in the same tongue. He was on the wall of his school. Now, keen to hear details about the Chifteh, I ask to meet his French teacher.

The sky breaks into cataracts and we rush to the entrance of the seminary where our new friend receives us. We are soon sitting by the desk of the principal, lamps are brought in and glasses of tea, while more than fifty great boys surround us, each with a question on his lips. We spend a splendid hour surrounded by their eagerness: it reminds me of the devouring curiosity that sometimes forced me on my way to school, to stop foreigners in the street and ask them where they hailed from.

A popular tradition says that the Persian Shah Katouivah ordered the building of the medresseh in the thirteenth century and that he is buried there. (If not a saint, I would like a Shah of Persia to have the sober round tomb I like so much!) But according to the archives relating to the building, it was founded in 1258 by Hundi Katun, daughter of Alaeddin Keykubad the Great, son of Keykusru I, Seljuk Sultan of Konya. In the seventeenth century it was turned into a foundry. During the Turco-Russian war of 1827, the Russians looted the place in the hope of finding gold ingots. But they only discovered old arms, casques, shields and swords, and Chaldean inscriptions. The splendid doors of the *liva* went to adorn a church in Georgia.

We left Erzerum disappointed: neither the chief of police nor the mayor would let us photograph the Chifteh: such was our lot for travelling without recommendations.

Armenia was cold, monotonous and unforgettable; a heavy wind raced over the wide plain that lies six thousand five hundred feet high. So short is the summer that wheat has to grow in sixty days, barley in only forty.

The silvery waters of the Arax meandered eastward along the high valley: they would soon glide out of sight, passing north of the Ararat, marking the border between Persia and Soviet Georgia, then ending in the Caspian.

Women armed with mallets were crushing wheat in a mortar. One of them (displaying an impressive set of false teeth) mocked my bare legs blue with cold though it was summer. She pinched them, showed me her wide bloomers and advised me to follow her fashion! In traditional Turkish style another woman had her eyebrows linked with black powder, but I took her to be Armenian or Kurd because of the small pill-box cap she wore under her head-cloth. In front of their ample yellow-red dresses, these three witches tied an apron round neck and waist; behind it the skirts seemed split to facilitate riding.

We were alone on the road except for a few "nightingales"— ox-carts with wheels clipped out of a single block of wood. They crawl at a snail's pace, their melodious axles heard over great distances. The aged atmosphere of the country was enhanced by the humpbacked bridge of Koprikoi built more than seven hundred years ago by the Seljuks. Nearby, five pairs of oxen dragged a plough as in the old days; but the machine bore the red Sovietic trade-mark "Krassni Zavod".

Even in summer this was a melancholy country: I shuddered to think what the long winter must be like. Here the first stanza of the *Vendidad* seems most appropriate, in which Ahura Mazda says to Zoroaster:

"I have made every land dear to its people even though it

had no charm whatever in it; had I not made every land dear
to its people even though it had no charm whatever in it, then
the whole living world would have invaded the Airyana
Vaego (the paradise of Zoroaster)."*

It was befitting to see rain pour down day after day, for we
were near Mount Ararat where the Ark is said to have landed
after the Flood. But such storms were out of season: the
Armenians were worried about their crops and we feared for the
track near the border where the road was not yet built.

We passed outside Taslichai where, arriving from Makou,
I had spent a noisy night two years ago. The abominable roads
had broken a spring and it was pitch dark as I walked in the
mud in search of a lodging. At a loss I shouted at the
middle of nothing: *Qui parle français par ici?* A voice free of
accent offered shelter nearby. A wonderful welcome awaited
us in the dormitory-refectory of half a dozen engineers of the
road. Immobilised in their wild "Far East" they felt like exiles
having visitors at last: raki flowed, coffee was made to the
accompaniment of a raucous gramophone. And the rickety
room soon shook to our marking time to the waltz:

Trink, Brüderlein, trink!

The chief's name was Adnan Bey. He said that already in
October the snow stopped their work. In winter the cold
sometimes reaches 50 degrees Centigrade below zero, Armenia
being for its latitude, one of the *pôles du froid* of our earth.

Finding myself driving once more through the same country
and supposing that Adnan Bey was still working here, at every
turn I expected to meet him again.

Another storm worthy of the Ark threatening the valley, we
stopped at a lonely police-post. Rough men in high boots and
leather jackets were camping there, road-builders whose food
we shared. We conversed in Russian, one of them being a
Georgian from Batum. Though an old man he was "too active
ever to retire". His son had a garage in Trebizond; his
daughter (he proudly showed us her photo) was studying
medicine in Paris, and he was sending her money regularly.

Our new friend Chorukh bore the name of the river that flows
between Turkey and Batum. He had studied mechanics at

* J. Darmesteter: *Zend Avesta.*

"Peterburg", had been chauffeur to a Russian general in Persia and now he was the chief of the twenty-two "zylinders" or steam-rollers used on this part of the road.

A rough and jovial fellow, the next morning he sat at the wheel of our Ford to drive us along that virgin road still closed to traffic. "You are my guests, I must look after you as long as you are on my road," he said. And when the car sat in the sand while we were fording a river, he whistled for men who seemed to spring up from among the reeds. In every sentence he used the words "my road" or "my daughter the road", proud that she was so expensive and had so many men at her service—(approximately 2,000 per kilometre.)

To the north-east and quite detached in the wide plain, the large conical base of the Ararat was now in full view, flanked by the small Ararat; but clouds hid the summit of the great mountain. When Noah came down these slopes still wet and softened by the Flood, what a fine day it was for a budding humanity: a new life was being started on a spotless page! Will it happen again? Shall we all depart but for one who will try to succeed where Noah failed?

Like abandoned toys in the grass, torn rails and discarded locomotives strewed the plain, remnants of the line built by the Russians during the 1914–1918 war. In this country devoid of any kind of industrial atmosphere (and where trees are a rarity) rails serve as joists, girders, transoms, railings around gardens and war-memorials. Along the road, here and there, boiler-plates replace a missing culvert.

Through the immensity of that dreary land we were now nearing New Bayazit: the cubes of its few houses gathered about oxen and lorries, about crates and piles of mud bricks just out of the mould.

To the south, high up in a rocky cleft, the proud castle of Old Bayazit ruled over the gloomy steppe, its minaret like a lighthouse watching out for the tides of coming barbarians. Two years ago I had seen it from the road; since then that castle had been a living regret beckoning at me across the distance.

Welcomed by a few Turks, we were led towards a tent where *pilau* was soon brought. I asked my neighbour where was Adnan Bey only to find that he *was* Adnan Bey and had recognised me at once! (I have seldom felt such a fool.)

Adnan's progress in two years was a hundred and forty kilometres.

He explained how interested the Persians were in his road, their shortest link with Europe; so far they could only use the roundabout way through Syria or the Caucasus. Knowing this, the Russians had charged such a high price for the transit of rails lately landed at Batum and which the Persians wanted badly, that the Shah had refused to pay it. These rails had then to come through Irak, since the five hundred and fifty miles of the Trebizond-Tabriz road could not yet take them.

With the trans-Anatolian railway reaching Erzerum from the West and the Iranian line soon reaching Tabriz, it is probable that these two towns will one day be linked by rail. Then Teheran will be the terminus of the railway system of south-eastern Europe.

Chorukh drove the car towards Old Bayazit over the five miles of steep track that was often nothing but rock polished by centuries of use. Bayazit was framed by cliffs showing beautiful streaks of green and red. But the eyes were drawn back to the promontory with the domineering castle bathed in light where the minaret points indefatigably towards the sky—Islamic Montserrat proud and alone in an Armenian sierra.

We left the panting car in the small village. We walked on and for a while were accompanied by a population rigged out in depressing cast-offs. The men were thin, long, with sad faces. Only one boy was well clad: his Georgian father owned the unique patch of green we saw, a walled-in garden squeezed half-way up the gorge. He was a pupil of the Erzerum seminary and knew some French.

We reached the level of the long wall of that ruddy-coloured fortress. Built of stones beautifully joined together, the great castle was said to have three hundred rooms—nowadays all ruined. I found no trace of enamelled tiles, the only touch of fantasy being a chequer of black and white slabs on the walls of a reception-room with splendid windows. I enjoyed the simplicity of courtyards linked together by arched gates. Panels of richly sculptured leaves gave a note of sumptuousness. Canals showed that once upon a time water must have flowed in from the mountain. The vast kitchen had a vaulted ceiling where two great arches crossed two others at right angles.

The mosque had a domed roof where stones were russet with old age; and ninety steps above it was the top of the striped minaret. From the tiny round balcony that shook in the great wind, the view was bewildering. Beyond the hovels of Bayazit cowering at our feet, the huge plain lay prostrate before the magnificence of snow-covered Ararat. Near us rose a wall of red cliffs whose crags were crowned with bold fortifications. And in the cliff-face, as if to remind us that we were in Asia, the square gash of a tomb like those of Persepolis; but hewn at its sides two bearded men evoked Assyria. I scrambled up to it with great effort only to see that there was nothing inside. I could only wonder who it was who had wanted to be buried in the wall of that eagle's nest.

In our excitement at exploring Bayazit we could not rest till, among the screeches of protesting choughs, we had reached the top of the cliff. From there, among rocks devoid of vegetation, the palace seemed to be on a level with the houses of the village. We tried to guess where the cannon-balls that had scratched the castle had been fired from. At last we tumbled back and landed by a plain mosque—minaret by a domed cube—that seemed very ancient. Resting against its wall, we looked at the sunset.

When I fall in love with a place I want to know who planned it, fought or lived in it. I wondered who was responsible for those stone cypresses in relief, symbols of immortality; for the cartouches set above square windows surmounted by arches in high relief, for the flat-faced lion whose raised tail winds among leaves and fruit; for a balcony-beam shaped into an elongated greyhound above a cantilever carved like a human face.

The fortress was first built by the Osmanli Sultan Yildirim Bayazit as a defensive measure against the ambitions of Timur the Lame, Emperor of Samarkand. The Sultan was defeated in the plain of Ankara in 1402 and taken prisoner by Timur; he died in captivity a year later.

In 1805 the officer Jaubert, under the orders of Napoleon, was sent to Armenia on a secret mission. He was arrested by Mahmut Pasha, a Kurd who ruled at Bayazit "in a palace (adjoining the old fortress) whose luxury astonished all who saw it." The tyrannic Pasha died of an epidemic of plague that nearly killed Jaubert too. But he had found a passage from his cell to the servants' quarters of the harem and escaped.

One traveller, J. Brant, wrote of Bayazit in 1835 that it was the most splendid palace of Anatolia. Another mentions the gilded drawing-rooms decorated with arabesques, the rare furniture, the precious carpets and treasure gathered there. The mosque, named after Belhul Pasha son of Mahmut, was famous for its proportions and the marble of its colonnade.

The Russians conquered Bayazit during each of their three wars with Turkey during the nineteenth century.

Ararat was still in full view, its dark flank brightened here and there by spangles of running water. We felt so much at the end of a world: a new world was bound to begin soon. In fact it is only when one has seen Makou—counterpart to Bayazit in the crack leading to Persia—that the full meaning of these two forts becomes clear.

As we rose to go, we were brought back to ourselves by the Georgian boy. "You must take more rest," he told me, "your son is very tired!"

As we left it at dusk, a pungent smell of burning dung floated above Bayazit. For once we did not discuss whether Armenians or Turks descend from the Hittites, but which style had inspired this palace.

10

AZERBAIJAN

WE limped along some thirty miles of bad track that separate Bayazit from Bazergan. These border-posts had not changed: at the Turkish one I recognised a starved cat, and a suckling woman with her towering head-gear reminiscent of Turkestan. She was squatting by the same stack of dried dung-cakes; but her child was noticeably bigger. The same idiot dragged a cart carved out of carrots, the same felt rugs were stretched to dry on a wall.

At the Persian post, a sort of great school-hall, we feared we should not be allowed to travel further. Though it vexed him, the official had to admit he did not know what to do with a *tryptique* and *carnet de passage*. So Christina filled up all the entries in his book. We saw that we were car number two entering Iran by this road.

Then our man discovered that the Egyptian Minister in Paris had delivered our visas; and he did not understand that this diplomat could act as substitute for the Iranian Minister away on leave. (Diplomatic passports can only be handled by a minister.) Having an ordinary passport, I had applied to the Iranian consul—only to learn that no visas were given at that moment. As a last resort, Christina had taken my document to the Egyptian Minister so that he might deal with us both, for she could not travel without me. In this way our papers had been provided with the indispensable formulas.

Convinced by our explanations, our border-official was at last prepared to let us go; but exhausted by our feat of eloquence, we were incapable of correctly counting our European bank-notes (the amount had to be entered in the passport). This error, discovered later when we wanted to leave the country, filled an hour with disagreeable tension.

We rolled down towards the Makou pass.

Like the wings of a stage-setting, two pink cliffs flanked the defile that even Timur could not conquer, though he had subdued fortresses like Van, Erzerum and Bayazit. Later, the great Shah Abbas decided to get rid of the Khan of Makou, a robber-chief who was spoiling with impunity the trade promoted by his efforts. With one soldier per trunk, two trunks per camel and four thousand camels to his caravan, Shah Abbas, disguised as a merchant, asked the Khan to shelter his goods within the gorge for the night. The Khan agreed and no sooner were all the camels brought in than the soldiers jumped out and conquered the place.

Whereas Bayazit contemplates the northern hemisphere from its rocky ledge, the flat houses of Makou facing south hide half-way up a concave slope where the sun never lingers for long. In their different ways these two villages are astonishing. Both had fulfilled the medieval requirements of life—ability to shelter people and defend them indefinitely. But nowadays adapting themselves to the demands of modern trade, they tumble helter-skelter to the level ground near the high road.

Though it was only five-thirty in the afternoon, for no particular reason we decided to remain in Makou.

No sooner had we reached the inn than out of a blue sky burst the most violent storm that I have so far seen. Night came. It went on pouring as if some wilful act were being performed. Uninterrupted lightning showed ominous violet clouds and sheets of pale water falling from the edge of the cliff. I don't know which was the more awe-inspiring, the noise of this new flood or the sight of that white cataract falling on the dark village from a height of two thousand feet.

By then our courtyard had become a deep reservoir (we were near the bottom of the slope where the gorge flattened out).

Raging torrent, shouting voices, crashing thunder and rumblings of the avalanche were all united in a mighty and terrifying roar. Dishevelled, dripping, muddy, livid creatures with their trousers rolled up above the knees soon invaded the inn. They wailed that they had lost everything: a river of pebbles had filled the main lane of the village to a height of six feet. Hammam and mosque had collapsed first. Cows were trapped or killed.

Meanwhile, unperturbed by this disaster, the son of the inn-keeper had seized my fountain-pen and was writing at my dictation the French translation of his long list of Persian words.

The new road was going to bring a stream of travellers to Makou and he was getting ready for them. He sat by the green-shaded oil lamp under which a reserved German had once told me that Hitler was the only living statesman not afraid to speak the truth.

Calm reigned once more by the time we went to our staved-in spring-beds—to fight sandflies above the sheet and fleas below.

In the light of the new day the cliffs were superbly scarlet against a deep blue sky. We scrambled up through the village where, among broken walls and fallen shelves, people were rescuing grain and their poor household articles. The mayor had decided not to rebuild the houses where they had been, but down on the flat by the new road. The sky had helped the times to move on. . . .

We dawdled under the overhanging cliff, trying to detect its secret: Makou is famous "for its gigantic cavern twelve hundred feet in span, two hundred thick and eight hundred deep. Immense granaries and room for three thousand men are said to exist inside the cliff. Within and carved on the rock, are inscriptions in an unknown language. The possessor of the stronghold received it under an oath never to permit strangers to mount into the interior or see the caves".*

We managed to enter a spacious inhabited house with two flagged courtyards of fine proportions; everything was decrepit, but traces of fountains and flower-beds spoke of past opulence. The front rooms had a lofty view of the amphitheatre: one felt near the eagles that swung along the cliff.

Makou is a natural border. Beyond it, no cloud, no rain, no mountain any more, but an undulating country, open, fertile, sunny. No longer the Latin characters now familiar to modern Turkey, but the sweeping curves of the Arabic alphabet. Tiny cups of syrupy coffee are replaced by big glasses of tea; and no more oxen and carts: from Makou to China the whole of Central Asia resounds with the spasmodic, strangulated braying of the ass.

No longer women in national costume or men with ample seats to their trousers and narrow sausage-like legs. Not a single stone house, but mud walls, wattle roofs; and everywhere the

* Lt.-Col. C. M. MacGregor: *Central Asia*, part iv.

sign of countries poor in wood—the dung-cake plastered on even surfaces. Except in towns, you will not find a door or window that locks: your privacy belongs to the past. Nobody would understand what you meant by it or why you could possibly want it—though you are in the country of the *anderun,* the room reserved to females. You belong to your host: his family and neighbours want to see and touch what you possess. You soon learn to comply with a good grace, remembering that it is the only contact travellers can have with Persians since, afraid of compromising themselves, their cultured compatriots in Teheran avoid you as a Russian avoids you in Moscow or a Japanese in Japan.

As for the Persian gendarmes, they show too much interest in your genealogy to be really charming. Water from the wells is often too brackish: to train your system to cope with it you are advised to eat raw onions with buttermilk. And the millions of flies are far too sticky and affectionate. But once you have risen above these small inconveniences, Iran is yours.

Turning and twisting among rounded hills, the road brought us to a river. We made our way nervously ahead: it was an opaque blood-red liquid whose depth could not be judged. Far, very far away, the high land was bordered with lilac and buff undulations.

We left behind us the region where red villages evoked those of the distant Atlas.

At Khoi the gendarme took me for the lady with the diplomatic passport, while Christina was addressed as my chauffeur!

Green Marand was even more beautiful than my memory of it. With its whitewashed houses and young poplars alive as pale birches, it might have been a rich Ukrainian village. It is said that the tomb of Noah's wife is at Marand: we did not try to see it. But we thought that many myths are at home in this part of the world, that the province of Azerbaijan where we found ourselves looks as ancient as Armenia. Only, her tired low hills appear *joyfully* old. We had admired the great Ararat: at the convent of Etchmiadzin on its northern slope they show a piece of wood said to have come from the Ark. It is also said that Noah is buried at Naksivan, the oldest city in the world. But the fame of Ararat is contested by the Muhammadans: they maintain that Noah's ship landed on Mount Djoudi in

Irak where dervishes have kept a lamp burning ever since. "The Ark rested by tradition on rising ground near Karbela— not on the mountain of that name miscalled Ararat by the Armenians" writes Sir Arnold Wilson, and he adds that this statement is endorsed by Sayce of Cambridge. "Jezirah ben Omar is an island on the Tigris at the foot of Mount Ararat and four miles distant from the spot where the Ark of Noah rested. Omar Ben Al-Khataab removed the Ark from the summit of the two mountains and made a mosque of it." (Travels of Rabbi Benjamin of Tudela, 1160–1173.)*

As for Zoroaster, one of the greatest among those who travelled along our road, he was born in Media, perhaps not far from where we were. He preached as far as Ghazni, south of Kabul. In the twelfth year of this renovated faith he converted King Vishtaspa of Balkh who ordered two copies of the sacred writings to be made.

It was not far from our Marand that Zoroaster, at thirty years of age, as he was sitting on the shore of the Vanguhi Daitya, a river of Azerbaijan, received a revelation from Vohu Mano, the Spirit of Wisdom, the Iranian Logos. This river, flowing north of Khoi, is the same Arax we had seen higher up in Armenia. The paradise of Zoroaster, the Eran Veg or Airyana Vaego, with its sacred mountain where Ahura Mazda answered his questions, was also not far from here. It was in the Eran Veg that the Maker Ahura Mazda told the good shepherd Yima:

"In course of time the earth shall be laid waste by the snows and rains of three long winters." In order to repeople his earth with superior races kind Yima is ordered to build an underground palace, the Var of Yima, where the finest specimens of human, animal and vegetable species will live till the moment when, the evil days being over, they shall open the doors of the Var and repeople the earth.

"There shall be no humpbacked, none bulged forward there: no impotent, no lunatic, no one malicious, no liar; no one spiteful, none jealous; no one with decayed tooth, no leprous to be pent up nor any of the brand wherewith Angra Mainyu stamps the bodies of mortals."†

---

* Contemporaries of Marco Polo, Komroff.

† J. Darmesteter: *Zend Avesta*.

Yima is said to have carried out these instructions. Looking at our wicked world, I wonder, then, what can have happened. Could the Maker have been deluded or did Yima make some mistake? Perhaps "kind Yima" was too kind and let into the Var his best friend who had a decayed tooth that made him jealous of Yima and so the trouble began all over again?

The latest effort at creating a small paradise was made in the Elbruz mountain which we were soon to see. In the eleventh century, a friend of Omar Khayyam, a learned Shia doctor named Hassan bin Saba, chief of the Ismailians, captured the castle of Alamut from the Seljuk Shah Melik Jelel-eddin. He became known as the Old Man of the Mountain and was the first Grand Master of that sect of missionaries; there his devoted Assassins or Hashishins, eaters of hashish, were given a glimpse of heaven. This garden of paradise was destroyed the following century by Hulagu the Mongol Il-Khan.

"The third Grand Master al Kabir bi Akham Allah Hassan openly ascended the throne in 1164 and proclaimed the great Resurrection. To his followers he prescribed spiritual worship, reducing the importance of the 'zahir' (sheria) as it is suitable to those who are saved and have entered the spiritual paradise. This paradisial state of the faithful is most probably the real basis of the well-known legend about the garden planted by Hassan bin Saba on the barren rocks of Alamut to imitate Paradise and dupe his followers."*

This third Grand Master was a descendant of Nizar. Through him as well as through the eighth Grand Master Ruknal-Din Kurshah is descended the present Aga Khan, who is thus the hereditary representative of Ismail, the seventh and last revealed Imam. In this sect of the seven Imams it is believed that the office of Imam would be held henceforward by a hereditary unrevealed Imam descended from Ali through Ismail.

From the top of the Arg we were looking at Tabriz, a wide expanse of flat houses within a dark circle of gardens in the middle of a yellow desert plain. At the horizon rose fluted hills of a purple which at sunset became splendid and intense.

I was interested to read what Marco Polo said about the

* Encyclopedia of Islam, suppl. vol. art, *Ismailiya*.

"large and very noble city" of Tabriz: "The merchants concerned in foreign commerce acquire considerable wealth
but the inhabitants in general are poor. They consist in a
mixture of various sects and nations, Nestorians, Armenians,
Jacobites, Georgians, Persians and the followers of Mahomet
who form the bulk of the population and are those properly
called Taurisians. Each description of people have their
peculiar language. The city is surrounded by delightful
gardens producing the finest fruits. The Mahometan inhabitants are treacherous and unprincipled. According to their
doctrines whatever is stolen or plundered from others of
different faith, is properly taken, and the theft is no crime; while
those who suffer death or injury by the hands of Christians are
considered as martyrs. If therefore they were not prohibited
and restrained by the powers who now govern them, they would
commit many outrages. . . . They have succeeded in converting
to their faith a great proportion of the Tartars, who consider
it as relieving them from restraint in the commission of crimes.
From Tauris to Persia is twelve days' journey."

Arg, or citadel, is a wrong name for the great wall we had
ascended: built under Ghazan Khan at the beginning of the
fourteenth century, it is the ruin of the Mosque Ali Shah which
must have had one of the biggest vaults that have ever been
built. The bricks are of such a quality that during the revolt
of 1933 they were not broken by machine-gun fire. The wall
on which we stood, twenty feet thick and more than a hundred
feet high, was fascinating me: the way the bricks were laid gave
the huge tower a spiralling movement that made me giddy.
The sharp shadows in spaces left free on either side of every
brick enhanced a pattern like the coarse side of plain knitting.
Below, at the far end of the open courtyard, spotless in daylight
stood a huge cinema screen. Below us where the arched
mihrab stood once to indicate the direction of sacred Mecca,
was throned the fire-proof cabin of a cinema-projector, new
god, and bestower of oblivion to our mass civilisation.

From our perch we could also see the church of the Lazarist
mission, belonging to a very much smaller sect of devotees.
There are not more than twenty-five thousand Christians in
Persia, mostly converts from the Armenian and Nestorian-
Assyrian faiths. The Superior, a Frenchman, told us how much

Iran had lately progressed: in the past, when a Father prepared to leave the town he used first to thrust two or three pistols through his girdle. We remarked how curious it was that France had no Minister in Teheran when it was so important to loosen the hold gained by Germany.

"I'll tell you" he said, "a Minister has been appointed but the Persians don't accept him: he has the 'evil eye'. During his stay in Afghanistan, King Nadir Shah was assassinated and when he served in Abyssinia, Ras Tafari was dethroned."* The priest continued: "One must add that, very susceptible like all parvenus, the Shah takes it as an insult not to be thought worthy of a Minister having served in one of the great capitals of the world."

That frame of mind was responsible for many incidents. The Americans of Iran had their newspapers confiscated for a long time because a crime of *lèse-majesté* had been committed in Washington, a Persian diplomat having been inadvertently imprisoned for driving too fast.

Paris too had been guilty when a gutter-sheet had published the pun: *Il n'y a pas là de quoi fouetter un Shah!* There was such a to-do about it that ever since the Quai d'Orsay trembled to think what might be published next day. To such an extent, in fact, that my editor in Paris had made me promise to have my articles passed by the Quai. In spite of my efforts at being a good girl, they did not pass. I had avoided the well-known crime of saying that veiled women had disappeared, though happily not all the camels. But this compliment of mine had perhaps been thought too indirect: ". . . lorry-drivers, those heroes of modern Iran, work sixteen hours a day. They lose no time for a midday meal: during the torrid halt they only pass around the opium pipe which gives them the needed calm to rattle along these infernal roads shaped into corrugated iron by the tearing on of overloaded trucks." How dare I mention opium in connection with the progressive kingdom of the modern Aryans!

Such was the xenophobia of the Shah that he had all posters bearing Latin or Russian script destroyed. So the cosmopolitan

---

* That minister ended by coming to Teheran and once more something happened to the ruler of the country, though not at once: Reza Shah Pahlevi was deposed and exiled. He died at Johannesburg in 1944.

inhabitants of Tabriz were adopting picture-posters that all could understand. A huge drawing of a jaw, for example, indicated a dentist. But the Shah could not prevent various foreign languages from being used orally in that big town. Had I not been awakened that morning by a roaring *Maroussia! Banya yest?*—a Russian asking for his bath?

Tabriz was the capital of the Mongol Il-Khans when the Polos arrived with their Mongolian beauty. But in the meantime the prospective husband Arghun Khan, had died. So they brought their precious charge to his son, the small Ghazan Khan who was warring in the East and who established himself on the throne two years later.

The famous Blue Mosque of Tabriz was built in the fifteenth century by Jehan Shah of the Black Sheep dynasty of Turkomans. Its brick walls had suffered greatly from invasions, earthquakes and wars, but nevertheless they moved me deeply. (I am no expert: I speak as a tourist comparing details seen at Khiva, Bokhara, Samarkand, Herat and Meshed.)

Its dark tiles are enchanting. Where traces of gold-painting sparkled over deep blue, it evoked a night sky. One great panel of faience-mosaic made me think of the time when one is in love, when one feels that never before has one really seen the splendour of the midnight heavens: the stars, no two of them alike, burn with such intensity they seem to come towards you. Imagine a corner of that sky but every star a coloured flower, then you have a hint of what I saw. This dark enamel has nothing in common with Prussian blue and its cold green afterglow: it is of a dark, dense ultramarine with a faint touch of deep red in it. I saw sculptured alabaster blocks with such rare jade-like shades that I should have liked to stay much longer to enjoy them.

II

ROADS

WE were in a bad temper.

The previous evening we told our policeman that to take advantage of the cool morning, we should leave the hotel at the crack of dawn. He had promised to bring in time the *javass* or document allowing our departure. But he never turned up. At nine o'clock we went to the police-station in search of a scapegoat. At eleven, rage having eaten away all our strength, we said nothing when at last the right man came and opened a drawer where our *javass* had been ready all the time. With an apology for his delay, he said that this document would save showing our incomprehensible passports at every post of control. So far we had been compelled to stop at either end of every village even when the two posts were within sight of each other—a law which had put a stop to the activities of brigands.

Because of that late start we were speeding along. I saw a white disk barred by a line (the sign meaning "control") but decided not to warn Christina, thinking that nobody could run after us. But yes: men in a side-car overtook and stopped us, read our *javass* and then commanded us by gestures to go back to their office. They skipped back thinking we were following them.

Seeing their mistake, they once more overtook us. These rascals were showing too much zeal: had they not seen we were provided with the best of documents? We went on. They yelled, cursed, drove alongside, took hold of our steering wheel. White with anger, Christina hit the arm that had caused a dangerous lurch. But with such mad men it was better to stop. The atmosphere was frightening. Something had to be thought out quickly! Yes, it worked: one of the gendarmes spoke Russian. Our inarticulate gibbering ceased, viewpoints were exchanged, the tension fell. In the end we all apologised, the man saying with great feeling:

"You are our highly honoured guests. It was very wrong of me to become so wild!"

Uncannily, the exasperated voice of that man seemed to pursue us though we were alone at last. It reminded Christina of another shouting scene in her home some fifteen years ago. Her grandfather came out of the room in which he had received a certain Adolf Hitler, complaining with his hands over his ears: "*Um Gottes Willen,* why must the man shout like that all the time?"

Because lorry-drivers gave us a hand when we changed a wheel, we also stopped whenever a truck had pulled up by the road-side. Once, as we gave some patching material, we were astonished to see a tube covered with many layers of repairs: we learned that tyres and tubes were as rare as gold.

For the wedding of the Crown Prince which had taken place two months before, all the cars in Teheran had been requisitioned by the Shah. They were punctually returned but their tyres had been replaced by worthless ones! There is such a lack of tyres and lorries in Iran that even the trucks of the Anglo-Iranian Oil Company—the uncrowned queen of the country—were sometimes seized by army officers and stripped of what they needed. Such dealings would continue until the manager of the A.I.O.C. warned the Shah that since his work was being interfered with, the much-needed oil-royalties coming to the Shah would be diminished at the next pay-day.

Blankets used to cover the wheels of lorries during the mid-day halt. It was to preserve the tyres from a possible sun-burst. We followed that example.

In a good inn furnished with tables and chairs there was an original collection of oleographs—many European kings and queens, naked beauties pinned on either side of stern Hindenburg, a geisha beside a bishop raising his hand to bless; and, best of all, a superb calendar showing Jesus, the Aga Khan, Edison and other great men grouped around Ataturk and Reza Shah in the middle of the scene. We were told that the Shah was undoubtedly a great man. Nevertheless he had always postponed a journey to the industrialised countries of Europe—afraid to discover perhaps, that all he had built in Iran was not so perfect as he would have liked to believe.

In that room I found the explanation of something that had

been puzzling me since 1937. Many lorries dragged a thick chain between their front wheels as if escaping from prison. The chain was meant to prevent an accumulation of electricity on cars whose shiny bodies have for hours rubbed against the fast, compact wind of these flinty and calcinated highlands: a shock might hurt the first man to step down from a vehicle overcharged with electricity.

Mercilessly driven lorries that have a merciless three-ton overload; jolting lorries that get deadly exhausted after two years' service (having then earned the price of a new machine, why worry?); trucks rumbling day and night ahead of their evanescent plume of dust; roads that bring resurrection to places thousands of miles away. . . . "To me it is the multitude of rough transport-drivers, filling all the roads of England every night, who made this the mechanical age," wrote T. E. Lawrence to Robert Graves. This is also true of Iran. Dozens of textile and flour-mills, of ginning—cement—soap—and cigarette-factories, sugar-refineries, wireless stations—each of them before being assembled, had been imported bit by bit over these long roads of Iran.

We came to an overturned truck. On the road stood grim-looking boxes of great size marked ELEVATOR! Two men sat in the shade of the chassis—the only dark spot in the heart of the immensity. They had already been here for forty-eight hours, waiting for a rescue party. The Persian driver cried:

"It is not my fault, what could I do? It is bad luck. God willed it. . . ."

The Russian mechanic who had accepted a *papiross* from Christina's tin of "Camels" retorted:

"God? Poor fool, what are you talking about? You know as well as I do that God exists nowhere but in your silly head!"

Thus Soviet ideas are imported too, not only machines.

I think that this sudden growth of transport facilities, especially in Turkey, Iran, Afghanistan, Russia, Manchoukuo, China, countries I have visited, discloses the background of our time: fear of too mighty neighbours. Roads are needed to build up industries. But this development—ultimately good for the people of the country, let us hope, though nowhere do men look more harassed than in our industrial lands—is primarily meant to increase the strength or the revenue of the state. And this revenue goes first of all to building a strong army, an army much bigger than the internal policing of the country would require. That army is urgently needed, for powerful neighbours notorious for their grabbing propensities might walk in at any moment. Fear! Fear of war is the pivot, the mainspring of activity in all awakened countries—and not only there.

Without oil, the mainstay of transport in Iran now that caravans are no more, the people would starve. Luckily there is oil in the south, though it is owned by a British company (that used to pay a yearly average of two and a half million sterling to the Shah). Oil is also, by far, the main export of Iran. All this means that in spite of the one thousand nine hundred very active Germans living (then) in the country and in spite of a powerful Russian neighbour, Great Britain still controls the destiny of Persia.

In a dark and low *chai-khana* we were once more sipping glasses of hot tea in the hope that it would wash away the dust that parched our throats. All of a sudden two strong men speaking Swiss-German rushed into the hut, eager to meet the owner of the Swiss car, a rarity in Iran. They were soon showing us the way to their camp, having decided to let their work look after itself: they were building the railway from Kazvin to Tabriz.

Over tankards of beer we spoke about the trans-Iranian line. It was not only finished but working along its eight hundred miles, from the Persian Gulf to the Caspian. According to some critics it was an expensive luxury (it cost forty million sterling) that would not free Iran from the economic hold of Russia: hundreds of miles away from the main traffic such a line was useless. I remembered how two years ago people who pretended to be well informed had said that technical difficulties were insuperable: the line would never be finished. "Only a miracle could make this line a reality," wrote G. Reitlinger in 1930. The miracle took place: one has to admit it and own it to the Shah!

But I have often noticed that Westerners have an inborn tendency to minimise or ridicule whatever the Persians do—

not because it is badly done, but simply because they are exasperated by the pride of the Persian who boasts that what he has done is "the best in the world". They do not see that among Asiatics this attitude is the inevitable reaction to the condescension with which Westerners brought their mechanical progress to the East as if it were a revealed religion capable of healing all ills. "Europeans know everything better than everyone else and can do everything better than anyone else. For a hundred years they have been nurturing in 'natives' a feeling of inferiority owing to their own attitude of superiority. It has been one means of consolidating their power. Nowadays it is turning on them and showing itself in an inferiority complex that is manifested sometimes in a hatred of foreigners, often in suspicion and always in great sensitiveness. . . .

. . . Modern European invasions are carried out under the banner of humanity and progress: to bring poor, pitiful backward people out of their state of darkness. The "poor things", who feel themselves to be infinitely superior in mode of life and in courtesy to their blunt and unceremonious invaders are nevertheless nonplussed by the fact that these people can speak into a black tube and carry a conversation across miles of intervening country."*

Two years ago I had met a few Swiss engineers at work, so I have some notion of the difficulty of building roads in Iran. On the Chaluss highway, the most direct link between Teheran and the rich provinces south of the Caspian, there was a workers' camp nine thousand feet up near the Kandevan pass. That impressive road was one of the most cherished constructions of the Shah who felt that the Pahlevi-Kazvin road was dangerously near the Russian border.

Dug under the pass, a tunnel not only avoided a few zigzags of the road but it dodged the heavy snowfalls that stop all traffic in winter. I have seldom come across steeper, longer and more barren hills than those near Kandevan where roofed galleries protect the road from landslides. Though apparently built on a safe shoulder of the mountain, part of the workers' camp had been swept away by a snow-slide; as for the car of the chief-engineer, it could be seen at the bottom of the huge ravine, a small, discarded, rusting toy.

* M. Boveri: *Minaret and Pipe-line.*

As a full-blooded autocrat, the Shah had ordered where he wanted the tunnel to start.

"Your Majesty's decision might perhaps be slightly altered considering that the yearly avalanches crash down just at that place."

"I have spoken, it is enough."

Disobedience was out of the question: engineers had to rack their brains to cheat avalanches rather than the King of Kings. To enforce the will of one man, six hundred workers and thirty-four European specialists were fighting a mountain armed with such weapons as loose shale, dangerous scree, slime and mush, or sulphurous infiltrations that disintegrated the cement-work of the tunnel. All that was part of the game.

But unexpected man-made obstacles were wearing out the energy of our engineer and with us he could unburden his heart at last. "The previous engineer made an error of three metres in his calculation of the level of the northern and southern heads of the tunnel—to say nothing of the phantasy of his budget." Each day brought a new problem. No work was possible without materials and no materials without transport. But no transport could be had, for the Army had seized the twenty-three lorries allotted to the Chaluss road. "Meanwhile the tropical dampness of a Caspian harbour was spoiling our cement heaped up in the open. Since the wrathful Shah may condemn someone to death if the road is not finished in time, we had no alternative but to annex a passing procession of lorries on their way to fetch coal. So the situation has been saved—this time!"

The Swiss engineer had had enough of Iran: even if the Shah's government were ready to pay him a new contract entirely in European currency, he was determined not to stay here a day longer than he could help. He would rather kick his heels at home than sign on here for another three years.

In the living-room at night, I found the specialists reading their newspapers. One look at these sheets made me think of the Tower of Babel: side by side on the long rough table were the *Province de Namur*, the *Volkischer Beobachter*, the *Feuille d'Avis de Neuchâtel*, the *Politiken*—not to mention Czech and Spanish names unknown to me.

A placid little man holding up the *Neue Zürcher Zeitung* told me: "I only read it to know who died!" Quite so.

12

NIKPEH

BADLY begun, the day did not end very well.

We stopped at a tiny oasis. Near a derelict caravanserai, a single wheat-field was glowing softly in its setting of coarse desert.

The tent was hardly pitched when two gendarmes in bright blue uniforms made us move to the small garden in front of their hut. Against our will we accepted their invitation, the tent was struck and carried there in a lump. We were soon preparing our supper while, all in a flurry, the good men tried to make themselves useful. The petrol stove was refilled. To one gendarme who had held his match-box ready for the last five minutes, a bit too soon I gave permission to light the burner.

Flames spurted from the earth, from my foot, and then from my hand when I threw shoe and sock away: robed in a blue flame, that hand burned like a plum-pudding. Then the sleeve of my blazer caught fire: I clearly saw myself entering into death as a living torch. It was a rare experience. I was so interested in watching every thought that rose in me that I had no time to feel anything. When would fear come? Was this not one of those occasions when you tear down the nearest curtain to roll yourself in it? I did the next best thing and wrapped myself in our small tent.

Then I had to console the little gendarme who was genuinely weeping: "Ayah! It is all my fault! O Allah!" or words to that effect. No: I alone was guilty. In the failing light I had spilled so much petrol that the earth was soaked with it. (Though this did not prevent my thinking to myself that too much dancing attendance is most upsetting.)

After all there was little damage. The swollen back of my right hand looked like a glove filled with water to bursting point. At one place raw flesh showed—from the tent-wrapping exercises I had performed to satisfy the demands of "tradition". A greasy dressing was tied around it; our supper was cooked and eaten; and soon we were lying down under mosquito-nets belonging to the Iranian Police.

Once more I had the proof that I can look at myself with detachment and that curiosity is uppermost in me. In my greatest moments, in danger, in love, I remain a spectator of myself. I shall never suffer so intensely, then, as Christina suffers: I cannot become entangled in the show I am witnessing. (Of course there is this possibility: that Christina deliberately chose to play a tormented part during her lifetime. If so, my clumsy advices and simple verdicts were useless.)

I slept a massive sleep, helped no doubt by a formidable swig of brandy. But Christina (who felt the need to drink the other half of the flask) hardly slept at all—imagining that I was heroically bearing torture in silence. (Pain came, thick and hard, two days later: the doctor carved away the rizzled skin and showed me how to sprinkle the red wound with tannic acid once every fifteen minutes. He wisely left me (he had to go to church) and I performed that infernal spraying while tears and perspiration rolled down my body. It was the quickest way to build a scab and without it the journey was impossible: for two days my hand had been trickling so much that I kept it outside the car to let the lymph drip on the road.)

As Christina mentioned her night spoilt by a worry that was groundless, in a flash I knew for certain that heaven and hell are here and now—the consequence of what our ignorance leads us to think. And what fools we are to let the projections of our own mind shape a vale of tears! I could prove it to Christina: the beauty of a wall, the joy of a symphony can, most probably, not be felt by my milk-boy. Beauty, pain, joy, are not intrinsic to a thing, an event, they are nowhere but within me. Therefore, since these latent feelings dwell within me, I can learn to bring forth from my being pure and unconditioned joy, . . . I can shape my world.

But it was useless to speak to Christina along that line: first I must discover why again and again she chose the complicated, cruel way of hell. Could it be that she preferred it to an easier mode of living? Did she believe it was a quick way of exceeding the limitations of her individuality? Having lived with Thomas Mann and his family she perhaps agreed with the hero of

The Magic Mountain when he says: *Zum leben gibt es zwei Wege: der eine ist der gewöhnliche, direkte und brave. Der andere ist schlimm, er führt über den Tod, und das ist der geniale Weg.* Was suffering something so wonderful that though conditioned by the mind, it miraculously helped to transcend the mind? Probably she knew more than I. I was only sure of one thing: she was wrong in identifying herself with a being obsessed by fear.

But if grief had taken her to the threshold of a world unknown to me, would she have been in such despair?

It is very likely that she herself did not clearly see the path she was following. The first time I saw her—how well I remembered the impression she made on me!—she had climbed the worn-out steps of the Baer Hotel in Zürich, a quaint, silent inn where my uncle the engineer had a *pied à terre*. It was a bright summer day. Hatless, smart in a grey suit, so thin that she was almost ethereal, she sat most of the time drooping and silent. At first I thought she hearkened to some inner music. Then I knew she was searching: she listened beyond the words just spoken in the hope of catching a lingering resonance from a world endowed with more significance than ours: she was waiting for a fundamental note. Or to use another metaphor, she looked beyond us as if we were so many prisms, trying to catch a gleam from the original undifferentiated light.

One thing was certain: she believed in suffering. She worshipped it as the source of all greatness. And that day for the first time I asked myself if she was able to bear her misery because something in her enjoyed it? If so, would she be able to complete that movement, thus turning hell into heaven?

When she begged to be helped out of her vicious circle, it was probably only a part of herself that longed to live normally. Thus the crises that composed her life were exhausting her. She was a sober violin whose cords had been made of her own heart-strings: while she played she was wearing herself out. Unable to transcend her torment, was she not doomed like modern Europe, enacting a suicide in successive instalments? To fall in full awareness from one gehenna into another was

* "There are two ways of life: one is the accustomed, safe and proper way; the other is hard and illegitimate, it leads through death, and that is the daring, the enlightened way."

the only way she knew of bringing head and heart simultaneously to life. Thus she waded through self-made trials that no one else could have borne.

And she was torn, as well, between the desire for that intense living that enlarged her consciousness and the fear of not obtaining it. The slave of her want, she was impatiently forcing the process of her life. And in the trough between two waves of intensity she felt so numb she thought that she was dying.

"Do you really enjoy life?" she would ask me again and again, or: "How do you live?" She meant: How can you bear the worthless trough? Where is the source of your patience? Are you sincere when you say that life is good? I hid from her that the moments of perfect fullness that show what life could be are desperately rare, but I seek that fullness in joy, not in a gulf of woe.

Once more I tried to change the trend of her ideas; but I knew how childish my effort was, for every day I saw more clearly how our inner life conditions all things belonging to the objective world. I emphasised the "shout" of a red flower against the blue of the sky, the joy of every step of ours that we had freely chosen. We had just met two proud beggars, young fair-haired Russians escaped from Soviet Turkestan four years ago. They had to "kill" two years more before they could become Persian citizens and thus be able to live otherwise than by hook or by crook. At present they could only work for a few days in a garage or on a farm—as long as their employers had not discovered that they had no passports. The handsome boy came from the Kouban, the other from Ashkhabad where he had worked in a printing press. They had risked their escape because "the bread was too sour and pay-day too rare". There were many like them. Near Shahrud they had built shelters where they were dying of malaria or dysentery; and their women could not stand the cold winters. Long ago they had sent their names to an organisation in Teheran, but what of that?

These boys had so few hopes, but they went on struggling. They had no books, no news of the world. The printer had started a diary which had been a great help; but in its fear of everything Russian, the police had taken it. Two friends of theirs had lately hanged themselves. When we parted the printer said:

"You go towards friends who are waiting for you. You do not know what a happiness that is!"

His remark had deeply moved me. We never appreciate enough what we have. And I used the incident to show to Christina how lucky we were.

Though we differed much we had much in common. Both of us were trying to earn a living—I since I had to, she because she would have been pleased to forgo her allowance. Each of us lived, as a rule, by herself. We had deplored the poor quality of the love we could offer; we knew that love should be a full and complete movement of the heart and so far it had always miscarried. Very thoughtfully she had asked me once: "Kini, what is wrong with me? Those I loved most, X, Y, Z, Mother even (I would have given my life to 'find' them again)—how is it that I could not settle the practical side of our relationship? Though at first they are devoted to me, I soon scare them, torture them with my love, with my impetuous demands . . ." "You are perhaps like me" I suggested, "in love with your idea of love and not at all with persons!" "They tell me I destroy their lives . . . And after some time they even hand me over to strangers or to doctors. Unwilling to submit to their silly rules, I end in the strait-jacket. Yet every doctor has begun by saying that I am absolutely normal . . ." "Yes, I have seen how you exhaust them. You want a love that is not compatible with our present limitations."

We were both travellers—she always running away from an emotional crisis (not seeing that she was already wishing for the next), I always seeking far afield the secret of harmonious living, or filling up time by courting risk, caught by the clean sharp "taste" it gives to life. Both of an active type, but while I repeatedly challenged myself to convince myself that I am not a worm, she on the contrary felt so unimpeachable that she could not imagine how any excess or experiment could touch either her health or her innocence. "How can a drug tried out of curiosity ever harm me, Christina?" That is what she had said in Berlin years ago.

Mentally we were very different. She was a poet moving among ideas shaped and enlivened by her imagination, her moods changing the world. Whereas I still believed in the reality of facts as such, thinking the external world responsible for my subjective life. Thus my rate of vibration was much lower than hers and when I try to explain her as I do now, I betray her by dragging her to my level. And I could the less elucidate her contradictions since I avoided questioning her about herself. I thought it important to turn her attention elsewhere. Only when she sent me a shattering letter from New York a year later, did it cross my mind for the first time that she might leave this world without warning.

But we were akin in our devotion to something we could not name. We had both wanted to remain free the better to fulfil in due time a paramount obligation towards ourselves, a trial or obligation whose nature was still hidden. This might be called selfish, but I was beginning to see that our total allegiance could be offered to nothing but an absolute before which we should disappear.

13

SULTANIEH

As we moved towards Kazvin, a flicker in the plain was our first glimpse of Sultanieh: the glazed bricks of the high mausoleum were reflecting the sun. Leaving the road, bumping over dried-up irrigation grooves, we approached the former capital of the Il-Khans, abandoned since an earthquake had choked its water-supply.

When a tree or a rock stands alone in the nothingness of a desert, it partakes of the surrounding greatness by centring upon itself the radiations of immensity; this is the charm of Tibet, this void around the simplest object. How much greater is this charm when in the middle of an empty plain the old tomb of Oljaitu stands aloof in simple grandeur—a gigantic egg in a massive hexagonal egg-cup towering above the land of Media.

When you reach the monument, the turquoise cupola becomes invisible: you see only the stern walls, each hollowed at the top by a triple-arched loggia. Above each of the six angles, a small round tower gives lightness. In style it is a Persian version of the Seljuk tomb built for Sultan Sanjar at Merv in 1157. It bears the date 1316 and was commissioned by Sultan Oljaitu of the Mongol dynasty of the Il-Khans. Panels filled with raised geometrical patterns are coated with a turquoise glaze that shines like charmeuse silk against the wall of rough salmon-coloured bricks.

The intense turquoise of old Persian monuments can be compared to nothing else. Against the sky it looks green, against the foliage of Samarkand it is blue. It is to the raw turquoise stone what the kingfisher's feathers are to the azure of the sky; I want to call it Central-Asian blue because of a glacial lake of the T'ien Shan which displayed that irradiant saturation of sky-blue tempered with green.

At Sultanieh, no arabesque, no tender note like the flowered panels of the Blue Mosque. Except, above a door, elegant motifs of thin stucco-work looking like crochet-lace.

When I entered that ruined and desecrated building, the simple structure at once conveyed its meaning: I stood still, with respect for something great. Slowly my mind rose towards the peace, the fullness of the inner dome some hundred and fifty feet above me. Form alone counted now, for delicate paintings and inscriptions had become mere shadows. The mellow light from lofty windows was like the promise of a wide, rich outlook—if only one could rise to their height!

I was captivated: here was a very simple monument that had suddenly become important to me. I was eager to learn details about it.

It was the tomb of Sultan Oljaitu Khodabendeh who ruled from 1303–1316, though it had been built to contain the remains of Ali, the son-in-law of the Prophet. To-day nothing can be seen of the grave, but in 1637 a member of the Duke of Holstein's embassy to the Safavid court saw "the reliques . . . preserved by a grate of Indian steel, polished and wrought Damask-wise, the bars being about the bigness of a man's arm."*

In Mongol, Oljaitu means "fortunate". The name was given to the Sultan to commemorate his birth. His mother was at that time crossing the waterless desert of Merv and though the caravan was afraid of dying of thirst, it had to stop for a few days. Happily a most unexpected rainfall relieved everyone's anxiety. After his wife had converted him to Islam, Oljaitu was also known under the name of Khodabendeh, Servant of God. During his childhood his mother, Uruk Katun, had him baptised into the Christian Church under the name of Nicolas.

Oljaitu succeeded his brother Ghazan (who had married the Princess Kogatun brought by the Polos). It was of Ghazan that King Haithon of Armenia wrote: "It is astonishing how so many virtues can reside in so diminutive and so ugly a person." Poor Kogatun, so beautiful and so young! Had she been unhappy with such a husband and may that have been the cause of her premature death?

Ghazan Khan had been converted to Islam in the company of his hundred thousand Tartar soldiers—which reminds me of the Christian General Feng Yu Hsiang who some years ago

* Filmer: *Pageant of Persia.*

Bulgaria: road wide open ahead . . . free to travel with car, tent and companion (Chap. 3)

On the Black Sea: landing at Trebizond (Chapter 7)

Istanbul: Sultan Ahmed mosque . . . drawn up from above . . . (Chapter 6)

Kurdish Armenia : motherhood (Chapter 9)

Minaret of old Bayazit (Chapter 9)

Tabriz Blue Mosque: the best mosaics I have seen (Chapter 10)

I evoked the Tower of far away Ghazni (A.D. 1080 or 1114) "Remember King Kabus of a thousand years ago" (A.D. 997) (Chap. 15)

Curing a 'kanat' of its mud (Chapter 16)

Golden dome and blue mosaics of sacred shrine   (Chapter 17)

Tall driver of my Afghan lorry (Chapter 16)

Kirghiz refugee at Herat (Chapter 20)

A country where women's faces are not seen

At the foot of the great Buddha (Chapter 26)

Family of Mandozai nomads high up on the Hazarejat plateau (Chapter 26)

Radiant manhood of a fair-eyed shepherd (Chapter 27)

"We saw at our feet a huge surface of polished bronze . . ." (Chapter 27)

Cock and hen are taken along too (Chapter 27)

baptised his Chinese army with the hose of a fire-engine.
Ghazan Khan died in 1304, the first Mongol sovereign to make
his burial-place known: so far, in accordance with the custom
of their people, Mongol rulers had always concealed their
tombs. Oljaitu—a descendant of Genghis Khan in the fifth
generation—heard of the death of his brother Ghazan when he
was twenty-four: he kept it secret until he had killed a possible
pretender to the throne.

Sultan Oljaitu knew a good deal of what was going on in the
world. He received embassies from China, one of them
announcing a truce between the two rulers. He corresponded
with Philippe le Bel, Edward the Second and Pope Clement V.
His ambassadors must have concealed the fact that he had
become a Muhammadan, for his royal correspondents expected
his help in "extirpating the abominable sect of Mahomet".
Oljaitu used seals of State bestowed by the Great Khan and
otherwise called himself *daruga*, Governor.

Reading of his conversion one gets a glimpse of the life at
Sultanieh where the court resided in summer time, after the
winter in Baghdad. Belonging to the Sunni sect, the Sultan
had put to death a man who tried to convert him to the Shiite
doctrine. But later, witnessing a dispute between Sunni
doctors of the Hanafi and Shafii sects who in the heated argument "brought against each other abominable accusations,
Oljaitu was greatly annoyed with both and even the Mongol
nobles, who were by no means squeamish, professed disgust
and began to ask whether it was for this that they had abandoned
the faith of their ancestors, to which they now called Oljaitu
to return". The Il-Khan was further alarmed by a thunder-
storm "which according to the Mongol belief is a signal of
divine displeasure. He adopted the Shiite creed after having
had a vision of Ali's tomb which convinced him that the
homage of the faithful was due, after the Prophet, to Ali and
his descendants".* He had the names of the Imams engraved
on the money he coined.

At thirty-five Oljaitu died at Sultanieh from an attack of
gout. "Virtuous, liberal, not readily influenced by calumny;
but like Mongol princes addicted to spirituous drinks and
chiefly occupied with his pleasures." His obsequies were

* E. G. Browne: *Literary History of Persia.*

celebrated with great pomp. Intrigues among his ministers gave rise to the accusation that he had been poisoned.

The twenty-year-old Abu Said succeeded Oljaitu and reigned for twenty years. Life was stormy at Sultanieh during that period. Chouban, Amir of Public Affairs, who had married Abu Said's sister, was becoming every day more powerful. Arrogant and immoral, his son Dimashq was engaged in an intrigue with one of Oljaitu's former concubines. Found out he failed to escape. His head was exhibited over one of the gates of Sultanieh.

The moral laxity of Sultanieh was held responsible for the great famine of 1319. Abu Said closed all brothels and allowed but one wine-shop in each district, and that for travellers only.

Abu Said died in 1335 from a fever caught while fighting an army from Kipchak; or perhaps he was poisoned by his wife Baghdad Katun, jealous of her younger rival Dilshad. He was buried in Oljaitu's tomb.

In 1335, too, was born Timur the Lame who was to put an end to the dynasty of the Il-Khans after having destroyed most of Sultanieh.

In the seventeenth century, Tavernier wrote that Sultanieh was again a large city where "many Christian churches were converted into mosques; and if you will believe the Armenians they will tell you that there were in Sultanieh near eight hundred churches and chappels".

As I left Sultanieh, the proud tomb reminded me of a Persian saying, quoted by Upham Pope: "Great art makes one strong and young and glad." Standing silently at one of the cross-roads of Asia it was the symbol of a time when rulers were of Mongol character though baptised in the Christian faith and converted to Islam—strength, new faith and ruthlessness were blended in this unique monument.

14

TEHERAN

THREE different houses, three ways of living, three swimming-pools (translucid trembling hearts of tidy gardens)—might summarise our enforced stay at Teheran.

First we went to Dr. Davies' bungalow tucked away in a corner of the British Legation at Gulhek. Our weariness was welcomed by a home open to us with simplicity—soft light of the lamp-shades on the veranda, silky blackness of a cocker spaniel on the rug, quiet euphoria imparted by tall glasses of pale whisky offered before and after dinner. The golden marmalade throned over the breakfast-table in the morning while noisy children splashed in a clear pond lined with sky-blue tiles. We had gone straight to the good doctor in order to show him my hand. After a few days we made room for other visitors.

We then found ourselves in the Persian summer-house of the Vernazzas—a narrow building with an elevated veranda where three stylised arches opened on to a symmetrical garden. Its venerable pool was not accustomed, I suppose, to see, lingering on its edges, so many women clad in skin-tight suits. The jade of its opaque water shone with a lustrous gleam where refracted sunrays penetrated the shaded regions. In the smart interior, small glasses of brown vermouth were drunk as aperitif, and "fine Champagne" after dinner. The good food was discussed during meals rounded off with velvety aromatic coffee. There, the parents tenderly watched their only child.

But the heat was so oppressive that we moved once more.

Our third tank, in the midst of a rock-garden, was breath-takingly cold: a *kanat* brought its waters straight from the Elburz range that bars the sky north of Teheran. These three gardens were all in Shimran, the great oasis in the desert of pebbles that slopes between town and mountain. They were only a few furlongs apart: the great variation of temperature between them was due to air-currents.

This last pool refreshed the park of the German Legation.

In the shade of stately plane-trees, five point-nosed dachshunds were fretting about like so many baby seals. The house was in European style and solidly built, fit frame for the frothy beer drunk at all hours of the day and night. After dinner everyone settled in the "bar", a depressing place *à la Turque* where the Herr Minister sampled schnapps. His son used to take leave early for he was working at a thesis on the Bahrein Islands, those juicy apples of discord of the Persian Gulf.

We had been installed in the *Kavalier Haus* or guesthouse, with the words: "You can stay here till you decide to go home, for you won't be allowed further East."

All the servants, gate-keeper, gardener, and sempstress included, made the Hitler salute whenever we passed; some of them felt obliged to tell us in pidgin-German that the English were *Bssiar harab*, very bad—not knowing, I suppose, that we had just been staying in the compound of the British Legation. The cook, an energetic Persian whose badly dyed hair was painful to see and whose roars (worthy of the kitchens of the Carlton) too often hurt my ears, showed us the *Breslauer Zeitung* where his name was mentioned in connection with his fifty years' faithful service to Germany.

By our first pool I was unwell, upset by a throbbing hand. By the old tank in the Persian garden the heat was such that we could not sleep at night. Near the cool German waters I toiled at my articles or worried about my friend, a prey to that alternate movement which, during the whole journey, swung me from the objective to the subjective world.

At Dr. Davies' the talk was mainly of itineraries, camping-grounds or travelling improvements.

At our French friends' the habit was to review the gossip of the town. Charming Prince Firouz, the owner of Christina's house at Farmanieh? The poor man had "died" in prison lately; he had the bad luck to be related to a pretender once supported by the British. What was being said about Maud Rosen's book? She had flattered Sardar Akram, her faithful and witty guide, and then took down every word he said. He belonged to one of the two families who could with impunity mix with foreigners—which meant that they must be informants of the Shah. Others who followed their example met with disgrace or death. In our enlightened century there was more than one country whose subjects did not dare meet the Europeans who longed to know them otherwise than through their poetry. Yes, the Shah saw, knew and willed all that took place.

Had we heard the latest? He was to visit an out-of-the-way village. The mayor had not obeyed the royal order to plant young trees; to replace them he had newly cut branches stuck along the high street. The Shah came and departed, having said nothing in particular. But a week later, like thunder out of a blue sky, he returned when all the branches had withered. They say that the mayor was shot for having tried to delude the King of Kings.

In the vast rooms of the German Legation the talk was of power-politics. Yes, the Persian people were shockingly poor, but so were the Prussians before they became strong. Only a tyrant could obtain results in a country as rotten as Iran. "The liberal ideas that flourish in the West are out of place here, I assure you, said Herr Sment sharply, and you would see it too if you were not blinded by preconceived ideas. It is the Shah's duty to amass a great fortune as quickly as possible: he thus assures the future of his dynasty and makes a new revolution impossible."

Though the Germans in Iran were ten times more numerous than any other foreign colony, they had no political views on the country, only commercial ones, the Minister wanted us to believe. Their goal had been reached at last, but only after the best businessmen had come in person from Germany.

During a dinner we sat near the brothers Mezzaforte, twins who, long ago, had been made Counts and Persian subjects at the same time. Pianoforte and Whiskyforte, as they were nicknamed, laughed at England's courting of Russia, the clay-footed colossus—an alliance that would be helpless against the strong Italo-German block. Taking our silence for approval, someone added that Hitler was a saint who was saving Europe from the Bolshies. Christina calmly remarked that a saint would never use the methods of a gangster. When the man retorted that she was simply a victim of press-propaganda, I saw my friend stiffen under the fierceness of her anger.

Our host did not hide his Nazi ideas. But his son was at that moment affected by the periwinkle eyes of the daughter of the British Minister, so he affirmed that the English had one mission on earth—to polish and refine the Germanic race. (Convinced that we could not continue our journey, he nearly went away with our car to follow Periwinkle, who was camping on the slopes of the Demavend!)

The father thought we should never get our papers. He, a most influential person in Teheran, was unable to send on four very busy businessmen who were on their way from Germany to Kabul; for the last three weeks they had fumed in their hotel in Teheran, cursing Herr Sment for the delay, not believing that the authorities could be opposed to their journey.

The cholera broke out in Eastern Persia, a gift from "these impossible Afghans" across the border. The Meshed road was closed and seventy thousand ampoules for inoculations despatched with a few doctors towards the endangered area. European travellers who were already beyond Firuzkuh were sent back to the capital.

We interviewed officials. Since we could prove that we were not returning to Teheran but had decided to plunge among the "Afghan barbarians", and since there was no time to fall ill between reaching the infected zone and our leaving Iran, we supposed that no-one had the power to stop us. But we had to obey the rules and be vaccinated at the Institut Pasteur. The three injections meant a week's delay.

We called on Mahommed Navroz Khan, the Afghan representative, to make sure his Government would not send us back. Though we interrupted his belated siesta, this charming man was positive about it: once on the soil of his great country all our difficulties would end: no-one there would want declarations asking for the birth-dates of our parents, for the political party we belonged to or for the amount of our monthly income!

The depressing forecast of Herr Sment reminded me of similar ones heard in Moscow or Peking where I had overcome greater difficulties. But they seriously frightened Christina. She began to say she could not leave until all her notes had been made use of. I thought it was pure madness. Our first objective was to reach a "positive environment" where work and health could go hand in hand. In any case her indifferent articles did not warrant a delay and our three weeks in Teheran had already much shortened our intended stay at the Hackins' excavation. But as I write these lines I feel that if she had no time to let her impressions settle quietly down it was because some part of herself foresaw that she had not long to live.

One day working hard, announcing joyfully that she was rid of her obsessing fear; the next confessing that she could not live much longer in such dismal unhappiness—it was obvious that she was not nearing a well-balanced state. Her health, too, oscillated from fever to inflamed throat, from headaches to weak knees. Dr. Davies saw it all as the result of low blood-pressure: sugar and sympathy were the remedies.

But I felt an atmosphere of danger: we were in a big town which might offer dangerous temptations. Had she not been inexplicably upset when the chemist recognised her and presented an old bill? I was continually uneasy: did she want to go to town alone? Was she planning it? Together we had already visited the beautiful museum where we studied the potteries so as to have a basis of comparison in case the Hackins should find something similar. But if that was her plan she could easily find pretexts for slipping away. Once I went alone to a Swiss tea-party while she searched for the platinum and emerald ring she had lost near the tank. When she joined me two hours later I did not dare ask if she had gone to Teheran, but I was so absorbed in my thoughts that I never knew what people had been telling me.

I carefully avoided speaking about the past. I never asked about beautiful Yalé who had died in the nearby Legation. And we never went to her former house. But I knew that Christina was very moved to be back in the land where her distress had been acute, the country that had made her write:

"Each nightfall, a farewell—and morning finds me near to the unknown. Adventure is over and gone, but a thousand realities are still to prove. I grip them, hurl myself upon them, love— and there is nothing I forget. Behind me, cedars, olive-groves, songs, columns, tents and sails. And the hoof-prints of mounted peoples on the march. O further yet, far off unknown horizons! How many a white night it costs me to reach them . . . Like a shying horse my patience would start to right or left—and plunges ever forward. The roads are veiled, meandering, like Milky Ways. Cold, hunger, thirst: I have what I desired, and nowhere to lay my head. No helping hand. If now, out of but one of these nights, I were to step forth into your streets, the neighbours would no longer know me. I should be no different from the blind, the dumb, the beggars. And 'Welcome', I should hear; but I should disdain the soup your pity offers to the wretched. Hunger is my friend. I welcome every weariness. I lie down beside the spring—unable to quench my thirst. What matter? My impatience has already crossed the mountains. And I go forward, light of heart. My heart so light, so empty, that every kind of force finds entry, all energies stream into me—the spiced night airs and salt winds of the sea, and then the sap mounting in plants, the soundless rain, the breath of branches, animals, of men asleep—every pulsation. And it rises from the rivers, hovers over the fields like the dawn mist, glides above the flocks, drifts down from the vineyards, caresses the crest of tents and trees, gathers about the shepherds' fire—'Fear not!'; and it is as if, on either side of the way, legions of angels I saw and had to weep with tears of joy."

Sometimes at dusk when the trees of the park seemed to invade the Legation drawing-room, Christina would delicately touch the keys of the grand piano. Her silhouette was hardly visible in the twilight but I could feel something of the reverence that filled her as the elegance of Mozart's music summoned from distant Europe danced out of the room to fill the Persian night. The contrast between the feverish entanglement of her life and the perfection of that music which moves with the ease and clarity of snow crystals falling now near a radiant summit, then through a muffled forest of dark firs, moved me to tears.

That night I was once more awakened by the wolf howling in his cage, howling and ululating like Palazi my great husky when he sits in the snow and yells, pointing his shiny dark nose straight above him at the stars.

The disquiet of that call made me feel that we must leave quickly before Teheran could undo us. I was half poisoned, too, by the vapidity of many after-dinner lucubrations: I was not armed for that fierce battle in the void called society-life. We must rush to Meshed before it could be closed. Our exit *javass* had been promised: within an hour of having received it we must on our way. We are already looking forward to seeing the German Minister's nose put out of joint when we take leave, thanking him for the rest he had given us on our way to Kabul!

15

GUMBAD-I-KABUS

"The start of a journey in Persia resembles an algebraical equation: it may or may not come out" remarked Robert Byron in his *Road to Oxiana*. Rolling once more towards the rising sun, we were happy to slip out of the meshes of red tape that might have immobilised us.

A letter we had just received from the Hackins advised us to go north beyond Herat: along the usual way south through Kandahar, the bridge had been carried away by the swollen Helmand. We had to swallow quinine, for Afghan Turkestan was full of malaria. We began to feel as if Afghanistan were ours for the taking, though as the crow flies Herat was still eight hundred miles away.

The winding road took us through the hills that buttress the Elburz. Christina's happy valley was quite near in a fold of the great Demavend which, like all solitary peaks, has inspired many a legend. One of them tells that the great phœnix Simurgh lives there for ever, one eye gazing at the past, the other at the future. I remembered having heard about Simurgh years ago when, more than a thousand miles away, I passed at the foot of the Caucasian Elbruz which is also, like its Persian homonym, a huge dead volcano. I cannot help thinking that the ancients confused the two mountains, hence their bearing the same name.

By carrying him to the Demavend, Simurgh saved the life of Zal, an infant who though "as beautiful as the sun" had been exposed to die in the wilderness because he had white hair and his father Sam was ashamed of it. Later on, the repenting father, then governor of Hindustan, recovered his son with joy. Zal came riding back through the kingdom of Kabul preceded by the reputation of being an incomparable youth. As for Roubadeh, the daughter of the King of Kabul, she was known to be wondrously beautiful. They managed to meet: the princess let down her tresses over her balcony and Zal climbed up to her. There was a serious obstacle to their happiness:

the princess was a descendant of Zohak, the hereditary enemy of Zal's family. But at last the court astrologers discovered that everything was in order, for their son would be Roustam, the great hero of Persia, the champion of Iran against Touran.

It was under the Demavend that Feridoun the Just shackled the demon-king Zohak who probably gave his name to the proud ruins we were to see near Bamian.

We soon left the direct road to Meshed: we wanted to see the solemn Gumbad-i-Kabus rise in the steppe east of the Caspian. We turned north and beyond the Firuzkuh pass we climbed down towards the sea. The famous trans-Iranian railway that crosses the pass—the first in a country three times the size of France—had been inaugurated in 1938 and we saw three trains in twenty-four hours. The arms of Iran painted on each freight-car showed a lion holding Ali's Sword of Discrimination.

Pulled by two huge, shiny locomotives, a train crawled across a steep slope before worming its way into one of the eighty-five tunnels which enable the line to rise from sea-level to the six thousand eight hundred feet of the pass. Like some unhealthy fungus brought by the railway—symbol of progress if ever there was one!—a hamlet built of flattened petrol-tins rusted by the side of the road, its ugliness an exact replica of what can be seen in the "Zone" of Paris.

We were quickly losing height. In this barren world of shale, gravel and colourless rocks, the electric green of the first rice-field hit one's eyes as a yell of joy would startle one's ears after too long a silence. So evenly dense, so neatly crammed behind the crescent-shaped dykes of the terraced fields, that green was so intense that it was difficult to understand that it had nothing to do with chemical colouring. Lower down where the paddy was riper, the green was gilded and full of changing glosses like watered silk.

Lower, still lower through a gorge, then through the thick undergrowth of a forest, in the damp heat, till at last we rolled through the flat fields of Mazanderan, the richest province of Iran. There thatched cottages were supplanted by the standard lodges lately imposed by the King of Kings.

With a central square and crudely modern houses, Shahi was the first town we reached; it was difficult to realise that a nearby jungle sheltered deer, tigers, leopards and wild boar.

Christina proposed a new definition: "One is really abroad when for no particular reason one goes a roundabout way to meet a compatriot."

We spent the night with the family of a Swiss engineer who was managing a textile mill of two thousand workers. Certain remarks of our host agreed with what the German Minister had told us: it is not wrong that boys eight or ten years old work in factories: they are taught a job, they get some schooling and learn the rudiments of hygiene. We cannot arrive from the West and think we can apply our rules of conduct to Iran. These boys would otherwise work in sweat-shops where there is no pay and much beating.

The law forbids a European to touch a worker. But when the Persian inspector on his rounds saw a fool or an idler, he did not hesitate to lift his hand and hit hard: it was the only way, he said, to get results in a country like Iran. At first opposed to beating on principle, our engineer had slowly changed his views. When for the second time a man had been wounded by foolishly putting his hand into a machine and then complained that it was the foreman's fault, he gave the fellow a good hiding. "This will teach you", he said, "to leave the foreman out of the question!"

It was a fact that wherever crops were exploited and manufactured, boys and girls were good at their work until they were about eighteen. Then the boys took to opium and the girls to marriage and child-bearing.

Reza Shah was ruling almost as ruthlessly as Shah Abbas or Cyrus, but it was probably the only way to get what he wanted done.

We were continually mopping either forehead or oozing chin and I pitied the people who had to work in that hot-house climate. At night the heat was an exasperating blanket that could not be thrown off; we longed for the breeze that fanned us while driving.

On the sea-coast an hour beyond Shahi, we reached Babol-Sar which faintly evoked a newly born Trouville-Plage. A Casino and some bathing huts stood on the deserted beach. There, out of a primitive boat, slow Turkomans unloaded dark iron-wood. I paddled in a small but incredibly heavy dug-out;

when I swam, the tired sea brought no invigoration to my limp body. These pale green waters sheltered many sturgeons, some of them weighing half a ton; in a nearby tinning shed we heard that the local caviar was "the best in the world". So had the modern carpets been, and the new railroad.

The whiteness of a palace-hotel was shining in the sun. It had been hurriedly finished two years ago when the Shah had expected Kemal Ataturk to pay him a return visit; and there, concealed in the wall of the best suite, I had been shown (sh! sh!) a microphone that never served its original purpose, for Ataturk did not come.

The orange-trees of the neighbourhood had been uprooted because they sheltered malarial mosquitos; so Babol-Sar, just then, was more like a waste-land than a *plage à la mode*.

Our way led further east: through dense green woods full of chirping cicadas, through luxuriant fields dominated by rickety miradors; past hamlets protected from wild beasts by thorny hedges, past cotton-fields starred with pink or yellow flowers.

Through the huge plumes of silver reeds we walked towards what looked like a small oriental church among tombs. Covered with old tiles, the projecting roof sheltered a long veranda and built a skirt-like ornamentation around a circular tower. The construction seemed to have had an interesting past. The tower's roof was a flattened cone like a Chinese hat: it topped a bulging drum built above a white-washed blind arcade. Tucked away into a pigeon-hole, pages torn from Qurans showed that the place was nowadays used as a mosque.

I was interested in a group of women and children who had come on pilgrimage: I had never seen such people before. They all had something thick and ugly about them, almost simian, with fuzzy hair and enormous mouths. I remembered that according to the legend, demoniac races used to live on the shores of the Caspian, far away from the plateaux where the Aryans dwelt. A little girl with frizzy hair and thick lips looked as if she were snarling at me: it robbed us of the courage to ask these people who they were.

That church-like mosque was perhaps no precious relic of the past, but we enjoyed it because it was our own discovery:

no sense of duty towards a guide-book had made us visit it.

Every turn of the wheel took us nearer to Soviet Turkestan. We lunched at a village where our interpreter was a Russian retailing vodka. He had lately come from Baku hoping to get rich quickly in a capitalistic country. But the apathy and poverty everywhere in Iran made him bitterly regret his move.

We heard that a colony of Russian refugees lived at Malakan, while true Kirghizes wearing typical high-heeled boots and making good cheese inhabited Kargush Tepe. Many are the Soviet citizens who sought refuge in Iran; in 1934 about thirty thousand escaping Turkomans had arrrived in Meshed. But on the other hand many Persian subjects had fled into Soviet Turkmenistan, unwilling to obey the new laws that forced nomads to become settlers. When she visited the Gumbad-i-Kabus a few years ago, my friend Irene found in that great tower many tribal chiefs being kept as hostages till their sons returned from Soviet Russia.

When we had passed through the town of Gurgan, we looked with impatience towards the north where the Gumbad was to appear. As soon as we left the main road, the country changed completely: we entered the vastness of the steppe. The tall yellow grass bristling as far as the remote horizon reminded me of the solitudes on either side of the Oxus. But here there was no *kibitka*—the round felt tent I had seen in the plains that stretch from the Caspian to the plateaux of Manchuria. Here, where thousands and thousands of sheep, horses and camels used to roam, not a sign of life was to be seen. Nomads and their ways of life belonged to the past. Even if we had gone further afield towards Bujnurd, we should have seen none of the once famous Turkoman horse-breeders: they are no more.

Ahead of us and rising above an island of trees, stood something that looked like a lighthouse or perhaps a round silo. Coming nearer we saw that it was not smooth enough for either: with sharp longitudinal edges, it was more like a fantastic rotor left on this frontier of Central Asia by some forgotten engineer of genius. It was the tomb of King Kabus built ten centuries ago.

At dusk we reached what looked like an oasis—two streets meeting at right angles and lined with trees. There, on the roof of a house belonging to an Armenian commercial traveller, we spent the worst night of our journey.

The oppressive heat under low clouds made us long for a storm that never came, while swarms of invisible sandflies fretted our patience to breaking point. We waited three hungry hours till a snivelling boy brought the rice and kebab we had ordered at the inn. The usually equanimous Christina lost her temper and complained about everything as if she had never been in Asia before: why were people so silly, so dirty, houses so badly built, why was it impossible to wash oneself? I failed to make her smile by saying that such are the joys of travelling when you do not speak the language of the country you are passing through.

We shared our dusty belvedere with another traveller, a Russian-speaking woman born in Samarkand and married in a neighbouring village. For the third time she had tried to have her appendix removed at the Gurgan hospital. This time the building had caught fire just as she arrived there. She did not suffer from the innumerable sandflies that so plagued us. Seeing our misery, she volunteered the explanation that the pests did not like her Tartar blood: it had been saturated with vodka ever since she was a child!

The roofs surrounding ours, where reclining figures were also trying to snatch the breath of air that never came, looked like half-demolished attics: flimsy bulkheads and matted rush built a screen here and there. Little oil lamps moved about like heavy fireflies.

I observed a man who handled an opium pipe half the night through: he at least can no longer have been conscious of a sweating body!

Above the wretchedness of these panting people tucked away in a corner of Asia, rose the splendour of the great tomb touching the low clouds, motionless, domineering, forcing us to remember.

Remember King Kabus, according to Nidhami of Samarkand "a great and accomplished man, a friend to men of learning"— Kabus who protected the famous Avicenna of Bokhara and to whom Albiruni dedicated his *Chronology of Ancient Nations*.

King Kabus stood for perfect hospitality. One of the Daylami princes who had thrown himself upon his protection was pursued by vengeful brothers. Rather than to disappoint him, Kabus refused large rewards, endured the loss of his possessions and shared a proud exile with his guest whom he at last succeeded in restoring to power; and he deemed himself repaid by the gratitude of the prince he had so nobly protected.

"Kabus is celebrated for his extraordinary wisdom and learning. His words were repeated as maxims; and he appears in all accomplishments to have been advanced beyond the age in which he lived. But his virtue was stern and severe and not calculated to gain the affection of men, who, living in troubled times, desired to make amends, by indulgence in all their passions, for the dangers and vicissitudes to which they were continually exposed. He was murdered in Gurgan with his son's connivance by his own mutinous officers whose excesses he had probably desired to restrain."*

The sky was still overcast when on the following morning we walked north of the village, to the mound from which the hundred and sixty-eight-foot tower soars up: it is probably the remains of the ramp the workmen built to reach the top.

The tomb was like nothing I had ever seen. Massive, austere, it was the only salient feature in the dullness of a world devoid of relief. Though built of bricks it had the density of a monolith. Ten flanges, sharply triangular in section, protruded from what, without them, would have been a plain cylinder: absolutely parallel they rose to the top and melted there into the cone that formed the roof. The decorative band of Kufic inscription in the bays between the flanges announced that "This lofty grave was built by the order of Shams-ul-Mali Amir, son of Amir Kabus, son of Washmgir during his lifetime in A.H. 375 (997)."

An old couple were camping on a trestle leaning against the tower—probably the keepers of the monument. It was being repaired and a scaffolding like a stylised fin, reached all the way to the top. It was impossible to bake bricks equal in quality to the original ones. For the conical roof, new tiles were needed which must fit into each other exactly: it was a very difficult work, for one had to account for their diminishing size.

There was nothing inside the tower. But once upon a time,

* Sir John Malcolm: *History of Persia.*

high up there, the coffin of King Kabus hung from the roof
where a small window faces East. Prof. Godard in his *Survey
of Persian Art* says that it was left open and carefully decorated—
facts which show that it had a special purpose, "probably
connected with the age-old custom of having the tent-opening
facing the rising sun. Kabus doubtlessly specified that his body
be exposed to the first sunrays of the day. This would explain
the exact orientation of this window and also the glass coffin
of which Jannabi speaks." His successor had it lowered.

I read that in the twelfth century the Supreme Commander
of Persia, Sultan Sanjar the Seljuk, visited Susa and its famous
bridge; at one end of it lived the rich Jews, at the other end, all
the poor of the town. The poor thought that this great difference
of fortune was due to the fact that the remains of the Prophet
Daniel were buried among the Jews. After a long strife it was
decided that they should remain alternately for a year on each
bank of the river. But Sultan Sanjar declared this to be
derogatory to the honour of the Prophet. He ordered the coffin
to be put into a bier made of glass which was to be suspended
with iron chains from the centre of the bridge. Rabbi Benjamin
of Tudela who visited Susa at the end of the twelfth century
saw this coffin. I have a strong feeling that Sultan Sanjar
was inspired by the Gumbad-i-Kabus.

We walked a little towards the gloomy plain, passed a
pondering camel (the right beast at the right place) and sat
down on the earth. The monument was grand, unforgettable.
It seemed full of repressed energy—a fabulous paddle-drum
that some hurricane from the desert would set revolving in a
great noise of mown gravel—a rocket with straight rifling that
might be bolted one day at some far planet!

And I remembered the Towers of Victory of Ghazni—
one of them built in 1030 by Mahmud of Ghazni, the founder
of an empire that stretched far into India. They are elegant,
much more slender—and less vigorous—than the Gumbad.
I remembered that some of King Kabus' blood went East and
with it, perhaps, the inspiration of those towers: it was his
grand-daughter who married Mahmud of Ghazni, the con-
queror of India.

At first I felt astonished to see a perfect monument like the
Gumbad alone in that plain as if it had fallen from the skies ten

centuries ago. But now I know that a golden age was flourishing then in that part of the world—in spite of wars against Seljuk invaders from the North. Not only was Avicenna about to write his *Sum of all Knowledge*, and Kei Kaus (a grandson of King Kabus) his *Kabus Nama*, but Firdausi had just finished his immortal *Shah Nameh*. The eleventh century was made famous by Omar Khayyam the "tent-maker", Hassan bin Saba the Grand Master of Alamut, and Nizam-ul-Mulk, vizier of Malik Shah, who organised the empire so well that the same monetary system prevailed from the Mediterranean to the Oxus. The fascinating circular tomb of the Forty Daughters at Damghan was built then, a lovely monument which reminds me of the small Cheshma Ayub, a mausoleum rising among the billows of rounded tombs about Bokhara.

It was to be a great century. At its dawn, Kabus the king-poet had written:

"My love is enkindled in thinking of thee,
And passionate thrills through my being do dart:
No limb of my body but speaks of thy love,
Each limb thou would'st think was created a heart!"

And I cannot help feeling that he cannot have been so severe and rigorous who also wrote:

"Six there be which have their home in the midst of thy raven hair;
Twist and tangle, curl and knot, ringlet and love-lock fair;
Six things there be as you may see which in my heart do reign:
Grief and desire and sorrow dire: longing and passion and pain!"*

---

* E. G. Browne: *Literary History of Persia.*

16

KHORASSAN

STORMING the mountain pass south of Gurgan, we escaped from the Turkish-bath atmosphere which had sapped us during these three days near the Caspian: bodies are not meant to go on oozing like a bag of curds.

It was cold near the top of the wind-swept pass; to the west the crests of the Elburz range frayed the rag-like clouds. The new road soon petered out and we had to climb down in low gear. Long before we reached Shahrud, a rider galloped wildly towards us, keen to find out who we were. With a big chin under a big felt hat, he was the Greek engineer in charge of the road-building. He tried to persuade us to sup with him; he felt lonely and depressed. He longed to go back to countries like the Congo or Abyssinia where he had worked before.

Like deep carbuncle wounds in the soil of the sloping country, small craters gaped at regular intervals. We had already seen many of these *kanats* near Teheran. You find them further on in the desert of Eastern Persia, too, where they are called *karez*, and in Turkestan, Afghanistan, Baluchistan. They always awaken my enthusiasm.

When a reserve of percolating water has been detected at the foot of a hill—sometimes as deep as eight hundred feet—an underground channel is built to bring it to the surface miles away. At given times it has to be "cured": across the top of narrow shafts about fifty feet apart, windlasses creak, hoisting to the surface a leather bag full of stones or mud according to the nature of the channel.

Down there where it is cool even in the hottest summer, a digger builds his sloping tunnel with a hoe, a wooden level and a string. Tucked away in a niche, a tiny oil lamp lights the darkness. We gave cigarettes to the men at the top and they lowered some to their mole-like companion. When they change shift, the new man slips one foot through a loop of the rope and standing stiffly, sinks down the muddy chimney.

When a new *karez* is needed they build many shafts at once and by some uncanny aptitude always manage to make these burrows meet exactly. Such costly but indispensable work is generally financed by the rich man of a village which either needs more water or must replace a dried-up channel. The gangs dig from November till March. It is almost always the same tribes which deal with this delicate and sometimes deadly dangerous work.

In the remote past, *kanat*-workers seem to have been Arabs and Gabrs. And Strabo already mentions *kanats* at the beginning of our era. Long ago I read that wonderful canals still exist under the sands of the Sahara: these *foggara* are said to be very ancient. I imagine that this kind of engineering has always been known to men in need of it.

Though it meant a tiring day, we decided to cover in one stage the three hundred and twenty miles between Shahrud and Meshed: there was no pleasant camping-ground on the way. It is true that being self-contained we could use our special bag for drinking-water (it used to hang outside the car where it kept icy-cold by evaporation, its sides caked in mud, dust having stuck to the damp cloth). But a bath and a clean bed at the British Consulate of Meshed was a goal worthy of some effort: we might not find such comfort again for a long time to come, especially if the Hackins were still working on their "dig".

We were beginning to adapt ourselves to the country and we had reached the stage when we involuntarily mixed Persian words with our French. For instance we had long known the words for *man, yes, madam, very expensive,* and quite unconsciously Christina would say to me: "A nafar stuck to me repeating 'Baleh, Khanum: this is not kheili gheran', so I ended by buying his soap-stone cigarette-holder." From her previous stay at Teheran she remembered *Lazim niist* (not wanted), an expression we often used in garages where mechanics were always keen to tinker with the car.

I could utter one curse which worked like magic whenever we would not accept *farda!* (to-morrow) in response to an urgent order. For a long time I did not dare ask what it meant: I was just repeating what a German tourist had used with success at Isfahan in 1937: he spoke Persian fluently and could boast of an underworld knowledge of it, for all he knew had been learnt in the Berlin "tube"! Later on, I found that that wonderful formula meant nothing worse than "son of a dog".

The car was also persianised: Christina had fixed to the radiator a few of the charming blue beads one sees about the neck of animals that are to be preserved from the evil eye. To combat a more definite kind of bad luck we now carried with us two pieces of iron grooved like roof-gutters in case the heavy Ford should get embedded in mud or sand.

Another kind of foresight had made me persuade Christina to buy a skirt: I had convinced her that as long as she wore her grey bags she would be taken for a man and Afghan harems would remain closed to her. I was also convinced that when difficulties are encountered in Asia, women are more readily helped if they are seen to be without a man.

Khorassan is a dull part of the world, a succession of immense waterless basins separated by hills of grey gravel or by the rocky ribs of a skeletal earth. The whole region looks more barren and forlorn than Russian Turkestan. But for a while, morning and evening, a glorious display of changing lights turns this mournful stage into a world of unexampled beauty.

Gold and blue, blue and gold, such was the scene that morning—a few gilded bushes rising against a far-away background of hills, dusky blue like a ripe plum, while golden dust and golden light throbbed in the depths of the azure sky. It is because of their sky that deserts are so moving—that vast, total sky, the greatest amount of space we can behold at once, a sky into whose subtle landscape of thin vapours all the charm, the very essence, of a once fertile land has risen and taken refuge. Yes, Christina, life is beautiful!

In the fields near a village we saw huge coffee-coloured "ice-cream puddings": wondering, we explored the nearest. It was a high mud dome built over a deep pit full of last winter's ice. Thanks to one of these *yakchal*, our next lemon-sherbet was surprisingly cool and pleasant—so long as we avoided looking at its muddy residue.

At Sabzewar we greeted the gaunt minaret of Khosrowgird erected in the year 1111 when Sultan Sanjar the Seljuk was governor of Khorassan—long before he went to Susa and saw

Daniel's coffin. The monochrome brick-pattern of the monument reminded me of Bokhara where a tower two hundred feet high stands at one angle of the Kalyan Mosque—a "death minaret" of imposing proportions: people condemned to death by the Amir of Bokhara used to be hurled from its top.

Before noon, the heat was already lording it over our world. Every detail of the country quivered as if at the point of boiling. Each blast coming from the oven-like desert was so searing that we wound up the windward pane, regretting that it was not fitted with a curtain to prevent the sun from scorching me. But our hood had been lined with red flannel, a device supposed to be very cooling.

We did all we could to maintain a speed of forty-five miles an hour: as soon as we slowed down the wheels ceased to skip over the corrugated waves of the road and once more the bouncing was infernal. Another discomfort was the dust: there was enough traffic for a high hem of dust to be continually curling down to the leeside of the road.

Our backs as well as the leather seats were soaked with perspiration. When we stood for a while in the great wind we felt chilled till we were dry, the evaporation of water in this very dry air being almost as rapid as that of petrol.

Nevertheless our progress was more comfortable than my overcrowded bus journey of two years ago. After days of rattle-trapping along that same road, my back had rubbed so much against a plank that I found my clothes worn through when I reached the garage at Shahrud; at that time my back was "steeled", for a lumbar pain obliged me to travel with a metallic corset. That inconvenience added to the heat of a Persian summer made things a little difficult; and camping for days together by the road-side where breakdowns had stranded us, it was impossible to undress. I tried to cheer myself, remembering what Irene had told me about her father Lord Curzon who journeyed to the Pamirs encased in a similar contrivance, for he suffered from a chronic sciatica.

Travelling by bus had been most interesting, though not so picturesque as with an Afghan lorry. The Persian vehicle contained no invocation to Allah sweepingly drawn on gilt-edged paper, no polychrome transfers on its body showing a recognisable Lake of Geneva with the Château de Chillon, no splendid Afghans who said their prayers in the desert while the engine stopped at their request, no long turban-ends floating in our wake like Isadora Duncan's veil, no hidden women who could hardly see how to climb up and down our high running-board, no babies' nappies stretched to dry on the back of one's seat, no shocked tribesmen beholding for the first time Persian women's unveiled faces and bandy legs with cork-screw stockings.

When we had left our pilgrim's garage in Meshed and when we drove past the Imam Reza shrine, all the passengers yelled in perfect unison the usual yell of the pilgrims—an invocation to Ali which sounded full at the same time of fervour and of threat. That bus stopped only when it had breakdowns: since this happened hourly, those who were religious had plenty of time to kneel and bow.

Once, as I was admiring the little curtains that protected us from the sun, a pair of pliers cut the wire that held them in place: it was needed to steady our exhaust-pipe, now trailing on the ground. Then the footboard dropped and soon after-wards a short-circuit cut off our headlights. When the next puncture happened nothing could be done till one of the passengers lent his torch; the driver went to sleep in the ditch while his young mate performed. The skin of that boy was rat-grey with grease and dust. Later a spring-shackle got lost and some contraption or other was fixed in its place. Until then not a grumble had been uttered.

But the peak of the journey was reached when our mud-guards threw a man off his donkey. Picked up by the driver and taken to a lonely *khan*, he wailed and pretended he was dying. Meanwhile his companions refused to let our driver go unless he paid a large sum as "blood-money". The palaver and bargaining lasted for eight hours.

The *khan* was a dark vaulted inn where, stretched on a mud platform, a few tired customers inhaled opium. No food was to be had. My hungry companions tried to shorten the entangled discussion. Some of them went a few furlongs away in search of food—and came back with one egg, the only eatable they could find!

Except for a schoolboy going back to Teheran, all the passengers seemed to be pilgrims returning from the holy shrine of Meshed. One very fat man (he managed to wear and keep in place a wide leather belt below his voluminous paunch) was a tea-merchant from Baghdad; another dealt in carpets at Karachi; a third characterised himself by holding a bottle between his knees during the whole of the five days' journey. It must have been holy water that had run over the padlock of the Imam's tomb: I cannot imagine arrak or oil being carried with such care and ostentation.

Most of my neighbours wore the Arab cloth with its head-band of woollen skeins; they called each other Hajji, so had evidently been to Mecca. A pock-marked man who spoke English was a tailor in Hamadan. His brother, a mullah in Meshed, had been angry at seeing how westernised he had become—clean-shaven and wearing a smart blue pullover above a tennis shirt which was tucked inside his trousers! (East of Istanbul shirts denote what latitude one has reached, the Muslim smock, Russian *rubashka*, Indian *djibba*, all float over trousers or dhoti: it allows the air to reach the skin.) But my tailor's greatest short-coming was that he had not yet taken a wife!

His brother the mullah knew for certain that though Reza Shah's policy attacked the priesthood, he had a priest as adviser: and following his counsel, the Shah had just postponed a long-advertised visit to the holy town of Meshed. The place was still unsafe for him.

In 1935 the Shah's soldiers had fired their machine-guns at a fanatical crowd massed in the wide courtyard of the shrine. A few hundred people were killed. This had happened because an important mullah had cursed the new law enforcing western hats: they prevent the forehead of the faithful from touching the ground during prayers (Muslims are forbidden to go bare-headed). "It is an infamy" the mullah said: "even the British have never imposed so ignominious a law upon our Indian brothers! Look what I do with this hat: I tear it to pieces!" Anger was quick to rise in the hearts of the people who thought they were safe, the shrine having always been an inviolable sanctuary. But that day they learned that their religious world was being crushed by the State. After that catastrophe many mullahs had to seek refuge in Iran or in Afghanistan. Since then pilgrims are counted by tens of thousands where before they were hundreds of thousands; new money regulations in all the middle-eastern countries, also, make the journey difficult.

Thanks to that bloody repression, we, though unbelievers, would be allowed to enter a shrine said to contain the most beautiful mosque in Persia.

For Shia Muslims, Meshed is the fourth most important pilgrimage—after Mecca, Kerbela and Nejef. The Shias do not recognise the three first successors of Muhammad and disagree with the Sunnis who do.

"In Persia the power belonged to the King, the Son of God, by his heavenly origin invested with the divine glory—*Farri Yazdan*. Through political revolutions, Persia transferred on to the head of the Arab Ali—and the legitimate heir of Muhammad excluded from the caliphate—all the splendours and sanctities of the old national monarchy. He whom she had formerly called in her protocols 'the King Divine, the Son of Heaven' and in her sacred scriptures 'Lord and Guide' (Lord in the things of the world, Guide in the things of the Spirit), she now called by an Arab name, Imam, the Chief— the simplest title imaginable and at the same time the most august, for all sovereignty both temporal and spiritual was contained in it. Over against the caliphs set up by the blind clamour of the masses, by intrigue or crime, she proclaimed the hereditary right of Imam Ali, infallible and sanctified by God. At his death Persia turned to his two sons Hassan and Hussein and afterwards to their descendants. Hussein having married a daughter of the last Sassanian king, the Imamate of ancient Persia and of Persian Islam was sealed with the blood of Hussein on the plain of Kerbela."*

There have been twelve revealed Imams. The last is to be the Mahdi who will reappear with the Prophet Elias at the time of the second coming of Christ. The eighth among them is Imam Reza buried at Meshed. He was a great saint and is said to have performed miracles. According to tradition, twenty thousand happy angels hover continually above the shrine.

As I once more came in sight of the golden dome of Meshed, this time with Christina at my side, I envied the state of mind of the faithful who believe that:

* J. Darmesteter.

"On the day of the resurrection, four of the earlier holy men, Noah, Abraham, Moses and Jesus; and four of the later ones, Mohammed, Ali, Hassan and Hussein will be in the highest heaven and will draw a rope across the front of the throne of God. All those who have made the pilgrimage to the tombs of the Imams will sit on the ground at the foot of the throne; but those who have made the pilgrimage to the grave of the Imam Reza will sit nearest and the favours shown them will be greater than any other.

The person who makes a pilgrimage to the Imam Reza will on resurrection day which is of seventy thousand years' duration, have a pulpit of his own placed in front of God's throne and at this pulpit he will sit until God has finished his accounting with mankind. God will then take him to Heaven."*

* Mullah Noruz Ali *Tuhfat al Rizawiyah*, quoted in B. Donaldson: *Wild Rue*.

17

MESHED

WE were walking towards the shrine, our cameras hidden under our arms for we had no permit to take photographs in Persia: the authorities in Teheran must have been too overworked to deal with us in spite of our reiterated calls. If I were caught I thought of trying to prevent confiscation by displaying a document two years out of date.

The broad avenues reminded me of Tashkent. Tired women, hatless and in drab overcoats, went to market with a basket over their arm. Droshkies gave a Russian touch to the scene; the white manes of their paired horses were tinged with flame-colour like the beards of old men—a sure sign that they had been bound with henna. At the cinemas, films were advertised in Russian and Persian and in shops every third man understood Russian. The new anti-religious propaganda also contributed to an otherwise superficial resemblance: like Kiev or Bokhara, Meshed had built its modern hospital with money levied from religious foundations.

Officially the shrine was open to non-Muslims but in practice there was much reluctance to enforce a rule that hurt the feelings of the majority. We didn't feel inclined to stroll through the great buildings: passed within the iron gates we felt nervous and self-conscious. We crossed the first court unobtrusively and went quickly towards the offices.

The main court, more than four hundred feet square, was enclosed all round by double rows of arcades. This courtyard was built at the beginning of the seventeenth century by Shah Abbas: coming from Isfahan on foot as a pilgrim, that cunning Shah had decided to advertise a shrine on Persian soil: it was unnecessary that a continual flow of pilgrims should enrich only the sacred places of Arabia and Irak.

In the middle of each side was a splendid *ivan*—the arched portico typical of Persian mosques. Every inch of the walls was shining with enamelled tiles. But the main feature of the courtyard was the gold that covered the tall minarets, lined the arched hollow of the *ivans* and shone with opulent bright-

ness on the bomb-like dome above the sacred tomb. The joins
of the square plates of gilded copper were clearly apparent:
slightly convex, they reminded me of a sumptuously quilted
upholstery. On the golden cupola, naked pink copper showed
in a large band bearing historical inscriptions. How unearthly
such gorgeousness must seem to the peasant who knows
nothing but the sun-baked clay of his village hovels, nothing
but the sun-scorched gravel of the desert!

The entrance to the actual tomb, a gold-vaulted recess in a
great portal, was like the dark mouth of an ogival cave: it led
to the heart of the golden summit.

We asked one of the officials to take us to the tomb-chamber;
dallying, he first showed us the treasures of the library. Among
the eighteen thousand books were some five thousand Qurans,
many of them famous masterpieces. Every page of each of them
displayed original designs and colourings, the margins filled
with enough gold and azure arabesques, green and ruby floral
entrelacs to inspire a cohort of modern artists in search of new
patterns. Bound in snake's skin, Ali's Quran showed great
Kufic writing. Walking along the shelves, I was astonished to
see such books as Thiers' *Révolution Française* and even Dumas'
Les Trois Mousquetaires.

In a big room hung with a portrait of Ali, we were shown
rare carpets, among them "The Four Seasons" made in Kerman
in 1650; it was full of lovely changing sheens as the attendant
directed different parts of it towards the windows. The shrine,
indeed, must contain many treasures: pilgrims have brought
their offerings to the saint for ten centuries.

Ali ibn Musa ur Reza was born in 770. He became the head
of the house of Ali, and thus Imam of the Shias, in 800, when
Harun al Rashid was Caliph in Baghdad. The Caliph died
of illness on his way to Samarkand to put down a rebellion.
Trying to unite Shias and Sunnis, Mamun, the son of Harun,
nominated Imam Reza heir to the Caliphate and married him
to his daughter. Shias rejoiced. But the Sunnis of Baghdad
revolted against so bold an innovation. Mamun was in a
difficult position. But luckily for him Imam Reza died in 819
of a surfeit of grapes. Shias maintain that the fruit was
poisoned, and when they visit the holy shrine they curse Harun
and Mamun whose tombs are in a nearby cell.

Our chief wish was to enter the tomb-chamber on the ground floor, but our guide was deliberately slowing his conducted tour. From the choked uproar that reached us we knew that the number of pilgrims was great; but as I once more moved towards the narrow staircase, the attendant said it was now too late to go down and dangerous to mix with so many people.

We had been warned beforehand about the elusive ways of the shrine officials, but we did not know how to counter them. Through a bull's eye, Christina took a plunging view at a dark hall that seemed full of pilgrims. And I told her what I had seen there two years ago:

Four warders having taken me in tow, I was asked to imitate their gestures. We then entered the humming crowd of pilgrims, the huge crowd that moved like a stream, the crowd that wailed, chanted and prayed all at the same time. The noise grew into a loud clamour as we entered a resonant hall whose walls sparkled with innumerable mirror-facets. I progressed, squeezed within an avid multitude, a seething mass of hallucinated eyes. We reached the tomb-chamber.

Like my neighbours I had kissed a great silver door splendidly worked in repoussé, then a dark door of carved wood; like them I pressed my forehead against a wall of pink marble. Beyond that I could no longer imitate them. They were in a trance: they looked but seemed to see nothing. I, I was still able to observe details. The tomb, under a canopy in one corner of the room, was surrounded by a silver railing and covered with a pall of blue satin. In that confined space the uproar swelled, thundered and bounded back like the mighty sea in a cave. The silver bars were caressed, kissed and clasped in an outburst of adoration that devoured the whole being of the pilgrims: they were partaking of the holiness of the saint.

They mumbled, yelled and cried without knowing it. They shuffled along, rubbing their bundles along the sacred walls. Between a turned-up collar and a battered felt hat pulled down as much as possible, a woman's eye burned with fever. Turbaned men evoked wild, starving animals. They were not looking at this world: carried away by passion they had approached and touched something greater than themselves.

I had no place there. To observe them as I did in a relatively

cold way was indiscreet, sacrilegious even. This must have been
the greatest moment in their lives, a moment during which,
wondrously, they went beyond themselves. Who was I to
scrutinise them as I did?

Instead of looking through me as most of the pilgrims did,
two bearded veterans watched me, saw me for what I was:
they were so hurt, their faces expressed a pain so acute that I
felt sorry. Had they lynched me I think I could perhaps have
agreed with them. . . . I slipped out with undignified haste.
I had seldom been so moved. I wondered if any of the great
pilgrimages in Europe were causing such religious fervour.

In spite of my excitement—and this shows how detachedly
one's mind works—I had been continually aware that,
impassive, ugly and Japanese, a wall-clock had trivially ticked
away second after second.

Leaving that confused roar behind us, Christina and I
followed a narrow passage that took us to the peace of Gauhar
Shad, the delightfully simple courtyard of that perfect mosque.
Among the mass of shapeless clay houses of the great town,
Gohar Shad was an unexpected pool of blue light: we basked
in it, felt refreshed by it as by a dip in the clean high seas when
the water is of a dense navy-blue with a white plume rising
joyfully here and there.

Double tiers of arcades formed the sides of the court, each
side enriched by the portal of an *ivan*, every surface covered
with deeply coloured faience mosaics.

The main *ivan* was flanked by two minarets decorated with a
network of dark lozenges; above the shaded entrance of the
greatest portal, the spandrels were filled with a mass of light
enamelled flowers. "From her private property and for the
benefit of her future state, Gohar Shad built this great mosque"
was the inscription inlaid into the façade. "Baisungur, son of
Shah Rukh, son of Timur Gurkhan, wrote this with hope in
Allah, dated 1418." (Gurkhan—universal Khan—is the
supreme Turko-Mongol title that had been used by the Kerait,
the Kara Khitai, etc.) Behind the main *ivan* rose the ellipse of
an exquisite turquoise dome with sinuous white arabesques.
A foam-white calligraphic frieze ran around and bound
together these glazed walls of splendid hues. A tank for ritual

ablution mirrored the radiant vision—happy proportions, good colours and lasting harmony.

Timur died in 1405 and the same year his daughter-in-law Gohar Shad started the building of this mosque. At Herat we were to see the tomb of that remarkable woman.

These mosaics were nearly as good as the much-ruined panels of the Blue Mosque at Tabriz. They were much more attractive than the tiled ensemble built by Shah Abbas for the great court of the shrine. The process adopted by Shah Abbas is called *haft-renghi:* it means that as many as seven colours may if necessary be applied side by side on a tile before it goes to the kiln. The result is that each coloured detail not being sharply separated from the next as it is when incrustation-mosaic is used, the general impression is more diluted, weaker. In the seven-colour process it is impossible to obtain a gamut of the densest tones since each colour has a different maximum firing-point.

I sat by the edge of the square pool.

That morning we had visited a carpet workshop. And now I felt that a richly coloured prayer-rug is a version in wool of the mosaic façade of an arched portal; and that in its turn is intimately related with the gorgeousness of Quranic illuminations. These three summits of Persian art can perhaps be traced to the bright flower-beds of Persian gardens—compact geometrical fields of multicoloured flowers that frame every moment of life in this sun-scorched land.

I felt I could grow fond of the place. And that raised a problem that interested me. So far I had always fallen in love with robust three-dimensional art—the Tower of Kabus, the charioteer of Delphi, China's Great Wall, the purity of Vezelay, the solidity of the Parthenon, the deep-rooted joy of Romanesque Tournus, the Trimurti of the Elephanta cave. What had I to do, then, with an Asian mosque, a lidless box whose inner surfaces alone are seen, shining with paint and lacquer?

I knew that Gohar Shad was "good" and it was casting a spell on me. Nevertheless, I still preferred the turquoise and ultra-marine glazes I had seen in Samarkand. Probably because it was there that I had first seen the rich glow that emanates from these two enamels when they are used side by side. There, near the Reghistan square, I watched the dying sun from the roof of the Tilla Kari medresseh where "Sovtourist" had allotted me a cell. An intimacy had grown between myself and the stubborn dome above its high drum girthed with huge Kufic characters. My Tilla Kari seemed to be a weak imitation but I was within a stone's throw of the perfect Ulugh Beg College named after the astronomer, son of Gohar Shad.

The old monuments of Samarkand have pathos, most of them being in ruins—the audacious cupola of Bibi-Khanum still challenging the bluish-green of a sunset sky, the vestigia of a beautiful arcade before Timur's mausoleum, the lane of tombs at Shah Zinda, palaces and hunting-boxes in the country crumbling into dust. Do we cherish better what is on the eve of vanishing? Would the Parthenon affect us equally were its paint and gilt still shining? Time, wars and earthquakes have badly mauled the Herat monuments, but the little that remains —a tomb with minarets in a wheat-field—touches me like the last smile of a friend.

In its good state of preservation, the mosque of Gohar Shad has none of these appealing qualities. I had to read Pope's *Introduction to Persian Art* to understand what was moving me. And I clearly see how knowledge "does both train and supplement the eye":

"Though it concerned itself with an art of design, the Persian æsthetic genius cannot therefore be relegated to a secondary rank. For in the same sense both music and architecture are arts of design, proof enough that design of a supreme quality attains a high seriousness and deep meaning that make it one of man's greatest achievements. The arts of design have no immediate appeal to sentiment and make no direct reference to nature; but their very abstractness, their detachment from a specific ideational content or emotional entanglement is a source of tranquil power. Nor are they merely a series of enticing forms. Like great music, they may characterise and reveal ultimate values and give expression to the basal and universal forms of the mind itself. Great design has the authority of logic. Design bears, indeed, the same relation to beauty that logic does to science and philosophy. It is the proper introduction to art, its indispensable framework, and perhaps also its finest achievement."

18

ABBAS ABAD

IMAM REZA is the patron saint of travellers and I like to think it was he who helped us the day we left Meshed for the Afghan border.

The country we crossed was vast and dull but for two clay lions that welcomed us at the entrance of the village of Fariman, an estate belonging to the Shah. These gilded statues waited patiently for a master who had been expected for the last three years.

At noon we rolled into depressing Turbat-i-Shaikh-Jam. Many ruined mud houses were slowly and surely returning to the earth they had been moulded from; carpet-slippered men shuffled along, a shapeless cap over one ear, a dead cigarette stuck to the lip; others sipped their glass of tea in a dusty *chai-khana;* a few sat on rickety chairs in the barber's shop; some stood aimlessly by a new petrol-pump; a dishevelled urchin dragged a pleading lamb. It looked as if Turbat would never recover from an age-old slump.

It fitted that dreary day that we should be hailed by a policeman just after we had retired to a half-demolished room in our *chai-khana* to escape from the dazzling glare of the street as well as from the pursuit of indiscreet bugs. Before lunching on bread and melon, we had been to the tall shrine of Sheikh Jam, an island of shade and cleanliness at the foot of a great arched portal. Beyond the flagged court and marble tombs I photographed a woman wailing on a fresh grave. Now the policeman, looking at my permit, wants to know if we snapped other scenes.

He takes with him my out-of-date document and tells us that we are confined to the inn. Then returns and snappily asks for a better permit. I play the fool and threaten to complain about him to his superior. Not at all shaken by my attitude, he goes away to prepare his chief for our coming: a colleague is left in charge of us.

We work out an escape. Christina walks to the car and when the guard tries to stop her, drives away, saying she needs petrol. I simulate a colic, vanish clumsily behind one wall and then another, hiding on me our mugs and satchels. Leisurely hurrying, I join Christina and thus, trembling with excitement, we run away.

Such was our short visit to the village that gave its name to Jami the poet, scholar and mystic translated by FitzGerald and of whom Emperor Babur wrote that he was "too exalted for there to be any need for praising him". Jami died at the end of the fifteenth century at Herat where the great men of the time used to gather.

That evening we were to be passed by the Persian customs at Karez. Of course we should empty our cameras beforehand; if they were found we should say that they had not been used, but devoid of seals, the cine-camera was bound to be confiscated. If Turbat rang up Karez about us, we were done for.

The country looked even duller than before. The *kanats* seemed dead: their craters had disintegrated, eaten away by harassing winds. The hamlets we passed were different: instead of flat roofs made of poplar branches covered with earth, we saw mud domes on which sun and shade played splendidly. This roofing had the advantage of being cool and, had trees been available in that desert part of Khorassan, the beams could not have withstood the legions of white ants.

Some of these hemispheres had their top shaped into a kind of broad chimney like a prompter's box. It was an air-shaft opening towards the northerly "hundred and twenty days' wind" which alone makes life bearable during the summer These wind-funnels are completely different from the ventilators with lofty canopies that give to Haiderabad-Sind the most astonishing sky-line a town ever had—immense lozenged kites which tower over every house of the city and can be trimmed according to the changing wind.

From fields where I could see nothing but gravel, the harvest was brought in and laid out to shrivel on these domed roofs— crescent-shaped slices of melon which are the staple food during the poor winter months. Under long smocks, women wore trousers that fitted their ankles; a narrow head-band kept their wide kerchief in place; their full round faces reminded me of the Afghan Hazaras, of the Kazaks and Kirghizes of Turkestan.

We halted in the shade of a ruined *khan* where the mass of the burning wind was inter-woven with unexpected threads of cool air. Escaping from the glare of the world, we sat in the twilight of a covered cistern. Christina had something on her mind and what she was to say was typical of her sensitiveness.

At Meshed we had met a young French couple. They had cycled all the way from Paris, their intention being to reach Indo-China. She had left the Bar for the handle-bars; he was an alpinist. I discovered that it was he who had once written to me asking if one could bicycle to Kashgar across the Himalayas. (I had somewhere written that camels, though aristocratic, were cumbersome companions and that there was no reason why a cyclist should not reach Tibet from Peking.) Splashing at each other in the swimming pool of the Consulate, dawdling together through the lanes of the bazaar, bargaining over carpets, jewels, cheap perfumes and gloriously gaudy socks, we had freely joked and laughed.

Christina's French—we spoke French together—was not very colloquial, her mother-tongue being German, and she had been surprised to see how gay and clownish I could be with Nicole and Raymond. She inferred that she bored me and that I should prefer to travel with our new friends. She very much wished she were already able to journey alone.

I admitted I had much in common with these young people. But I asked Christina what would Nicole think if I told her that I chose to study Afghanistan (a country so far hardly altered by the West) because I actually want to sum up Europe from a new vantage-point in order to understand the deepest cause of our craziness. And that having thus sounded our continent, I hope to grasp why my contemporaries have ceased to live from the core of their being.

On the other side of the border ahead of us, we were to see a way of life that was simple, patriarchal and harmonious, probably because it still left room for an unknown agent called divine; while at home where, Prometheus-like, men have wrested all the powers of nature to themselves, life drives everyone to insanity.

And what would Nicole say if I confessed that my paramount

wish is to get rid of my tiresome self, of my wanton desires so devoid of wisdom? I did not want to do that by killing myself or by plunging hastily, as before, into new countries, nor even by working in a leper-house of some kind, a way which, I admit, must certainly help towards getting rid of one's pre-posterous ego. There must be a less sentimental way of doing it, a way of rationally transfixing that self, even of transmuting it.

"No, Christina, I am grateful to have you at my side because I know you understand me."

Fear was still alive in her, Christina said: only for two or three hours had she been free of it during the past months. She was not pursued by desire for the drug (it gave her no pleasure, only a long moment of the only peace she knew) but by the fear of becoming the slave of it.

Trying to be helpful, naïvely I said aloud what I had so far kept to myself:

"Are you sure this is not your way of living fully, marrying at last intellect and emotion in that particular kind of suffering of yours? Even pain is joy to be more alive. . . . But don't you think that so long as you wallow in pain you are bound by it? Pain can only be great if it is transcended, if it has made you aware of your depths, I feel sure of that . . ."

Calmly, as a doctor speaks about an anonymous patient, Christina said that as a rule people take a drug to sharpen or widen their consciousness. But she took it only to forget her torment and this was a very limited experience. Then why was it that she took to it again and again after having been off it for months?

"One day you will face your fear boldly: in it, through it, you will grasp your real being," I replied. Then I read aloud this passage from Sri Aurobindo Ghose's *Thoughts and Glimpses:* "Consciousness of being and Delight of being are the first parents. Also they are the last transcendences. Uncon-sciousness is only an intermediate swoon of the conscious or its obscure sleep; pain and self-extinction are only delight of being running away from itself in order to find itself elsewhere or otherwise."

I also asked her if she had not learned much: she must have found by now the limits of the drug. She was no longer interested by the integrality of the experiment, I thought, but by its form—the perversity of pursuing what a part of herself condemned as anti-natural. She was keen to reach the end of perversity in order to see where it can lead. Through the practice of something negative she hoped to obtain a positive result. At that moment she would know that nature and its laws cannot bind us, she would begin to feel in herself a freedom beyond nature: she would enter the realm of the spirit, experience its actuality in herself.

Then she would no longer be obsessed by the need to fight her daemon. Having been beyond it, having tasted the savour of pure being where Love is the active force, she would have something to cling to during her relapses: at least she would have snapped the vicious circle of constantly remembering that she must forget her fear! Until then, every time she remembered her obsession, she forged a new link in the chain which bound her.

As we drove once more on the flat road, the dead land ahead of us was like an empty screen on which we projected the silhouettes of T. E. Lawrence and Alain Gerbault.* From what we knew it seemed as if, unable at times to bear his thoughts, the first tried to chloroform his mind by becoming a private who need not think; and the second, having no use for such thoughts as are awakened by life in Europe, chose to become a Polynesian occupied with wind, sea, sun and poetry. Both acted as they did because they would no longer tolerate the kind of thoughts their minds were milling.

Christina too.

We reached Karez late in the afternoon. There were no lorries in the yard of the custom-house. The chief or *reis* kept us an hour in his office trying to discover what had happened to thirty pounds sterling of ours which, against the law of the country, had disappeared without leaving any trace in our passports. Producing our accounts on the day we left Geneva and then adding our road expenses, we tried to prove that we had never had that sum. Whether he ended by believing that a mistake was made when we entered his country, I don't know; but dropping the question, the *reis* moved towards our

---

* Gerbault died on Portuguese Timor of a tropical fever in December, 1941. According to Perreira de Costa, his yacht disappeared later on, sailed by a Chinese who was obeying Japanese orders.

Ford. After the incident at Turbat, this interlude contributed to tauten our nerves long before we reached the Afghan border, one of the climaxes of our journey.

Relying upon her diplomatic privileges and pretending that all the luggage but one suitcase was hers, Christina hoped to save our box of negative films from being seen so that there would be no enquiry about our photographic equipment. Assuming that excise-men like hidden corners, we had simply pushed our cameras under my low seat. After my suitcase had been locked again, there was a pause, unbearably long. What was going on in the head of that man?

At last he merely asked if we had a medicine for inflamed eyes. Yes, we said triumphantly. He called his little girl from the terrace where I had slept two years ago, and we gave her a tube of ointment.

We breathed more easily: it looked as if Turbat had not yet communicated with Karez. One more hedge remained to be cleared: darkness had fallen and the *reis* took it for granted that we would spend the night on his terrace. We told him we were going on. "But you can't cross these twelve miles of no man's land now! Even in daylight you can hardly see the track!"

Fear that delay might endanger success so near at hand made us lie—may the Imam Reza plead for us. We said we could not keep our husbands waiting for us at the Afghan border-post and that a drive by night through no man's land was just what we liked.

The *reis* stood speechless. Christina's toe set the engine whirling. Our beams of light showed the way beyond the gate.

19

THE BORDER

In mad exultation we rushed and bounced through the desert: we were no longer held back from a beautiful and little-known country called the land of the Afghans. Ours were its great mountains, its splendid people, its icy rivers, its ruins "as old as the world", the peace of its isolation. We gave out yells of victory, we congratulated each other, we giggled like fools, we said all the silly things that passed through our heads!

The hour was magnificent.

Our headlights thrust a tunnel of visibility through the dark of the night. Swooping out of the obscurity, huge white-breasted birds swam without effort on that moving stream. They floated, steadying themselves now and then with the tip of a brown wing; otherwise we saw nothing but the unearthly paleness of their wide under-span. Could we wish for a more sumptuous escort? And who knows if Simurgh the noble vulture was not among them, keeping watch over us?

An eerie sound accompanied our progress when stiff thistles scraped the belly of the car. Meanwhile we lit up the fantastic silhouette of gigantic hemlocks that stood guard over leagues of withered tufts.

All of a sudden we slowed down: two men—white turbans, shining teeth, white shirt-like smocks under tight waistcoats, trousers gathered into innumerable folds—were pointing their rifles at us. The moment and their attitudes were so perfect an introduction to Afghanistan that I burst out laughing: "Didn't I say so? Aren't they grand?"

We had come up with them. One soldier, for soldiers they were and thank goodness they had not yet been forced into tight khaki uniforms, crouched between our mudguard and bonnet. The other, having crawled like a cat over the back of our seat still holding his weapon, dropped plump between us . . . and on we drove.

Two right-angle bends in the track marked the border. In

my exhilaration I declaimed what raced through my head: "I warn you, though the desert is here the same as in Persia, though racially a Meshedi is much the same as a Herati, nevertheless we are crossing a border, a real border that separates two sharply contrasted countries. Different ways of living—mutually despised—account for it. The Persian *reis* pitied us because we had to travel among "savage Afghans" . . . and I bet you my ciné that the Afghan chief will pity us as he did two years ago, for having had dealings with "those Persian worms". Here, where the pattern of life remains unchanged, where the son thinks as his father did, men are still proud to be men. Meanwhile in the West where there is nothing but change, no-one knows what to think, nobody feels secure—least of all the rich—and that even in so-called peace time. Here, no more high-heeled sluts in short frocks: you've come to the country where women are not seen, where men are capped with snowy muslin and walk with heavy shoes like gondolas. You've come to a country that has never been subjugated— neither by Alexander the Great nor by Timur the Lame, neither by Nadir nor by John Bull. It is the Switzerland of Asia, a buffer-state without colonies or access to the sea, a country whose great hills shelter five races speaking three totally different languages, a country of simple hillmen and well-bred citizens who . . ."

I could not attend properly to my flight of eloquence: I was distracted by our new neighbour and by what must have been going on in his mind. He could not make out what these gibbering people were. Had they perhaps stolen the car that they were so excited? Could they possibly be females, the two of them?

The soft reflection coming from the dials on the switch-board lit only the lower part of our small chins which looked feminine. But there was short hair on both heads. . . . Attempts at conversation having yielded no elucidation, the Afghan decided to solve the mystery according to his means: very slowly his hands began to follow the curves of our ribs! Had there ever been a more ridiculous situation? We could not afford to be offended and thus perhaps antagonise these feline soldiers because after all, we were at their mercy. Explanations or sharp injunctions were equally useless. Repressing our frolicking mood, we hoped that our hurt attitude would convey our feelings. And by then we were in sight of our goal.

A modern rectangular building in the middle of nowhere, a long passage, an oil lamp, a sitting-room, curtains, plush table-cloth and chairs: our first night in Afghanistan! Having unrolled our sleeping-bags near the window where some coolness might reach us, with a smile of success lingering on our lips, we fell asleep. But soon to waken . . . uneasy . . . disturbed. Yes, there was the whisper of a man's voice coming from the window. Should we need a weapon? we had none. But then we had the last laugh of the day and perhaps the best: we grasped that the "bandit" was begging: *Khanum, shigret* (Lady, cigarette)!

It was true that the border was closed because of the cholera: nothing but a Turkish car had passed during the four last weeks. The track we followed next morning looked quite abandoned.

The Chief of Customs had been pleasant. He spoke Russian, wore a becoming grey astrakhan cap narrowing at the top and had blue eyes in a tanned face. The Afghan arms had been stamped in our passports: the front of a domed mosque between two minarets. Islam Kaleh had changed since I last saw it (kaleh is the name of the great fortified houses so characteristic of Afghanistan: one of them must have stood there formerly). The old caravanserai with its cool dark cells where I spent the hot hours of the day two years ago, had unhappily been rased to the ground. Was the Persian habit of demolishing what looks old already spreading to Afghanistan?

A radiant sun, a purring car all by itself in the desert plain, the yellowness of camels browsing near the green of feathery tamarisks, the feeling that hills were to rise ahead . . . I knew that Christina was as happy as she could be.

We approached a sandy ridge: spreading out like a pleated skirt, its base had covered the track and we launched the car through it since we had to reach a culvert forty feet ahead. It took us three hours to cover that distance.

Would we have started work if we had known our efforts would be so back-breaking? The peculiarity of this kind of floundering is that one keeps on thinking: "The next trick will see us out of it." We played with gears; the wheels backed, sank, whizzed; we sat studying the situation; we blistered our hands on our Yugoslav shovel; we pushed the Teheran gutters under the tyres; sweated like coolies under the hats from Trieste; we cursed in Russian and Swiss-German: each great offensive only gained us the length of the gutter.

I threw up the sponge first and sat gloomy, exhausted, while Christina went on shovelling. Where did she hide her strength? How useless the muscles I am usually proud of!

Then, O joy, I saw three men coming towards us. I greeted them smilingly, made explanatory gestures and offered the spade to the youngest. Two of them worked in turn for a few minutes. The third sat down, bored. Just as I was thanking our lucky stars, they walked away . . . I ran after them, convinced that the word *bakshish* would alter their minds. But no. They did not want my tip. Just like that. How far we were from begging Persia!

The hearty way they laughed as I retrieved my silk scarf from the neck of the bored one—I don't know when he had picked it up—was also a new experience.

Eventually we gripped the safe cobbles of the culvert.

And then, O reward! the parched desert was cloven by the intense indigo of a river flowing towards us. Half blind from the glare of a torrid noon, we rushed to the shade of a massive old bridge, jumped out of our sticky clothes and, poised on a rock, looked at the miraculous blueness that was to enfold us. But, damp with perspiration, we shivered in the great wind though the temperature of the air must have been above 115 degrees. And quickly plunged.

Up to our necks in the river, our bodies light as feathers, all our fatigue wiped away, we were in a kind of paradise, soft waters gliding smoothly around our limbs, eyes filled with the azure that surrounded us while hurried ripples raced each other eagerly, joyfully.

This pure stream had seen the Hazarejat range still invisible ahead of us, those hills of Central Afghanistan where the great site of Bamian breathes in peace. Under the name of Hari Rud the water had flowed past Herat, the goal of our day's drive. After marking the boundary between Iran and Afghanistan, that precious blueness would be lost in the sands of Russian

Turkmenistan. A yell from Christina interrupted my rapture: our velvety soap had slipped out of her hand, never to be regained. And this was the third cake thus unwillingly offered to the naiads of Asiatic rivers! There at the edge of the water stood Christina in her slim body asking to be forgiven—her thighs so thin that it was almost painful to look at them, reminding me of the slenderness of Indian adolescents.

Feeling sleepy, we looked for shade where we might lie for an hour. We drove to the wall of a ruined *khan*, but tramps occupied it already; so we hoped to find a tree or a rock. But on and on we rolled through a bleached world where nothing rose.

At long last, through our narrowed eyelids, we spied a yellow village one or two miles to the south. Or rather, we saw its fortifications—a huge wall with two round towers flanking the entrance, as at Ghazni. The only patch of green in our world, a walled orchard, grew at the foot of the northern wall.

Alone in the desert three towers rose, massive, square, with strange vertical slits in their walls. As we approached we saw a complicated rigging high up in the slits. But only when we passed underneath them did we see huge straw-matted blades on a gigantic wheel—the wings of a windmill. The construction had that ancient and ingenious appearance that Chinese water-wheels also possess. One wall was built at such an angle that it would send the great "hundred-and-twenty days' wind", the *bad o sad o bist ruz*, towards the wheel. Rows of perforations in another wall gave an elegant hemstitched effect to the simple building: they were probably meant to cause a draught or as an outlet for air-currents.

Prostrating herself on the soil of the desert in the shade of the northern wall, a veiled woman acted her prayers. Had we wished to rest near her we should soon have been disturbed: a flock of twittering children ran towards us, their long wide shirts flapping in the flowing wind; the reserve with which they met us was blended with a friendliness we had not encountered in Iran.

The same was true of their elders who surrounded us when we reached the end of the track near the fortifications. From a shallow pond, a narrow dike led to the main gate. A shepherd pushed his brown and white sheep along the foot of the beige wall. Under the deep blue sky, and among these sober tints, the garments of the villagers shone splendidly white. In time and space we felt remote from everything we knew.

I think the village must have been called Shahbash: that is all we tried to learn about it. From where we were it looked perfect and we were afraid that it might show nothing but tumble-down houses, if we entered, like the nails and glue at the back of a good painting.

On the mainroad again, and as soon as we were out of sight, we stopped the Ford sideways to provide us with some shade. And there on the earth we fell asleep at once, plumb in the middle of that international highway!

Waking up towards the end of the afternoon, we found that a peasant was looking at us. Three melons nestled in his arms: they were offered to us with a smile showing healthy teeth. A godsend for our thirsting bodies! The man walked away across a fallow field having refused the money we offered.

Afghans are not always so meek as our last benefactor. A few weeks later we were to find ourselves with two wheels in a ditch. Four robust tribesmen passed by. With black turbans and embroidered waistcoats above white clothes, the white of their eyes heavily outlined with antimony, they looked like brigands. When they had lifted the car back on to the road Christina put a five afghanis note in the hand of the tallest man; he looked at it, looked at her, returned the note and walked away without having uttered a word. Never have I seen prouder eyes or prouder countenance.

Had we been in the wilderness we might have thought that money meant nothing to these hillmen, but not on that main road south of Kabul where *chai-khanas* tempt the traveller at every village.

As we drove towards Herat, there was a deep gladness in us. Not only had we reached "our" country, the country we were to study with love, but the people we had met that day were kind, they knew how to smile, they behaved as our equals and not like wrecks: they moved with ease in a life built to their size.

20

HERAT

To find myself back at Herat in the rest-house just outside the rased walls of the Old Town brought back memories which I shared with Christina. The glass pane that used to rattle in the windy skylight above the dining-room was still banging as if all the jinns of Ariana were knocking to be let in.

My first stay at Herat had been a worried one. Because he had heard I was a journalist, the Persian Minister in Kabul had postponed the delivery of my visa for his country till he had heard from Teheran that I was persona grata to his government. When three weeks had passed and there was still no answer to our reply-paid wire, I had left, deciding to force my way through.

And in Herat, passing myself off as a tourist, I asked the Persian consul to let me travel to Meshed. He said "yes"— which in the Orient has many a meaning. When I called for my passport he delayed matters so much that I missed the weekly bus to Iran. Though I was used to the difficulties of modern travelling, this time I was nervous: in a month I was to start a lecture-tour in the wilds of Scotland and the delay robbed me of the time I needed to interview Reza Shah and Kemal Ataturk on behalf of my Paris newspaper.

At long last I received my documents; and just as I was thinking I owed them to my cunning, I learned that the visa had been telegraphed from Kabul.

Except for that incident, my stay was agreeable. I met the energetic young governor smartly dressed in Western clothes who invited me to a meal of varied pilaus. I also interviewed the only European, but for the Russian consul, who lived in Herat—a German engineer who found his loneliness unbearable: every day he told me what a treat it was to speak to someone. His wife was to join him but he was afraid he would go mad before she could arrive. Overworked and obsessed, his pale eyes were frightening and my attempts at making him talk about his work met with little success.

He was in charge of the new Herat. When he travelled about the province to build bridges, he lived with the nomads. Hearing that I searched the bazaar for a pair of "saddle-bag carpets" he offered to sell me his own: he could order them again from his nomads. Later he wanted to give them to me with other possessions of his; one day he produced a big roll of black satin which he thought would win him my heart. That comic scene decided me not to meet him again though I missed his town-gossip.

My afternoons were idled away near the tomb of Gohar Shad, the princess who built the perfect mosque of Meshed. I walked there along a road planted with pines. According to the German, death was the penalty for those who let their goats eat trees, so impossible was it otherwise to make Afghans understand the need for reforestation.

The dark row of pines bordered a pale wheat-field and above its shimmering surface stood the stiff remains of the past—six or seven minarets which, from far away, looked like factory chimneys. But as you came near you saw the sparkle of blue mosaics, the whiteness of great inscriptions, the finish of marble panels. Though very imposing, the two biggest were nevertheless like colossal round sausages; partly fallen down, the tracery of inlaid turquoise arabesques had left a rugged surface of brown terra-cotta.

But the minarets near the tomb were unbelievably beautiful. The density of the colours, the sharpness of the flowery designs, the radiance that emanated from these proud columns forced me to rush around, hopelessly trying to find the angle from which a colour-slide might do justice to such joyful contrasts. But a photo could no more reproduce the velvety tones of these enamels than it could catch the lustre of a rich carpet.

At the other end of the field stood a ribbed dome resting above the four walls of the simple mausoleum of Gohar Shad, a building that gave peace to one's whole being. Flashes of turquoise glaze gave a note of gaiety. The higher you climb on mountains, the deeper is the cobalt of the gentian, the green of the turf, the scarlet of the alpine rose. The same seems to apply to Asian mosaics the further one climbs back in time. Then, at a certain altitude, ice and rock prevail, all vegetation having disappeared. So, before the twelfth century, as far as

I know, there is no coloured enamel: ascetic plain brick reigns supreme beside the snow of stucco-work.

Christina and I sat against the ruins of Gohar Shad, a child and the wind the only things alive in our world. With a witty face which looked pale under a black turban, the boy explained with quick mimicry the reason for a worn-out hollow in a tombstone that lay abandoned before the mausoleum. With the help of a pebble, people with a throat-ache will rub a few berries in this improvised mortar; they eat the resulting paste and, O miracle, those who had no voice (here agonised throat-noises from the boy) can babble happily again. Of course the healing is attributed to the spirit of the saint who is buried there.

A town must always have existed here, at Herat, near the Hari Rud: called either Haraeva as in the *Vendidad*, Artacoana, Alexandria in Aria or Heri, it was once an important stage along the road that brought silk and jade from China through the Pamirs and from Balkh in the plain of the Oxus.

At Sultanieh we became acquainted with the Mongol Il-Khans who were annihilated by Timur at the end of the fourteenth century. The ruins where we now sat introduced us to the Timurids and to the golden age of Herat in the fifteenth century, after Samarkand had been given up as the capital of Central Asia. If we go on linking up centuries and inter-related dynasties, we see that Babur (who conquered India in the sixteenth century because he could not recapture Samarkand) in his youth visited Herat just before it fell to the Uzbek invaders (in 1506). And leaping once more through time and space, we read that the last of these Timurids, the Moghul Bahadur Shah II, was deposed and exiled to Rangoon in 1858 while his sons and grandsons were executed. Queen Victoria was the next ruler of India.

According to Chinese historians, the Timurids sent tribute to their emperors. One of them writes that in 1410 his embassy returned from Herat with a lion, a present from Shah Rukh son of Timur to the Emperor of China. I wonder what the lion thought of the cold Pamirs!

Another Chinese ambassador gives us a description of Herat in the second part of that rich fifteenth century. Every custom he noted differed completely from what he was used to in China:

"The houses are built of stone and resemble a high level terrace. The interior comprising several dozens of rooms, is empty. The doors and windows show beautiful carved wood adorned with gold and precious stones. They spread over the floor carpets which they sit on cross-legged. They shave their heads, wrap a piece of cloth about it; women cover their heads with white cloth and leave only aperture for the eyes. White colour is the colour of joy; black means mourning. They use no spoons or chopsticks at meals; they have porcelain vessels. Wine is made of grapes. Taxes on the coins stamped with the seal of the king are two out of ten. Two sisters are allowed to be the wives of the same husband. Mourning lasts a hundred days. Coffins are unknown: they wrap the dead body in a cloth. There are no sacrifices to the ancestors. They pray to heaven."*

There are few changes among these customs even now, except that modern houses are plain mud and whitewash. The old Herat had just been demolished to make room for modern streets. Showing the place to a Swiss engineer, the governor came to an old house and said it might be sold for the equivalent of £200. Inside, the Swiss discovered polished marble, painted glass, beautifully carved wood inlaid with brass and silver. He grew eloquent: "This must not be sold but preserved and restored by your French archæologists. Does your Excellency realise that this is the first example of skilled craftsmanship I have seen in Afghanistan? You want to awaken and build up your country so as to be proud of it, but we foreigners cannot do that for you. It must spring out of your own enthusiasm. This house is a thing to be proud of: give it as a model to your workmen, show them what their forefathers did. Tell them that men build with such skill and love when their country is great and free—as Afghanistan is to-day."

Who knows if the Swiss and the Chinese have not seen the same house?

After Timur's death in 1405, his son Shah Rukh ruled from Herat. Both his parents gave him some Mongol blood. His father belonged to the tribe of Berulass, the progenitor of which was a brother of Kabul Khan the great-grandfather of Genghis Khan; his mother Saral Mulk Khanum was a daughter of Kazan, a descendant of Genghis Khan. Gohar Shad, wife of

* *Medieval Researches*, Bretschneider.

Shah Rukh, was a sister of Kara Yusuf of the Black Sheep dynasty. Baisungur and Ulugh Beg the astronomer were her sons.

At Herat, Gohar Shad was responsible for the building of her tomb which still exists, but her college and her great Musalla mosque have disappeared. She died at eighty, put to death by the ruler Abu Said because she was intriguing in favour of her grandson. On her tomb were engraved the words: "The Bilkis of her time." And four hundred years later, Mohun Lal, secretary to Burnes, wrote that the people of Herat still called her: "The most incomparable woman in the world."

Sultan Husayn Baikara succeeded Abu Said and ruled surrounded by famous men like Bihzad the painter, Mirkhond the historian and Jami the poet. Under the name of Husaini, the Sultan himself wrote poetry. Emperor Babur gives details that show traits common to the Il-Khans and the Timurids. Sultan Husayn was ". . . slant-eyed and lion-bodied, being slender from the waist downward. He was of high birth on both sides, a ruler of royal lineage. He was abstinent for six or seven years after he took the throne: later on he degraded himself to drink. During the almost forty years of his rule in Khorassan, there may not have been a single day on which he did not drink after the midday prayer; earlier than that however he did not drink. What happened with his sons, the soldiers and the town was that everyone pursued pleasure and vice to excess. Bold and daring he was. No man of Timur Beg's line has been known to match him in the slashing of swords."

Babur was summoned to Herat by Sultan Husayn, probably because he had just captured Kabul. Having accepted the invitation, Babur writes in his Memoirs: ". . . the whole habitable world has not such a town as Heri had become under Sultan Husayn Mirza whose orders and efforts had increased its splendour and beauty as ten to one, rather as twenty to one."

After that Herat declined rapidly.

In 1885 the great Musalla and Gohar Shad's college were wilfully destroyed. Some Afghans had been defeated by Russian soldiers at Pandjeh, north of Herat. Amir Abdur Rahman, who was advised by officers from the Indian Army,

feared for Herat. It was decided to blow up these monuments
so that their roofs could not serve as platforms from which to
shell Herat in case the Russians came so far south.

I took Christina to another monument that had charmed
me: isolated on a vast gravel slope, it was the Gazur Gah shrine
where Kwaja Abdullah Ansari is buried. According to
Colonel Yate, the name Gazur Gah (bleaching place) is
explained by this inscription: "His tomb is a washing place
wherein the cloud of the Divine forgiveness washes white the
black records of men."

After a first huge enclosure reserved for caravans, a second
court welcomes you with its shady trees, flagged alleys and
shining tank. Wearing foam-white turbans, bearded mullahs
stroll along; some of them are probably refugees from the
Meshed rebellion.

Between its high walls, the third courtyard shines austerely,
bristling with the white headstones of marble tombs. Opposite
the arched entrance, the great *ivan* rises in the noble joy of its
enamelled mosaics, some showing a Chinese influence: dark
reds glitter among the classical shades of turquoise, indigo,
pure white. After inspecting one of the cells built in at the side,
I face the court once more: it has become gay with mounds of
yellow-red checks flaming among the pale tombs. They are
kneeling girls, all belonging to the same tribe, it seems. They
peep at us from under their cloth. They are young. Their foxy
faces express boredom but also pride to be seen here performing
their devotions.

Under a gnarled tree, behind a wooden trellis, by the side
of the tall pole that announces the presence of a Muslim saint,
the huge grave of the great man stands in front of the *ivan*. Tied
all over the place, many threads and bits of rag are tokens of
votive offerings; little oil lamps can be lit in their dark niches.
The exquisite carving of the tall fat headstone glistens. Also
beautifully worked but of smaller size, near by lies the grave
of Dost Mohammed, the Amir of Afghanistan who died in
1863.

Once more I am charmed by this atmosphere saturated with
a deep peace, and with a richness due, perhaps, not only to the
good proportions of the enclosure but also to the mood of pil-

grims who through the ages have been inspired by the character of the saint.

Abdullah Ansari died in 1080. The actual shrine was built by Shah Rukh. When Babur visited it he saw people fainting near the tomb when Jalal-ud-din Rumi's *Masnavi* was recited. Ansar means "faithful assistant" of the Prophet and it was the name of the sect founded by the saint. Like Abdullah Ansari, Jelal-ud-din Rumi, founder of the Maulavi order of darvishes, was a mystic who was convinced that there is only God.

One evening on our way back from the bazaar, we watched a thrilling game. Having pushed our way through hard-limbed spectators (nothing but men, of course), we saw a duel between two stalwarts. They were armed with what at first I took to be short rubber truncheons, but it was only the might with which they handled the stick that gave it that supple appearance. They feinted and side-stepped like boxers; now and then the stick crashed down with whipping power, the blow parried with a leather-padded fist. Having defeated successive opponents, a perspiring brave remained in the lists for a long time. In spite of his thick waist he was fighting with the swiftness of an infuriated mother-cat.

I also watched the spectators—their sharp eyes, joking mouths and narrow faces under the disorderly turbans that lent them such good looks. As opposed to a land like Iran where it has been discarded, this turban-wearing country has much in its favour: since men are influenced by what they wear, the heads of its people are proudly erect. If by winding a length of cloth around his skull the Afghan gains in dignity and beauty, would he not be a fool to adopt the ragged cap of the Persians? Even a skull-cap is a pleasant object when it is brightly embroidered. But considering what the Persian wears nowadays it is no wonder he feels sorry for himself.

We walked away: we were attracting too much attention and, for my part, I wished my skirt were longer. Overtaking us, the manager of the rest-house summed up the situation: "Remember that these men have so far seen the faces of only four *khanums*—their mother, sister, wife and daughter.

Now and then we passed a few of these hidden women—shrouded silhouettes guiding their steps from behind peepholes embroidered lattice-like before the eyes. Driving, we found them a public danger: they saw little and heard even less. We had to be right upon them before they would jump aside, frightened like cackling hens.

The caravan-roads of Central Asia are dead and the foreigner who visits Herat feels that he is far away from modern lines of communication: Baghdad or Teheran are many days to the west, while to the east the same is true of Kabul and Peshawar. Some seventy miles away to the north a branch of the Russian Transcaspian railway reaches its terminus at Kushk, but it is closed save for the mail and for some freight.

Ahead of us and about five times the size of England, lay a country of which we wanted to see as much as possible. We wanted to cross the Paropamisus, a range that rises between Herat and Mazar-i-Sharif. A rough road five hundred miles long links the two towns. But the Polish engineer, working then at Herat, told us that the Murghau bridge built by my German acquaintance of 1937, had been carried away last spring. A new bridge was being completed and we should wait till news came that the road was open. The last snowfalls were heavy and many other constructions were carried away when melted snows flooded the river-beds. Still, the Germans were also guilty, and the customs of Asia. Foreign engineers evaluate the cost of a work and that sum is one day paid by Kabul. But owing to the graft which has sometimes already started in high circles, the right amount of building material never reaches the engineer. If he is bold enough he will trace the leakage to its source, call on the culprits and persuade them to check their greed: a ten per cent commission, admitted all the world over, should be a maximum never to be exceeded. In this way work can be done for Afghanistan while the goose that lays the golden eggs is still willing and healthy; after a few years, profit will be substantial as with the old ways. But for such a method to succeed, the country must be free from revolution; otherwise the greedy ones try to make the most of it while they can. (By the time the engineer has said this, he may have been dismissed!)

From the Secretary for Foreign Affairs we learned that "our" bridge was finished, but not so the thirty miles of new road leading to it. Seeing how depressed we looked, he added that he would announce us to the governor of the province, temporarily at Kala-i-Nao: once there, we should know what to do.

I was keen to take the northern road to Turkestan and did all I could to get this move decided. The car not being mine, it was probably easy for me to forget how it might suffer.

BALA MURGHAU

AT last I had ceased to follow my old tracks. It was worth travelling so far if only to feel surging again that expectation, that deep excitement awakened by the unknown. Day after day I was going to get up with eagerness, knowing that every minute of the scenery would be fully new.

Our Herat factotum had shown us the way out of town, straight east and past the new government buildings: we could not miss the road to Karokh, he said. Having convinced the Secretary for Foreign Affairs that we had no seat for the escort he offered us, we were by ourselves. We had an Indian Survey map of one inch to thirty miles that gave us confidence, anyhow.

We took leave of Herat on the morning of August the second. The same evening, crestfallen, we were back in the house with the clattering skylight.

We had crossed a barren land with hills to the north; and after two hours we wondered why we did not rise towards the Sauzak pass, the "Zarmast", presumably, of our map. Though we passed a sleepy village with blind mud houses, where isolated square towers enhanced the clarity of the atmosphere with their deep and sharp shadows, not a soul did we meet who could have told us where this too straight road was leading us.

Hills had also risen to the south; and then, amazed, we saw between us and them a deep broad river splitting the earth, cañon-like. By its size and its blueness we knew it could only be our friend the Hari Rud. We were on the newest road of Afghanistan, the short cut to Kabul across the Hazarejat. Parts of it were very steep and so far only a few officials had used it—preceded by a lorry-load of petrol. When I was in Kabul in 1937, I was on the verge of following it: at the last minute, unhappily, the American I was to accompany met a compatriot of his and took her to Bamian instead.

Now we stood at the other end of that road and, though unreasonably tempted to follow it, we went back in search of the main highway to Turkestan.

A few days later Nicole and Raymond took that Hazarejat road. Bravely pushing their bikes up the steep gradients, they had a hungry journey. The hamlets were far apart and the people so poor that they had neither flour nor milk to sell. Long ago, and before he became emperor of India, Babur had also followed that road. He got lost and nearly died, for the track had vanished under deep snow; but with great determination he plodded on till he found caves where his men could sleep.

Because we could not find the way, we asked for an escort; we could not exchange a word with our man, and he was useless at the gesture-language. Near the square towers, which turned out to be pigeonries, he led us past a few walls and then straight into the steep bed of the dry Pashtan river. Twice we remained stuck in whale-backs of sand. Our man was not keen to handle the spade and since the car was in the way it was impossible to use it Afghan-fashion, a rope tied just above the blade being pulled by a second worker.

Higher up, when we had reached gentle slopes and a good road, we met veiled women riding asses, their pointed shoes dangling from stockinged feet. "The night is for sleep, the day for rest, the ass for work" goes an Afghan saying.

Suddenly, straight ahead, we saw a compact mass of dark vegetation that looked particularly dense in the heart of such a barren country. And there, behind a wall, rose a forest of pines surrounding a shrine. It was Karokh.

Shaded alleys led us to the tomb. Built last century, it was a simple box-shaped grave with the usual pole, rags and rams' horns. But the pines gave such relaxation and joy: Asia teaches you beautifully how to appreciate trees. The wooden columns of a veranda arrested me: I passed my hand over the elongated bulbous shafts, feeling that I knew them already. Yes, they reminded me of the great wooden pillars I had admired in the Khan's Palace at Khiva; I thought then that they must be descendants of a most ancient shape.

The mayor took charge of us (he was fat, round-faced, with

Mongolian eyes, wearing new knickerbockers) and led us to his little house. He gave us tea while we sat on a bright carpet. The room was bare, the window-panes of paper as in China. His water pipe went round among his followers but some of them exchanged tiny snuff-bottles. Christina was fascinated by the eyes of a beautiful but over-petted child with velvety lashes. The conversation was soon reduced to an exchange of smiles. In the end we went to the mayor's garden. Afghan vineyards are original—parallel rows of small steep slopes are built facing north and the plant crawls on that side, where the sun is less scorching.

In Karokh we hadn't seen a single woman.

According to the map, the spine-like ridge that rose to the north was the Paropamisus; driving up and down from one rib-like spur to another was like sliding along a gigantic scenic railway. We had no glimpse of the pass that gave exit from our narrowing valley.

Black tents squatted near a patch of turf. With a splendid movement, one arm erect and apparently motionless, two women whirled above their heads a long thread with a ball of wool at the end. Was it their way of spinning? Whizzing round very fast, it looked like a magic circle sheltering two rigid priestesses. Having approached, we found them ugly but for the way they carried themselves. They belonged to the Maldar Kutchi tribe that spends the winter near Shahbash, the village with the ancient windmills.

Driving along a clear channel, I remembered the words of the Herat postmaster, that the water south of the Sauzak is good. He did not mean uncontaminated. Good water is a boon that gives good tea and good bread. In China too, where tea is all-important, places and their waters get the kind of appreciation that the French give their vineyards.

At Charshambeh we rested under mulberry-trees by the side of a torrent. Three bearded hajjis sat near us, severe until, having dozed off, I nearly rolled into the river. They helped our ordering tea. The flat bread, thick, tasty, good-smelling, was the best we had ever had. The flesh of the melting peaches was as sweet as white honey. Two kittens gambolled on the carpet. And (welcome change!) walls were made with dry stones instead of dull adobe. The air, too, was good; I felt keenly alive, curious, courageous—ready to learn Persian even!

On the way to the pass we met donkeys loaded with pink and yellow logs—cedar, pine or juniper? Could a forest hide in this barren world? Had the Polish engineer meant it when he said he was to build a sanatorium in these forlorn hills?

The track opened out: a broad country rolled at our feet, barred far away to the north by the pink cliffs of a huge table-land. To the west it reared into a succession of knife-edged pinnacles of intense orange and purple, surprising and magnificent. Near at hand on our slope the blackness of a few old trees, twisted and full of character, enhanced these colour-values. Called *archa* or *archalek*, which means conifer, the trees must have been a kind of juniper. Between them, the earth disappeared under the dark round pin-cushions of dwarf bushes; sunrays played over their pink flowers.

Our descent was impressive. The track had been hacked out half-way down a sandy slope. Christina drove, sitting towards the mountain—which was lucky: from my seat it looked as if our off-side wheels turned in the void. At some places the crumbling soil was stiffened with a row of faggots. While we skidded round sharp curves, the glistening shale reminded me of the icy track the ski-racers had rushed down six months ago at Zakopane. I said nothing: to this day I am sure that Christina never guessed how soft that ledge was.

What a relief to reach a long hog's back yellow with ripening wheat, where three noble camels climbed uphill. The world was richly gilded by the last darts of the sun. But our lyric mood could hardly prevail against the sickness of our Afghan, unused to swishing round hairpin bends.

The scene narrowed as we reached poor, grey Kala-i-Nao. Villagers stood up hurriedly as we came—a mark of respect one still finds in Asia. A few, taking us for officials, gave a military salute: for some months there had been no private traffic.

A walled compound sheltered three mud-houses, one occupied by the governor of the province, the other by an office with crates of petrol, the third a *mihman-khana* or guest-house.

The yard was filled with square sunken flower-beds that could be flooded with irrigation-water. The favourite dark-purple petunias were trying to grow among flakes of clay.

Rice, bread and a dish of spinach were soon brought by a handsome servant: he studied us frankly with his virile, laughing eyes.

The small governor smiled as spontaneously as his servant. He wore plus-fours and on his head a straight *kola* of brown lambskin. Full-faced, almond-eyed, with a slightly aquiline nose and a skin hardly more tanned than mine, he belonged to the ruling clan of the Muhammadzai. For those who know, the fact is important, though government people in Kabul would have you believe that the tribal system has lost all meaning: when you question them about their sept they answer, "I am simply an Afghan!" This governor had no children and his wife being ill, he was without her—a most depressing state, he said.

He had been newly appointed to this poor province. Conditions and climate must have been better in the past when forests covered all the northern slopes of the range. Now only a few small pistachio-trees are still to be found, though they persist all the way to the Persian border. Further north, he said, we should cross the region of the *karakuli* lambskins that bring such profit to Afghanistan.

He offered us grapes so good that had I been told they were drops of dew from paradise I should not have been surprised nor called it a Persian floweriness. The peaches, sweet like ripe figs, came, he told us, from Khiva. While our host spoke in lively French (he was a pupil of one of the three foreign schools of Kabul) I wondered if apart from the nomad women who go unveiled, we were the first "open" girls he had seen outside his family.

Though the road was not finished, the governor was returning to Bala Murghau, his usual residence; so next morning our two cars started together. I sat in the governor's Chevrolet, having given him my place near Christina. I chatted with the Afghan chauffeur who spoke Russian. He did not think that with men like his compatriots who had no needs and ate only bread, Soviet propaganda would have any success. The Afghan is still under the sway of his mother, and being attached to Islam he is not likely to listen to the godless theories of his northern neighbours.

Great bumps in the track slowed us down but still we sent

grazing horses running for dear life. Round felt yurts mingled with black tents; Turkestan was not far off. When our boiling radiators needed a refill, the call of the governor was answered by men with water-skins slung over one shoulder.

At noon we stopped near the hamlet of Dareh Boum where a delegation of worthies was waiting for us. The Elders kissed the hand of the governor who, meanwile, looked charmingly unconcerned. We rode saddled horses as far as the white tents that had been rigged for us. After drinking some *doukh* (butter-milk, the most cooling drink of Asia) flavoured with mint, the three of us sat down cross-legged to a great repast eaten with our right hand—succulent kababs, pilau studded with nuts and spices, deep wooden dishes of creamy curds spooned up with a piece of flat bread. And as a finale, bowls of green or red tea at will. Ewer and towels were passed round for washing hands.

Some of the villagers who waited on us had carrot-coloured beards, the result of applying henna to white hair. According to an advice of the Prophet, to "bind" henna, to clean the teeth, to take wife and to use perfume are four things every believer should do. "The benefits are many that come from the use of henna. It drives out shifting pains through the ears, restores sight when weakened, keeps nose membranes soft, imparts sweet odour to mouth and strength to the roots of teeth, removes body odours as well as temptation from Satan, gladdens angels, rejoices believers, enrages infidels, is an ornament to the user and diminishes trials in the grave."* Far from enraging, these flaming beards always gladden me when I see them brightening a bazaar crowd.

The hottest hours of the day were spent in the tents. When we returned to the cars we found their bonnets hidden under rugs—as a defence against the fierce heat.

In its windy valley, the great Murghau pushed its tumultuous grey waters against the piles of the sunken bridge. The German construction was thrown down by an exceptional rise of the river, but it is an engineer's job to account for such possibilities, the governor said.

The river irrigates Merv in Soviet Turkmenistan, and ever since the Anglo-Russian convention of 1907 the Russians were annoyed by that border-line. Sometimes they accused the

* B. Donaldson: *The Wild Rue.*

Afghans of using too much of "their" water and the Amir had to prove to them that the snowfalls and not his subjects were responsible for such irregularities. Nowadays there is a great model village on the river, just on the Russian side of the border.

We found no real road. In ankle-deep dust we followed a track that much too boldly attacked round-topped hills. Just where climbing cars begin to fight, choke and gasp, men were embedding rough cobbles in that powdered clay. Twelve or fifteen workmen followed us from hillock to hillock, pushing the helpless cars or spreading rush mats before the wheels. By then the governor was impatient: he wanted to arrive before the time for the sunset prayers.

We were relieved to sight the new bridge, the square walls of a citadel and thin trees quivering above walled gardens.

Our great courtyard was filled with the usual sunken flower-beds. We spent the night on the terraced roof before our room on the first floor. There between earth and sky, the rustling of the poplar leaves lulled us to sleep before we had had time to feel drowned among the surging stars of a fathomless dark sea.

We spent a day at Bala Murghau, the governor having promised us two horses for visiting a camping tribe. But they never appeared. And so it happened that, having time to tidy our rucksack, we found a few onions from Trieste: the governor planted them at once, keen to see if they would do well in his province.

We had come down to an altitude of fifteen hundred feet and from now on a notion of heat was continually to occupy some part of our consciousness. During the hot hours, the governor took refuge in his *sardab* or cold-water room, a kind of cellar crossed by a rivulet. Joining him there from the oven-like upper world, I used to shiver, so great was the change of temperature.

Though a telephone had announced our arrival and though a disembowelled Ford adorned a corner of the garden, I felt as if plunged into the Middle Ages. Smoothly flowing, life seemed changeless. The bazaar was peaceful, even somnolent. Believers said their prayers kneeling on the platform of their booths. Subjects kissed the hand of their master. The dusty braying of asses filled the air. At the cross-road a dishevelled fakir held a beggar bowl.

It amused us to chat with the governor; and it was important to rest so that Christina should not get over-tired. Noticing that she was a great smoker, our host gave her many boxes of Russian cigarettes with cardboard mouthpieces. This was bad luck: I had just convinced Christina—or thought I had—that before attempting to master the weakness that caused her such remorse, she must train her will and gain confidence in herself through small victories like, for instance, controlling her daily smoking. And she agreed, partly no doubt because her provision had greatly dwindled!

The governor spoke about oil: "the world's best" had been struck in his province and the same quality was found as far south as Farrah. In 1936 the Inland Exploration Company of New York obtained a concession over more than two hundred thousand square miles of Western Afghanistan; the same "interests" had also secured a concession on Persian soil, thus insuring that no rival could tap their underground naphtha from across the border. But could the boring machines be brought so far and the oil be piped to Chahbar on the Indian Ocean across more than a thousand miles of desert? A five-year contract had promised twenty per cent of the benefits to the Afghans; but two years later the company had suddenly given up its claim. Some people say that the Americans were frightened by the oil-expropriation that took place in Mexico.

Shadows were lengthening across the garden. Conversation became personal.

The governor was puzzled. How could we live so long and so far away from our husbands and friends, how could we travel without them in foreign countries where everything, no doubt, seemed hostile to us or at least unusual? Once, when it had been his duty to go on tour, after two sleepless nights he had found that he could not bear to be separated from his wife: he went back to fetch her.

The following night, Christina's couch and mine were again side by side under the dazzling stars of Central Asia. Before dawn we heard quite near us the voice of our host calling "Madame!" (we knew he was camping in our wing of the house, for he had offered his apartment to a visiting official.) Tacitly, we postponed answering him till the sun rose. And then we told him how heavily we usually slept in a sheltered place, whereas in our tent even rustling leaves disturbed us.

The governor apologised for waking us. But the night was so long. He had not slept and would have liked to talk to us. Framed in the doorway, he stood in his European dressing-gown of dark-blue silk, his attitude at the same time shy and wilful. Then, with charm and simplicity, looking beyond both of us, he said: "I would have liked to breathe the flowery fragrance of your face!"

I decided that the remark was not for me, my face having been so far likened only to horse, ship's bow or wild grass.

22

SHIBARGAN

THE track took us round the western end of the Band-i-Turkestan, across a surprising world of steep round hills where I saw nothing but thistles. At one place they must have been cut in great quantities: the wind had piled them into a wall that blocked the sunken road near a pass. It was a new experience to dig into big balls of pins. Tall Aminullah, our new escort, helped willingly.

"Eastwards from Bala Murghau the Band-i-Turkestan forms the northern ridge between the Firozkhoi plateau and the sand formation of the Chal. It is a level, straight-backed line of sombre mountain ridge from the crest of which, as from a wall, the extraordinary configuration of that immense loess deposit called the Chal can be seen stretching away northwards to the Oxus, ridge upon ridge, wave upon wave like a vast yellow-grey sea of storm-twisted billows."*

We found ourselves in a dull, depressing, sand-coloured world. But suddenly felt alert, excited: a bright, untidy caravan was coming towards us. Riders, walkers, bears, monkeys, children were greeted with shots from our cameras. Then we dealt with the "whence and whither" questions. They were Jatts, or gypsies, going to Kandahar and further south. Opening his portable harmonium, one man forced his monkey to dance. Filthy children in red rags already showed the undauntable character of their people; one of them had huge and bold grey eyes. Fox-like but still somehow kingly, men rode past without stopping. Straddling a horse, a pair of kettle-drums followed. A rebellious white stallion was bleeding at the bit. By way of a ruby frontlet, a bay horse wore one of the reflectors usually screwed on the back of a bicycle. Bells, beads, necklaces, ample skirts—women just as impressive as the men—the scene was thrilling to watch, evoking similar encounters in another continent. We had seen the very brother

* Encyclopædia Britannica, 1875 edition: "Art Afghanistan."

of their dusty, moth-eaten bear two months ago in Yugoslavia.

At noon we rested in the clean little room built above the Kaleh Wali caravanserai. Kind Aminullah saw that grapes, curds and eggs were brought to us. It was market-day and men thronged the road at our feet. No trees, nothing but a world of yellow earth and yellow earthen walls in which the white of turbans and the red of kaftans vibrated joyfully as if in a composition by a master-painter. As usual, not a woman to be seen.

When we returned to the car, all the curious idlers pressed round us so tightly that our host—radiant yellow eyes enhanced by the wine-colour of his long coat—had to use a whip to clear the way.

Christina was growing fond of these men, strong, gay, holding each other by the little finger, sometimes irresponsibly trying to bump each other against the car as we passed and thoroughly pleased when their pal was frightened. Others laughed loudly when their mount bolted away, proud of their good seat on a horse.

We had reached a wide, flat, biblical valley: near huge haystacks, cattle were driven round and round to thresh the grain. The sun shone gaily and if I had not seen Kirghiz-like faces giggling at us over a wall, I could have thought I was near Kandahar where I loved to see a few peasants gather at the end of the day to dance their nervous, vigorous Afghan dance on the dusty threshing floor.

I was always thrilled by it, finding it wilder and more spontaneous even than the Caucasian acrobatics of a similar kind. The magic power of the drum commands the bounds, the leaps, the accelerating foot-work. Pirouetting at an incredible speed, the sun-tanned men throw their manes of shiny black hair now backwards, now sidewards—shocks of hair that reach to the shoulder. Living tops, they wheel out the fullness of their white skirts from beneath their tight waistcoats like a ballerina's tutu. Gathered at the ankle, the thick folds of the trousers evoke the elegant curves of the Græco-Buddhist sculptures that are found in this country. After the dance they re-wind their turbans and wipe their shiny faces with the long end that flows loosely down their backs.

They seem to dance just when they feel like it: there are no spectators, no girls to please, no alcohol to prime them up. In this beautiful and virile way they express their feelings, their overflowing vitality. Football matches, which may be said to be the Western way of doing the same thing, have only one of these two qualities.

It need not be the end of the day for tribesmen to dance, nor is the threshing floor indispensable. Once we drove through a small valley of northern Baluchistan; men were reaping wheat with sickles, all of them squatting in a line. Their leader stood singing and beating his hands to time their movements. They waved at us, we crossed the sun-scorched field to join them. They quickly formed a circle and with their crescent-shaped weapon in hand, bending now inside, now outside, moved with slow and complicated steps. The rhythm accelerated, the dust rose in billows, only their whirling hair was visible now and then while their arms were flung towards the sizzling midday sky. From time to time they uttered guttural growls, real roars. The dance over, they resumed their work, apparently not exhausted by their strenuous performance, obviously proud of having displayed their skill. Their bearded foreman—or ballet-leader—explained that they had performed the Tiger dance.

We have wandered from Sangalak-i-Kaissar, the village we reached on the day we met the Jatts. There we felt slightly linked with the rest of the world; people spoke of a regular service of motor-buses with the towns of Afghan Turkestan. I hoped it meant the roads would no longer force us almost to a stop at every humpbacked culvert. Like most modern cars, our "V 8" had too little clearance and a hundred times a day we grated these humps, accosting them sideways according to the best technique. If the hump sagged, show-ing its skeleton of wattle, matters were worse, for the water had made the road a quagmire in which our wheels whizzed angrily.

And it was on such a road that Christina tried to teach me the double de-clutch. I was keen to learn so that she would not have to do more than her share of driving. But she suffered so much when I crashed the gears, blocked the car or scraped our sump, she got so tense when a hump loomed ahead and I tried so hard not to exasperate her—that I was bound to fail.

I was worried to discover that her usual calm was a mere façade that hid so great a nervousness.

But it looked as if we could soon rest: Maimeneh, the end of our stage, was only half an hour away, so we heard from the mayor of the village, a strong man in khaki breeches who had blue eyes, a sign, perhaps, that there was Russian blood in the family. He wanted us to share the meal of his womenfolk.

We were soon sitting on a carpet under a mulberry-tree, surrounded by charming people. Old fashion-papers appeared, our opinion was wanted and, after some shy nudgings, a length of blue silk was brought which we were asked to cut out for the young daughter of the house. Our mimicry explained that since we wore trousers we knew nothing about frocks. I wouldn't mind making a dress for myself, but I could not run the risk of spoiling someone else's material. Bitterly regretting my ignorance of that kind of cutting, I found a solution: I gave our hostess a frayed linen dress of mine that could serve as a pattern.

Learning that Christina had been married for a few years, the mayor asked about her children. When he heard that she had none he exclaimed: "Then what have you been doing all this time?" Before Christina could think of an adequate answer, his wife, looking at my lean friend, announced: "She will have to eat a lot of rice before she can bear any!"

This little scene having broken the ice—if one can use such an expression with such a sweltering afternoon—we basked in an amiable atmosphere. Distinguished and quiet, all in white, the lady of the house reminded me of an Italian aunt of mine, petite, plump and black-haired. Her married daughter Zara— pink skirt, white blouse, white wimple—was rocking a fair-haired baby in a spotless cradle swung under a branch. A tall, handsome girl with a bold face framed by a softening white veil was the daughter-in-law, or so it seemed; she was nursing a brawny boy and when our hostess said he was "very black" and therefore not beautiful, a touch of contempt crept into her usually kind voice.

We shared a rich meal—a platter of rice in which were hidden bits of juicy lamb, followed by various vegetable dishes—and then felt very sleepy. Though still awake I was dreaming about Sinkiang: two faces with Mongolian eyes hovered in the background, an old woman and a girl called Hamitah. I thought they were of Kirghiz blood though with her soft and full face Hamitah could even be Chinese; her long gown with a big red flower-print reminded me of the loose *khalat* worn by the men of Samarkand; her little head managed to keep on the white cloth that hung all the way down her back. They were Turkomans and belonged to the group of the servants. Again and again my eyes went back to their impassive faces and, beyond them, to the wide stretch of earth they suggested.

On our way to Maimeneh we discussed a subject about which neither of us knew anything. I had noticed how often Christina's eyes had rested upon the handsome daughter-in-law. And now Christina asked if I thought it was perverse of her to be profoundly moved by the charm of a woman. It was a delicate question to answer, for it had roots and branches in every part of Christina's life. It would not be enough for me to tell Christina that she was the most straight and honest person I have met.

But my range of experience being quite different from hers, I could not analyse the cause of her reactions. When we had cross-questioned each other and talked at leisure, we reached certain conclusions which I reproduce briefly here because we had been so interested by them. For those who identify themselves completely with their bodies, it would be deplorable if they were to be mainly attracted by the qualities of their own sex. Physiological laws being by-passed, unfulfilment would be a first penalty followed by such mental consequences as morbidity and lack of balance. But with exceptional people who identify themselves almost entirely with their mind, who know that thought is foremost because where there is no thought there can be neither body nor object, the question is less important: the mind has no sex, or rather, it comprises both sexes alternately or even simultaneously. The body may grumble now and then at being forgotten, but since it is conditioned by the mind of which it is only a temporary tool, it will be unable to upset that mind. For such people it cannot be of grave consequence if they disobey the laws of nature: they can be said to have transcended them. But there is trouble ahead for those who are at one moment centred in the mind, the next in the body: the liberty the mind enjoyed is challenged, then, by natural laws that claim supremacy as soon as the body is given pre-eminence. No plane of being, in consequence, can learn its lesson: there is no way of coming to a conclusion or of finding a consistent line of action that could lead to inner peace. Unwillingly, unknowingly, people find themselves trying to ride two proud horses at the same time—the stallion Nature and the hermaphrodite Mind. They suffer, then, from being torn apart. As Christina was torn, perhaps.

We took two hours to reach Maimeneh. It was true that the mayor of Sangalak-i-Kaissar covered the distance in thirty minutes; but driving like the devil, he had already broken his bones once. It was late enough for charpoys* to be out in the middle of the street; men waited for the coolness of the night, using their inseparable snuff-bottles a last time. Put in the mouth the tobacco powder, mixed with lime, is hotter than red pepper: if you question the man who has just taken it he answers with a tongue paralysed by the burn. It gives him a woolly pronunciation rather like the English accent as it is imitated by music-hall artists on the continent. Pointing at a house with a wireless-mast, such a man told us that it was not the *mihman khana* but the "Rooshan Konshoolah-ti". He moved his bed to let the car pass and came with us to the guesthouse, a simple lodging in the middle of the sleepy town. The keeper had long drooping moustaches like a Mongol warrior and carried a petrol lamp that kept on petering out as if it protested at not being treated with proper respect.

In Maimeneh many things bore a "Rooshan" stamp—matches, sweets, cigarettes, tea-pots, sugar, petrol in crates called shellaks.

A bright boy who had attended the German school in Kabul interpreted for us when we called on the mayor—paunchy, bearded and yawning—to ask what kind of road lay ahead. Sand-dunes sometimes caused difficulties: one usually telephoned to a certain post so that men could stand by in case of need.

Like the dulled surroundings of Pekin when a storm-wind is heavy with the yellow dust from the Gobi, our earth and sky were choked with loess.

That day we knew for certain that we were in the country of

* Four-footed frame stretched with ropes, serving as a couch.

the "Persian lambskin": not only were sheep grazing at what looked like hills of sand, but we met cartloads of skins stiffened by their curing in a batter of salted flour. At a sorting-house near Andkhoi we fingered samples of *karakuli*—the black, shiny, smooth *nazuksha* with hardly any curl in it, small four-cornered skin of an animal eight days old, worth about £3; the "tackerr" or *breitschwantz* quality, rare, thin like moiré silk; the great-curl astrakhan skins, brown with flanks of café-au-lait colour or grey with a cool blue flash in their tight ringlets. The stories of pregnant ewes having their bellies slit to allow the pelts of the unborn offspring to be collected, were partly true: but it would only happen if the mother had a broken leg or was ill, a miscarriage impending.

The yearly export of *karakuli* skins to London and New York amounted to two and half million sterling—approximately half the total of Afghan exports.

I was keen to touch and admire these skins at their place of origin, for they were linking me with my adolescence: sometimes father had sold such an expensive coat to a customer abroad and I travelled to Paris to deliver it without delay. And it threw me back to the time when I planned to learn my father's trade while nevertheless escaping from the artificialities of town life: I nourished the idea of going to Canada or Asia to buy for him there the bales of raw skins he needed. And now I was on the spot, seeing how the bales were tightly sewn: piled together like a pack of cards, the skins were wrapped in one great piece of white leather.

Waddling along, the fat-tailed sheep were astonishing, their caudal appendix dangling heavily. It looked as if they carried behind them a big cushion tucked up in the middle of its lower side. A Turkoman embraced a couple of them so that I could study them. So far I cannot confirm the statement found in the footnotes to Marco Polo's book that some champion sheep carry their tail on a two-wheeled trailer.

Andkhoi was within sight of the barren Russian border. Its grey earth, grey camels, grey walls and cubic houses seemed bleached and asphyxiated by the heat. As if trying to dodge that climate, the covered bazaar was restfully dark. Though every booth was occupied, trade was not brisk. We teased a jeweller who would not accept our price for the traditional

silver necklace worn by brides—big round beads each with two
parallel pin-head motifs, a sober ornament sold by the weight
in ancient Chinese-looking scales. It is the carpet-hunt I
always enjoy most and though it is my desire, now ten years old,
to buy on the spot a good but cheap nomad rug, I was still
going from town to town without finding what I wanted. Most
of the men wore striped or flowered *khalats* and not a few the
mushrooming fleeced hat.

Young, gay and fat, the mayor advised us to travel to
Shibargan in the company of a passenger lorry so as to have
help if the sands were bad. By then, because of the difficult
road, we were reconciled to having an escort, though these
men were usually of low stock and not pleasant. They made
up for their enforced silence with us during the day by talking
the night through with the guestroom factotum.

One of them sighed and wailed without interruption and it
was really not surprising. Imagine him, in a temperature
approaching 115 degrees with legs pinched by sock-suspenders
and patent leather shoes squeezing his toes while his body
broiled in a black serge suit. When he stripped coat and braces
to help us through the sand, he displayed a shirt of pink, dark
green and violet stripes. Arrogant with inferiors and servile
with superiors, he was altogether ugly—and that in a country
where the simplest peasant is worth looking at.

The deep ruts of the lorries were too far apart for us, so we
skidded in the sand. Driving was so wearisome, we stopped at
Shibargan though it was not a usual stage. And our escort
having interfered with our camping-plans, a guide took us
across fallow fields and dried-up ditches to a gate in a wall.

Then things happened as if in a fairy-tale. In the first court
was a simple house and a huge tree in whose shade we left the
car to mirror itself in the *haus*, a deep square tank. In a second
enclosure—garden, drawing-dining-room in one—we met the
tall and elegant owner, Abdul Nahed Khan. He left his
friends to welcome us and asked us to sit under a pale plane-
tree. On the red velvet quilt and cushions which were brought,
our escort sat without taking off his muddy shoes, oblivious of
the most elementary rule of behaviour in countries where
people live on the ground; or perhaps he was too lazy to undo
his tight laces.

A meal was served where we were. By then we knew how to make a bolus of rice and meat with our fingers; but it was quite another matter to tackle bits of brinjal in a succulent sauce of oil and curds. After our dusty day, the cleanliness of that oasis where falling leaves made a soothing noise, did us good.

After sunset we moved to an elevated platform in the centre of the regular garden. The flowers paled in their sunken beds while stars were brightening up in the velvety dome overhead. But for ourselves, everything was like a Persian miniature. Rugs and quilts were brought before we were left to enjoy the purity of an Asiatic night.

Our host was a bachelor. He gave the impression of being completely at peace with himself. He was a friend of Shah Wali Khan whose portrait hung in the house, (the man who freed Kabul from the usurper in 1929, a brother both of Hashim Khan the actual Prime Minister and of the late king Nadir Shah,) and now Afghan Minister in Paris.

We decided to start very late so as to avoid the heat of the day. During the afternoon Abdul Nahed Khan brought out his chessmen at which game we were easily defeated. Then he fetched an album and showed us picture post-cards of Mont Saint Michel, the Eiffel Tower, ships in Port Said, domes in the Kreml. Among these views I saw the face of a pretty brunette signed "ta Lucienne". For some time I wondered whom it had been sent to: our host had not travelled further than Tashkent and I found it difficult to believe that there were Luciennes in that town. Was it possible to ask who she was?

But the time had come to take leave of our gentlemanly host.

23

TURKESTAN

At dusk we slipped through the mat of dust that hung motionless above the road. Under our headlights, riders clothed in white seemed to be moving silently through smoke. Later we thought with excitement that we were overtaking majestically pacing elephants, their narrow and sloping hindquarters ending in a tiny tail. But they were only tall camels, their grey bulk made of two vertical sacks that built a massive ridge above their backs.

Akcha loomed splendidly out of the night, a pale angular citadel surrounded by low flat-roofed houses. Men were stretched on their stringed charpoys; a group of brightly painted buses rested their tired bones, their bonnets touching. Once more we had that direct physical feeling of being in a remote corner of the world.

It was four in the morning, we had drunk our tea and wanted to start, hoping to reach Mazar-i-Sharif before the heat of noon. Since the road was now easy, we dismissed the escort who so cramped our style. But our man began to shout and soon we had many stalwart Afghans around us. Wearing a stylish *khalat* with brown stripes, an "old beard" who spoke excellent Russian tried to settle the controversy. He understood our point: we were giving a letter to our escort saying he was not to be blamed because we had left him behind. In such a heat, when the slightest pressure exasperated our skin, we could no longer bear to be squeezed three in front, especially when the man's dirty socks forced us to live with a handkerchief to our noses. (I do not know if all this was translated, but the sympathy of the crowd was certainly not with our horrible policeman.)

Meanwhile, because we did not want to lose face, the precious morning hours drifted away. The escort would only let us go if the mayor of Akcha ordered him. The interpreter went to the mayor. At last he returned accompanied by a new escort and a tray of figs for us! Defeated and impatient to start, we took the new man on board.

He was very tall and did not know how to keep his knees steady; he was prognathous and did not know how to keep his mouth shut. He had to keep it open anyhow, to be sick from the motion of the car: it was a change from his predecessor's spitting of tobacco-juice. This was enough to spoil the quaint charm of travelling through what looked like a lunar country asphyxiated by too much dry heat. It was the nature of the soil and the lack of relief, no doubt, that were responsible for the deadly whiteness of the light. Moving with the wind, the car was unbearably hot.

The country was quite flat, sometimes furrowed by great irrigation channels which distributed waters born high and far among the hills of central Afghanistan, in the cool lakes of the Band-i-Amir which we were to visit.

To give some respite to our policeman, we halted at a hut in the desert where an Uzbek tending his samovar sold us some thirst-quenching *chai sabz* or green tea. The shade cast by the hut was all that could be found. A decent Afghan was sleeping there on the beaten earth, and before we could prevent it he was kicked awake and sent away by our man. It filled us with anger.

And that on the morning when we were approaching the ruins of Balkh, Bactres, the Mother of Cities, known to have been twenty miles in circumference, but dead now in this plain of the Oxus which, in the sixteenth century B.C. so they say, witnessed the first Aryan migration on its way to India by way of Herat, Kandahar and the Bolan pass south of Quetta. Balkh, where the religion of Zoroaster was for the first time adopted by a king, Balkh, where according to Marco Polo, Alexander the Great married the daughter of Darius, the town whose satrap Bessus had killed that Darius while he was escaping through Khorassan.

In the second century B.C. Chang Kien was at the head of a Chinese mission sent to the Yue-chi of Sogdiana (which is the same as Bactria); his journey seems to mark the beginning of the silk trade across Asia. The Yue-chi were Indo-Scythians who had recently invaded the country, until then a great out-post of Hellenism. "It is because these successors of Alexander the Great were so forceful and active that you are going to excavate Græco-Buddhist remains," I said to Christina.

The white Huns were the next to invade Bactria in the fifth century A.D. In spite of their ravages, the country was still Buddhistic in style when two centuries later Hsuan Tsang the pilgrim arrived from China on his way to India "in search of wisdom"—Hsuan Tsang whose tracks I have crossed during three journeys to Central Asia and whose writings had so greatly helped me to appreciate what I saw. There were still, in Balkh, a hundred monasteries rich in relics of the Buddha when he arrived from Kunduz, the capital of the Western Turks who ruled over Afghan Turkestan or Tokharestan.

At Balkh, Hsuan Tsang admired "a magnificent plateau": there must have been more water in the country then than there is nowadays. The change may be due to the fact, affirmed by geologists, that the crust of the earth is still rising in this part of the world.

A century later the priest of the celebrated fire-altar of Balkh was converted to Islam and his example was followed by the landowners. In 1221 Balkh was laid waste by Genghis Khan. At first, the town that had sheltered Muhammad of Khwarezm had simply been occupied. But when Genghis Khan heard that the son of Muhammad had raised an army of seventy thousand men in Southern Afghanistan, he destroyed the town, marched to Bamian and later defeated the young man by the river Indus.

Fifty years later Marco Polo arrived at Balkh which he calls a large and magnificent city. "It was formerly more considerable but has sustained much injury from the Tartars who in their frequent attacks have partly demolished its buildings. It contained many palaces constructed of marble and spacious squares still visible, although in a ruinous state."*

Timur in the fourteenth century was the next invader and his example was followed by the Uzbeks who conquered Herat in 1506. It was one of their descendants, Abdul Aziz, who fought Prince Aurangzeb of Delhi, then governor of Balkh. The Moghul prince was brave, dismounting at sunset to pray during the battle, and winning the admiration of both armies. "To fight such a man is to court ruin" cried Abdul Aziz, and

* *Travels of Marco Polo.*

suspended battle. It was the last attempt of the Moghuls to
retain these far-away provinces.

We had no hope of emulating Renan and his *Prière sur
l'Acropole* by meditating over the ruins of Balkh, comparing
Asia with Europe: dreaming about the future of Paris, London
or Berlin: our escort would have annoyed us, standing near,
watching our movements, ready to forbid the use of our cameras
as he had already done before. Photophobia was the latest
affliction of Afghan officialdom—by contagion, probably, from
Persia which tries to nip in the bud pictures that show her not
yet entirely modern.

But we planned to outdo our gaping man.

Reaching the dead, bleached mounds of clay that had once
been the ramparts of Balkh, Christina walked towards them,
arming her camera and followed by the escort shouting
Mafi! Mafi! Meanwhile, my gaze was fixed on a tall
monument with a shiny blue dome that stood a few hundred
paces away at the entrance of the living town. Jumping back
into the car, I drove to it as quickly as possible, leaving behind
me a man on the verge of being split between us.

I had gained a few minutes during which I busied myself
with my three cameras, taking coloured stills, black-and-white
stills, and coloured "movie". The sun shone harshly on the
lofty ribbed dome and on the arched portal to which it was
yoked. The dazzle of glazed tiles brought an unexpected touch
of liveliness in a world that had fainted in the whiteness of the
midday glare. Most of these tiles were too pale to please me,
but that Green Mosque which stands by the side of the shrine
of Khwaja Abul Nasr Parsar stood proudly in the square and
I liked the thick spiral minarets that framed the great portal.

Khwaja is a name given to a sect of holy men who once
acquired sovereign power over the Khans of Turkestan and
whose tombs are found all over Central Asia. This name is
perhaps derived from *khojagian*, a teacher. They belonged to
the darvish order of the Naqshbandis and they developed
the "Power of the Will" through perfect concentration: "It
is impossible to conflict with an *arif* or 'knowing person'
possessed of the 'Power of the Will', is written in their books.
The 'Tarikh-i-Rashidi' informs us that 'they were workers of

miracles and healers of the sick and in these capacities obtained
a hold over the minds of the mass of the people'." The Naqshbandis (painters) were so called because their founder
Naqshband "drew incomparable pictures of the Divine Science
and painted figures of the Eternal Invention which are not
imperceptible."*

As soon as Christina joined me, shadowed by the policeman,
we speeded towards Mazar-i-Sharif. To silence the expostu-
lations of our man, I began to read aloud from the first booklet
I happened on—Mr. Ford's instructions to owners of his cars.
But I soon stopped: it was too disquieting to read all we had
done that we should not have done.

The deep pot-holes of the road were a menace to our springs;
but we forgot them more or less, in the question: "Is it possible
for our time to produce such mystics as the Naqshbandis?"
Born at Balkh, the most famous of them was Jalal-ud-din Rumi,
founder of the darvish order of the Maulavis. Like his friend
Shams-ud-Din of Tabriz known as the "Moving Spirit of the
Order, the Sultan of the Mendicants, the Mystery of God on
Earth, the Perfect in word and deed", he lived at the beginning
of the thirteenth century, the century during which Genghis
Khan brought one world to an end by destroying all its great
capitals—Balkh, Merv, Nishapur, Rey. Perhaps if a world-
war—the modern equivalent to a Mongol invasion—was to
destroy our present world, mystics would rise once more, eager
to deal with facts more important and less sickening than the
madness of men.

We travelled with a bookshelf fixed above the back of our
seat. The poor books were shaken madly during all these days,
but we rejoiced to be able to lay our hand on the right volume
at the right moment. Rubbing against each other were Marco
Polo, Pelliot, Evans-Wentz, Vivekananda, Maritain, Jung, a
life of Alexander the Great, Grousset, the *Zend-Avesta*. I picked
The Darvishes by John P. Brown and H. A. Rose, and read
aloud a passage about Jalal-ud-din Rumi. "When on a roof
with other youngsters, he was asked if it were possible to jump
to the next house-top. He answered: 'Woe to the human being
who should try to do what cats and dogs do. If you feel yourself
competent to do it, let us jump towards heaven,' and then he

* John Brown and H. A. Rose: *The Darvishes*.

sprang and was lost from their sight. The youths all cried out as he disappeared, but a moment later he returned, altered in complexion, changed in figure, and said that a legion of beings clothed in green had seized him and carried him in a circle upwards. 'They showed me strange things of a celestial character and on your cries reaching us they lowered me down to the earth' ".

Later whenever he became absorbed in fervid love for Allah, he would rise from his seat and turn round; and on more than one occasion he began to recede upwards from the material world. Only by means of music could he be prevented from disappearing from among his devoted companions."

Years afterwards I came to know of lines of his that might have been written for Christina:

> Knowing will, memory, thoughtfulness
> A hell, and life itself a snare,
> To put away self-consciouness;
> It is the soberest men who bear
> The blame of Drugs and Drunkenness.
>
> (JALAL-UD-DIN RUMI.)

24

POL-I-KHUMRI

THOUGH Mazar-i-Sharif is the main town of Afghan Turkestan as well as a centre of pilgrimage, we wanted to leave quickly before the authorities could get to know of us. Not in order to realise my plan of vanishing into the wilds of Kafiristan (I must first introduce Christina to the Hackins), but, to enjoy the beautiful valley of the Hindu Kush, it was essential to skip out of that escort-system. In our little hotel (tiled bathroom, metallic beds and long dining-tables) my ears were continually strained towards the telephone for fear the manager was announcing us to the police.

The name of the town—Noble Shrine—comes from a tomb which, so the Afghans claim, is that of Hazrat Ali, the fourth Imam, who had many Sufis among his followers. The shrine, a massive building topped by pale turquoise domes, stands in the middle of a flagged courtyard. Looked at from the entrance gate, it is a bewildering vision of flashes darting from every tile-glazed wall. But as you approach the charm wanes: there are too many pale blue and yellow surfaces and, as with Dulac's illustrations, there is something too exquisite about them. Heavy flocks of white pigeons landed noisily in the shade of the arched *ivans;* lines of beggars waited patiently for a donor to appear.

Built by the orders of Husayn Baikara who ruled in Herat in the fifteenth century, the mosque was re-tiled less than a hundred years ago. Genghis Khan destroyed an older shrine built in 1136. Hazrat Ali lives in my memory for the peaceful atmosphere of refuge that enveloped me as soon as I passed the limit of the sanctuary where a heavy iron chain hung in a festoon across the gate.

We were only two in the car when we left Mazar. In the late afternoon the heat was still exhausting, but we meant to spend the night on the heights of Haibak.

We crossed a pale desert where brown tents stood sharply

under dark-blue clouds. Overtaking us, a strong wind scudded along. Our floor-boards were so hot that my shoes no longer protected me: I drew my feet up on to the seat. A sandstorm was brewing somewhere.

At Tashkurgan we were to branch off to the south, following the Kabul road which climbs up over the Hindu Kush. I should have liked to continue straight ahead towards the source of the Oxus till I linked up with my tracks four years ago in the Chinese Pamir. I would have passed the ruins of Kunduz where the Hackins had unearthed the first Buddhist monuments found in Bactriane, except for the stupas of Balkh; I would have crossed the province of Badakshan whose hereditary kings, in the time of Marco Polo, still descending from Alexander the Great, held the title of Zulcarnein, Lord of the Horns, the Arabic epithet of the great Macedonian; Badakshan famous for its rubies and for the lapis lazuli that coloured all the dark-blue mosaics I have seen; Badakshan whose original people are "of a violent and coarse disposition" according to Hsuan Tsang who on his way back to China followed through their country the upper course of the Oxus. Hsuan Tsang also wrote that "for the most part they have greenish-blue eyes and thereby differ from other people"—a fact still true to-day.

At dusk we passed through Tashkurgan which seemed to consist only of garden walls. And there, just as we were turning towards the hills, a back tyre burst—its own way of protesting against the unbearable heat. We screwed on a spare wheel. It was deflated. Keen and intelligent, two tribesmen pumped it for us and left. No sooner had we packed our tools than the tyre was flat once more. The screwing on of the second spare wheel claimed the rest of our energy. Not only was I stunned by the heat, but our sweat falling freely in the dust attracted such a cluster of blood-sucking mosquitos that I could hardly see what I was doing.

Night had come, stifling. It was foolish to climb into the hills with no spare wheel: they must be repaired. We might find help in the rest-house we knew existed in the village. But unable to find it, we were helpless in a place apparently dead. We banged at wooden doors, tried to spy through locked gates. Muffled in dust, the world was silent. It was a queer experience: I had the feeling of acting in a dream when one knows that all one's efforts are useless. Were the inhabitants afraid of bandits?

Camping on the road was out of the question when a shower-bath and perhaps a driver willing to patch our tubes were within a stone's throw from where we stood. Then a gate lined with flattened petrol tins was unbolted: a dignified personage appeared followed by a servant with a lamp. Our difficulty was at an end.

By ourselves we should never have found the rest-house: beyond a huge wrought-iron gate, a *jardin à la française* sloped towards the palace of Jahnama built originally for Amir Abdur Rahman, the shrewd man who ruled Afghanistan at the end of last century. I imagined him solid like his palace.

It was here, at Tashkurgan, that Abdur Rahman tried to subdue the unruly governor of Badakshan. But his soldiers were disloyal: they began to run towards the governor Ishak Khan to surrender to him. Afraid of being taken prisoner, Ishak Khan decamped and so the victory that was within his grasp turned to defeat!

Before he became Amir, Abdur Rahman had been defeated by Shir Ali in Kabul. He took refuge in Samarkand where he spent ten years. Taking him for a country bumpkin, the Russians used to discuss all their political affairs before him, convinced that he did not understand them. But the future Amir had studied Russian secretly and learned much about Asiatic politics.

Walking through the empty halls of Jahnama, I thought of him—bearded, shrewd, wearing the astrakhan *kola*, corpulent, dignified, stiffened with rheumatism.

It was still early morning when, climbing out of a great ravine, we reached Haibak, the Samangan of Persian legend. The new sun filled an idyllic scene. The impressive ruins of a crenellated castle crowned a hill; at its foot sparkled a clear shallow stream where women draped in black filled shiny bulging water-skins and hitched them on the back of asses.

Sitting on a rush-mat and drinking tea from small bowls, we admired now the distant hills we were to penetrate, then the amber fields near at hand; or nearer still, the superb heads and aristocratic poise of three elders. There was a fruit-vendor, too, by a pile of mottled melons where each customer made a

careful choice before concluding his purchase. Further on, a
sheep hung from a branch, the butcher skinning it dexterously.
Behind us where a row of tea-pots glistened on a shaded shelf,
a boy was fanning the charcoal of his samovar. A few men
wore embroidered skull-caps, gay like a cupful of bright
flowers. Pigeons cooed, lost in a world known to them alone;
gazing at the strangers, a boy was absent-mindedly stroking
his tame partridge. From the flat roof where they were parked,
a few brown goats looked at the horizon.

And then, to make the moment magnificent, six slow camels
surged up, solemn under dark trappings and dangling tassels,
the first carrying a nomad woman of rank with Turkoman head-
gear and an orange shawl, the most joyful note in the blue
morning.

Joy, yes, and peace—peaceful flocks thudding past the great
castle where in the seventeenth century a king of Haibak
started a campaign in favour of Pashtu, the language of the
Afghan tribes; peace of the earth yielding its yellow wheat to
peasants clad in white; peace of a steady world that knows
nothing of our forty-eight-hour week, or "organised leisure", of
cylinder-presses that flood the world with innumerable
newspapers.

On the evening of the same day the scene was to be surprisingly different.

From the height of Haibak we slipped down into the great
valley of the Kunduz which we were to follow to the Shibar
pass. By the river we found reedy swamps, paddy-fields, a
warm dampness. It was with drooping eyelids that we continued towards a part of the valley that looked narrower.

All of a sudden, beyond a rocky spur, with marvelling, with
horrified amazement, our dazzled eyes beheld the white walls
of a mill-building whose numerous dog-tooth roofs cut into the
dusty air. Around it, tents and shanties for thousands of men;
and further on, not yet finished, a great dam of reinforced
concrete. Here in the heart of Asia and with no Sovietic
impulse, this time, to explain the miracle, this great monster
had taken root, modest Mazar, the nearest town, being one
hundred and forty miles away.

We stopped on an arched bridge, built perhaps seven hundred
years ago by Genghis Khan; though it had withstood the

tearing whirlpools of a wild river for so many centuries, it was doomed to perish now under the waters of the new basin.

The scene recalled certain descriptions of the Far West—barracks, tents, booths, dusty work-yards in a great wind, noise and activity everywhere, narrow-gauge waggons clanking along, rivets being hammered in, hills re-shaped, cement crunched—everything rummaging, flashing, transporting. We were at Pol-i-Khumri.

We drank and rested in a *chai-khana*. We learned that five hundred looms and eight hundred workmen, so it was planned, were to spin and weave ten million yards of cotton a year. The hydro-electric plant also furnished power to a beet-sugar refinery at Baghlan, further down the river. Thousands of workmen had already died of malaria. (The same thing happened with the great Wakhstroi built by the Soviets north of the Oxus seven years ago.)

The men differed greatly, though they all wore rags instead of turbans. The gentle Hazara, whose ancestors were left in the country by Genghis Khan, had high cheek-bones and narrow eyes. Flowing black beards and regular features marked the hill-Tadjik, who is probably our Asiatic cousin. Afghan faces were long and narrow, with aquiline noses and piercing eyes. The fat-faced ones were Uzbeks whose brothers live beyond the Oxus where Tashkent and Samarkand have been westernised long ago—where pioneers of socialism sometimes give a pitying thought to feudal Afghanistan. Persianised Turks are called Kizilbash. Hardy Turkomans from the desert plains of the north, with their proud straight noses, are known to be the only willing workers of the lot.

Some trained men had come from Kabul where factories are already functioning, but most of the workmen were from neighbouring villages. How did they react to a day of uninterrupted work? How did they like to be under the eyes of a foreman when, so far, most of them had been free to sit in the shade of their elm-tree when they had no pressing work?

Sometimes we heard a great rumour: a group chanted or rather yelled a word, always the same: *Yakh Chariah!* to encourage themselves at their work. It was also their war-cry, we were told. How significant—to attack one's work like an enemy!

Riding a Badakshan pony, a smart German called on us at the tea-house (looking at him with keen curiosity, I remembered that I had not seen a European for a long time), and that night we enjoyed the hospitality of Herr Kuhn while work went on in a wonder-valley flooded with electricity!

A portrait of Hitler watched over the coffee-table, the pet dog, the cushions, the fair-haired lady of the house. Were we still in Asia? Yes, without a doubt: our hostess announced she used only tinned milk: it was too risky to have anything to do with the cows of the valley!

The Kuhns knew Iran: he had built and occupied the veranda'd house where we slept at Shahi by the Caspian. And Frau Kuhn made a comparison which she intended to be flattering to the Persians:

"Afghans are impossible. During the dirty winter weather in Kabul they don't step down from the pavement when they meet me: they force me to wade through the slush, whereas a Persian will always make way for me."

"It is well known" I said, "that the proud Afghan thinks he is better than anybody else. Moreover, however much respect he may have for his mother, unknown females are mere cattle to him."

But, thinking of another grievance, Frau Kuhn was not listening. "Would you believe it," she said: "Frau Kirsten and I were asked not to bathe in the river, the only thing that helps us to bear this tropical heat!"

"It is difficult for us to imagine what it feels like never to have seen the arms or legs of a woman in the open, not to speak of her body in a bathing-suit," said Christina.

"But we don't exhibit ourselves, why do they look at us?" retorted plump Frau Kuhn. "Anyhow, Herr Kuhn made it clear to the Elder of the valley that the two *khanums* would go on bathing. He would submit to the laws of the country most willingly, but he was going to live according to the customs of Germany. He was not prepared to hide his wife under a shroud every time she came out of the house."

The two German engineers spoke of their difficulties. The Afghan officials were full of grand ideas but would not realise that they lacked the right personnel: they had no honest underlings that could be trusted to carry out their orders. And though they had no foreman in carpentry or masonry, they were starting an engineering university! Nothing ever got done, or the slightest achievement cost tons of wasted energy. Typical example: after months of effort, one of their colleagues in Kabul, despairing of ever having a broken window-pane replaced, went to the P.W.D. Minister to complain. "I am the only man here who is allowed to kick or use a stick: always come to me" remarked the Minister.

"Do you remember what we heard the other day?" someone else remarked: "Skoda sold mountain machine-guns to the army. When the soldiers have to carry the separate parts of a weapon, they find them too heavy and put them down. It is written in the Quran, they say, that heavy work is to be left to asses. These men had to be taken to task and taught that war against the invader, or training for it, excuses all infractions of the Quran."

Herr Pertsch added: "When I tell my carpenter that the new door is not perpendicular, the man laughs at me: 'What does it matter so long as it shuts?' How can I teach such men that every fraction of a millimetre is important when they have to build the foundations for a Diesel engine?"

" 'I allow you to deal blows as long as the dam is finished in time,' the Minister told me," said Herr Kirsten. "Coming to blows is dangerous in Afghanistan: it is forbidden by law. The principal of the German College had to leave the country within twenty-four hours because he slapped the face of the sentry who—obeying his orders—prevented him from entering the repair-shop of the Motor-Khana where he had left his car."

Trying to analyse what I had felt when I discovered these mills hidden in the folds of the Hindu Kush, I asked the Germans if they were not upset to think how much misery their grand construction had already brought to the valley? Were not the technical achievements of our civilisation a curse when they swept the Afghans off their feet, plunging them too suddenly into a life that was never meant for them? But these engineers were not willing to consider that their power-plant would spoil the indigenous way of life. Of course they mentioned Progress, our emaciated god that thrives on wars. Their job was to build: they were satisfied so long as they built. Happy the short-sighted who see no further than what they can touch.

We were allotted the dining-room with its two divans. The heat tormented us, we could not sleep, we talked.

We thought that it is not the machine in itself that is bad, but the way we use it. When man is master of a machine he feels more powerful, whether he is free-wheeling on a bicycle or climbing above towers of cloud in the skies. A skilled bus-driver shows a kind of dignity: master after God on board his ship, he is a hero to his twenty-five passengers. But when man becomes the slave of a machine that dictates the gestures he is to make, he soon finds that life becomes tasteless, even though his increased wages allow him more and tastier food. Yet taste is in you, not in the morsel. Such work does not call for initiative, decision, understanding or the joy of making. Men born in our monstrous capitals have little choice, they can hardly avoid becoming factory-hands; but to turn healthy peasants or independent shepherds into nerveless or up-rooted robots is nearly a murder. A day must come when machines will no longer be used to stifle half of what makes a man. It is the only solution, for in Europe we cannot go back to the patriarchal system by which the clan looked after the needs of all its members.

"In the meantime," said Christina, "there is a cry for quinine, schools, hospitals, roads and soldiers. To pay for these there must be factories, docile subjects and tax-paying workers. So, little by little, we come to the sort of development that charac-terises Europe, whose main effect on the rest of the world amounts to this: more machines and more specialised workers producing more and more every day."

Pol-i-Khumri grew into a symbol of our machine-age oppressing the heart of man, our machine-civilisation copied servilely by Asiatic countries in spite of the fact that all Easterners have nothing but contempt for the Western bar-barians. The nature, the climate and the character of Afghanistan were completely alien to what was already appearing here and there—not only factories and hurried industrial schemes, but houses of Western type with broad windows and thin roofs, and tailored suits, laced shoes, bicycles.

. . . When mill-woven cotton means a population of robots, is it not better to go on wearing homespun?

Men must certainly be fed and clothed, but in doing this must we strangle their most important faculties? In other words: Is it necessary that each Asiatic country should go to the bitter end of our materialistic experiment? Taking it for granted that Europe is now beginning to see the need of founding its life once more on spiritual values, when will Asia in its turn see through the mirage of "immediate industrialisation at all costs"? Will Hashim Khan the shrewd Prime Minister of Afghanistan see that by introducing too many Western methods among his people, he will upset them? They will be unable to fight the moral depression that crawls in the wake of our materialistic culture. Mines, oil, electricity, coal, offer quick and big returns. Cattle, fruit, lambskins, wool, wheat, forests, demand patience but they are Afghan products calling for Afghan activities: they provoke no rupture with the past, no forcing of an alien growth. They leave harmony and joy of being free to blossom normally.

"It ought to cause us deep concern that it is the material and acquisitive side of Western civilisation that has so powerful and revolutionary an effect on the rest of the world," wrote Dr. J. H. Oldham in one of his Christian News Letters. It is the answer to give to engineers who mention Progress.

It is not the modesty of our research scholars, the self-abnegation of our scientists, the honesty of our craftsmen that are known abroad, but our ways of making money, our sewing machines, looms, motor-cars, guns, movies and cheap text-books. Why does our civilisation disintegrate everything it touches? Why do most of Arabs, Japanese, Hindus, Chinese adopt the worst of our ways?

Besides two thousand lodgings for workers, Herr Pertsch was going to build schools. At Kabul in 1937 the Prime Minister had told me that half his budget was spent on education; his actual motto was a sentence from the Quran: "Seek knowledge though it take you to China." He believed that education was the best safeguard against being invaded by ambitious neighbours.

Schools! In Kirghizistan, Manchuria, China, India, the word is uttered as if it could solve all difficulties. Of course

I am glad I can read and write and tot up what I have spent when I see my purse is empty, but schools don't so much develop your faculties as choke them with tired facts and lame arguments that the Chinese student and the Hindu clerk will use like Gospel truth: "We know for certain that man descends from the ape." No, we don't. Tolstoy, who knew our Western culture as well as the ignorance of his peasants, writes in *War and Peace* of the "so-called advanced people—that is a mob of ignoramuses" living in "our conceited age of the popularisation of knowledge thanks to the most powerful weapon of ignorance—the diffusion of printed matter".

Our Western ideas will spread further with the development of education. It will help to make a young man more quickly free on the material plane: he will no longer need to obey Gholam Haidar, his father-in-law, or whoever was keeping him. But our kind of education is a dangerous solvent: it divides, it will teach him to criticise, he will think he knows enough to judge. He will augment the ranks of little Prometheuses and he will soon feel alone, paddling against the world in utter solitude.

The question is: are the advantages of hospital, school, newspaper or wireless at the disposal of the new factory-hand, worth the loss of the lingering smile that used to accompany his hard but well-balanced life? Soviet Russia answers: Yes, because the profits made by the factory don't go to a Shah or a plutocrat but ultimately return to the worker. I say No, convinced that if you spend the best part of your energy walking two steps one way, then two steps the other way eight hours a day year after year, mending the broken threads of devilish spinning bobbins, you have no inspiration or vitality left for living your own life during the rest of the day.

But before I say No with complete certitude on behalf of the Afghan, I should spend one or two years with him, sharing his life rich in great winds, sun, snow and hardships. I must be prepared to consider it possible that the confused tribesman might eagerly exchange his free skies for factory-life and a lousy wattle-and-daub room in Kabul so as to laugh once a week at a degrading "movie" made among cardboard settings; so as to have a daily shave while he listens to the town gossip; so as to "stuff wads of chewed newspapers" into the ears of his neighbours at the tea-house.

In the early morning we rode up a side-valley, then followed a track zigzagging freely across a wide country of gentle round hills barren and scorched like those we were to see beyond Bamian. Here and there in a far-away depression, animals were grazing—mere spots like nits sheltering in the hollows of an unbleached cloth.

We did not go far. The feeling of so much space was exhilarating. We drank in the impression of boundlessness that arose from the monotonous hills. And opposed it in our minds to the transient ant-heap stirring of the valley.

After lunch I felt ill. The heat had upset me, I suppose, or perhaps it was the wooden saddle of my jogging pony or the exciting talk of the previous evening. I felt so weak that Christina went without me to visit the great buildings.

Once more I wondered at her: it was the second time during the journey that this frail girl was showing more strength than I. Where did she hide it?

25

DO-AU

WE were approaching the most beautiful part of our long journey.

Haibak had been a threshold at the foot of the Hindu Kush, and now the valley of the Kunduz was to take us to its heart. *Hindu Kush* comes, perhaps, from the Greek name for these mountains, "Indian Caucasus". Or, according to the fourteenth-century traveller Ibn Battuta, it means "slayer of Indians" because "the slave boys and girls who are brought from India die there in large numbers as a result of the extreme cold and the quantity of snow. We crossed this mountain by a continuous march from before dawn to sunset. We kept spreading felt cloth in front of the camels for them to tread on so that they should not sink in the snow."

Camels are dwindling, replaced by grunting and clanking lorries that live on an oily juice from far-away Burma or Baku. No more do leaders of caravans gather at night around the fire in the *serai* to listen to a story-teller. The *serai* has become a garage where resourceful drivers spend part of the night at repairs under their machines. Their apprentices help them as soon as they have emptied the radiator—seizing the steam-hot screw with the loose end of their turban—and fixed a jack to support the far end of the overloaded floor-boards.

These modern beasts of burden lead a strenuous life. Ruts and pot-holes are so many in Afghanistan that some people even make out that they are part of its strategic defences. In winter the unwieldy "beasts" slide up and down the icy grooves of the ten-thousand-foot Shibar pass, between snow-walls that have been known to reach a height of ten feet. Brakes, even supposing they were in working order, are useless then: when the lorry must be stopped, the driver relies on his *batcha* ("child") who has to overtake the car and thrust a big mallet in front of one of the wheels.

Lorries die on the road like donkeys. I have seen them side

by side, the first wheel-less, showing its rusted heart, the other eye-less, the vultures having begun on him, his little hooves motionless after a modest agony. A metallic carcase can sometimes be spied down a ravine where it landed after a skid; or perhaps, turning the blind corner hacked out of a cliff, it collided with a bus and capsized. One of those I saw in 1937 was at the bottom of the Dareh-i-Shikari. There a wooden bridge gave way and seven passengers were killed. The driver escaped but was fined for "breaking bridges"!

Which poet will sing the lorries of Asia? the modern epic of the Gobi desert, of the Burmese ranges, of the Shensi hills?—sing the rattling convoys that cannot wait for their wounded and the couples that man them: the silent driver so used to his young mate that he speaks to him by gestures only, the driver who takes such risks that your hair stands on end and you need all your will not to jump out. The young mate is dead tired but his eyes are still shining with the pride of having taken to the road. The boy stands all day long at the rear of the lorry where there is room for one foot only. Stands with the big mallet on his shoulder, performing miracles of equilibrium, his sole reward to be cursed and ordered about at the halts.

Had I been born a boy in an Afghan village, I should pro-bably have started life as a driver's mate on one of the three thousand lorries of the country: it would have been the best way of travelling young. One day lacerated by the icy wind of the pass, gliding the next on the warm tarmac east of the Khyber; from the cool shades of the gorges to the throbbing sands of Andkhoi on the way to the awe-inspiring shrine of Meshed. So pleased to belong to such a manly world, that lack of sleep or food would just be one more way of living, another form of enjoyment.

Tooting, clattering, smoking, farting, scrunching, skidding, gear-crashing or free-wheeling lorries would have been my life . . . Until, having smuggled enough tit-bits, I might have bought my own car, being then, in my turn, the great master on board.

Christina was quite apprehensive: even private cars had accidents. Herr Kuhn had a broken collar-bone, his Chevrolet had fallen down a bank. But what was this wailing coming out of a black tent? We stopped. Interrupting their mourning, the women came out to us, unveiled, unforgettable in dark-red garments under black head-cloths. We inspected, fingered, questioned each other, till a man came along who tried to send our new friends away. We were at once all leagued against him in good humour: outbursts of laughter received my remark that "Women can well do without men!"

But, sure of himself, the man was so beautiful, sickle in hand, golden eyes glittering under a black turban, with his tiny moustache, the rich lips showing healthy teeth, that our meeting with the dark witches lost its interest. From the way he studied the car and questioned us, he showed his quick intelligence: he had no need to fall back on "How many children? how many brothers and sisters?" This Afghan might lie or kill according to a code of honour that differs much from ours, but first of all he was a man, a radiant masterpiece, fully alive, at peace with himself, every expression marked with simple nobility.

During our picnic in the mulberry grove of Doshi, we could speak of nothing but that wonderful man.

Nor was he unique. A few days later, miles from everywhere in the undulating world that stretches beyond Bamian, we met a solitary tribesman. We came upon him suddenly. His step was quick and sprightly while he sang to himself, playing on a small viol held against the waist. He laughed at us as we slowed down and he shouted the usual greeting: *Mandana bashi!* to which we answered: *Zenda bashi!* In a country where distances are so great, there could be no better words exchanged than "Don't be tired!" and "Be alive!" Not only was that man's body beautiful but his eye shone with a great light. Our whole day was bright and unforgettable for having met him. The same kind of light burns in the eyes of a girl when she discovers that love inhabits her, a love she feels so inexhaustible that it can inundate the whole wide world.

Long and narrow till then, the valley brusquely opened out and pink cliffs stood against a very dark-blue sky. They built a perfect table-land—surprising in this rocky world where every other line approached the vertical: an unexpected smile in an austere valley straining towards the sun.

That stony glade ended at Do-au, a hamlet at the entrance of the Dareh-i-Shikari, the gorge we were to follow. Two little motor-buses rested at a tea-house. We followed their example, ordering tea and hard-boiled eggs. While waiting I bathed an old man's abscess in permanganate; he was something of a wit and the whole atmosphere seemed very friendly. But no. Though I had seen eggs in the tea-shop, the inn-keeper said he had none; he advised us to go to the government rest-house. I flared up. We had never been treated like this before. It was contrary to the laws of hospitality. We were not dangerous animals to be set apart inside a sad stone-house. (Later, too late, it occurred to me that the man was probably obeying orders stipulating that foreigners must use the house that had been built for them.)

The fusty rest-house was opened in a hurry, its plush furniture revolting in this heat, though no doubt comfortable in winter; dull, prison-like the place was, after the liveliness of the bright inn. We had not crossed two continents to sit unwillingly between dreary walls. And the factotum brought us a price-list to confirm his saying that tea-and-eggs were charged at the same rate as a full meal. Having lived so long on the country, we had never got used to the prices of these Afghan rest-houses: there had been many a discussion already when the bill appeared. The point was so sore that later, in Kabul, I called on the Postmaster-General who runs these hotels. Your prices, I said, may suit the rare ministers who travel this way, or Englishmen earning good pay in India. But Europe is full of people like us, travelling as cheaply as possible. Since you build hotels for foreigners I suppose you want your tourist-trade to grow. Then if you don't want your rest-houses to be avoided like a plague you must remember those who are like us.

It is because we left Do-au banging the doors, annoyed quite out of proportion with this particular local incident, that we decided to give the Bamian hotel a wide berth. The decision was to have grave consequences.

The Hunter's Gorge or Dareh-i-Shikari, offered thirty miles of thrilling scenery. Sheer rock-walls rising either side of the torrent left only a narrow ribbon of sky. Bridges sent the road from one bank to the other. Dark overhangs threatened us, but being for ever in the shade they were deliciously cool. If we had felt inclined to search for it in the neighbourhood we might have found a great cave full of human bones, the cave where nine hundred, or perhaps nine thousand, people had been trapped during their flight from Genghis Khan.

Sometimes the mountain-sides opened out, the sun blessed the rippling blue waters, goats browsed among the stiff grass of the shores and hillocks were topped by square towers—a reminder that the armies that came this way had to defend their long lines of communications.

A bulbous samovar, a floor of beaten earth under a great roof, a row of gay tea-pots were a welcome hint to enjoy the moment.

A rider came down the hard road, clickety-clack. The suggestive noise reminded me of my life along the bridle-paths of Asia: had I ceased to long for it? The great wind howled down the defile, a colossal shaft whose draught fanned the furnace of Turkestan deserts.

We had greatly gained in altitude and I felt much revived. Moreover we were within an hour of Bamian, the peak of our excursion and the last stage before we reached the Hackins.

On we rushed, escaping from the cold of these rocky gorges (we had even seen snow on a triangular peak that peeped at us for two seconds), leaving the valley through a crack in its western wall. And we followed up the stream of Bamian in its riotous leaping from boulder to boulder. Greatest joy of Asia: clear running water—promise of fields, trees, grazing-lands.

A caravan of donkeys rested on a spit of land, their loads like rectangular slabs of pink marble. I knew them to be salt, for I had seen them before when the Hackins took me to Bamian.

There was a last narrowing of the valley where, like a ship's prow challenging the invader, the purple cliffs of Shahr-i-Zohak rose like a wedge above green grass lapped by scintillating waters; from there, by the side of the Kalu affluent, a track led directly to Kabul over the Haji Gak pass, the upper Helmand river and the Unai pass.

Then we beheld the whole of Bamian—a few miles of peaceful fields sheltered from northern winds by the Hindu Kush. Gentle slopes rose towards the Koh-i-Baba range in the south and in that direction we could make out the lonely hotel with its pale roof. Two dark openings as of huge sentry-boxes were the niches of the great Buddhas sculptured in the northern cliffs.

They belonged to our future. The present was our grey tent at the foot of a bank, and the perfect turf whose greenness enhanced the chestnut of the little cows. Across the small valley two cliff-walls met at right angles, fluted, serrated, eroded into castle-like shapes. They showed such vivid crimson, orange and grey that the eye went back to them again and again, to make sure of what it had seen. With the rays of the setting sun these walls became a vision of flamboyant velvet belonging to a world of legend.

The softness of the meadow, the radiant purity of the mountain air, the deep peacefulness of the rich valley, all contributed to our intense delight.

If only for that unforgettable moment of plenitude, it was worth having travelled so far.

The cosiness of the little tent enveloped us. Once more the Primus stove cooked soup, rizotto and fried apricots. Once more we spoke about the future.

Christina knew she would never become an archæologist: writing was her sole ambition. But the best thing she could do now was to lead a regular life with the Hackins for six months at least. I did not want to take her into Kafiristan and she was still too uncertain to live alone—though confidence in herself was increasing every day.

I remember saying to her: "If you are a born writer, a time will come when you will feel so full of inspiration that you will be completely borne along by your work. Until then accept the support which a member of an organisation receives. Any temporary work intelligently tackled can become interesting enough to ward off your moments of depression."

She felt sure of herself as never before in her life.

She could not understand why I wanted to become an ethnologist. Why didn't I go on writing books that gave *le goût du monde* to fettered young people? "If ever my books accomplished so much," I replied, "it doesn't satisfy me any more. What is the good of sending people round the world? I have done it: it doesn't help. It only kills time. You return just as unsatisfied as you left. Something more has to be done. It is childish to blame this dictator or that government for the mess we are in. Ethnology will give me an opportunity to compare ourselves with a non-mechanised society. You remember our talk on the frozen road near Neuchâtel? When did Europe begin to go wrong? When did we cease to be worthy of ourselves, cease to carry our head with dignity? Why are traditional cultures everywhere so weakened that they crumble before our materialism which has nothing to put in their place?"

My words were wiped away by a very cold blast of wind: I hurriedly pulled down the zip of the tent.

"I know that the Afghan hillman, the Tibetan, the Mongolian I have met has his troubles," I added; "but he is free of our tormenting urge to consider the misery of the whole world as if he were God. Why is it that no sooner have we enjoyed some beauty or goodness than we feel guilty, we remember with shame that our friends are murdering each other in Spain or China, that our charwoman's children are too pale under too scanty clothes?" After a silence I concluded: "Isn't there a middle way between the bitter knowledge of the Westerner and a tribesman's happy-go-lucky ignorance of the world?"

26

BAMIAN

THE early morning filled me with delight. The colours were bright but mellow, as if edged with mother-of-pearl—the emerald of the short-napped grass, the violet and orange of the cliffs, the yellows of the fields, the sparkling of poplar leaves; and above it all the incredible blueness of the sky, a deep rich blue as we have it over the snowfields in Switzerland.

The Koh-i-Baba floated grey and vaporous, as if very far. To the north, beyond the pink cliffs and their sculptured figures, rose high hills with velvety blue furrows dotted here and there with little blots of snow.

A great number of cells had been hollowed out of the sheer sandstone face and many were still inhabited, their edges blackened by smoke. The Department of Archæology did its best to preserve the caves or shrines that were adorned with paintings or mouldings. I remember one, the higher part of which was ribbed and conical; the flat ceiling—also hacked out of the mountain—reproduced beams in four lessening squares one upon another, the corners of one meeting the middle of the side of the next. (Germans call it "lantern ceiling"). I was interested: I had seen the same pattern in wood, in a house of the Taghdumbash Pamir where it formed the only opening of the central room. The Sarikolis inhabiting that part of the world are people whose customs can still be connected with fire-worship. Some of them had pale-grey eyes and Sir Aurel Stein writes that like the Galchas and the Wakhis, they have preserved the *homo alpinus* type in remarkable purity. The same kind of roof has been found as far north as the centre of Sinkiang, in the caves of Qyzyl.

We went to the small Buddha where he stands stiffly in his niche, his face partly sawn off, his mutilated right arm holding his robe of plastered drapery. At a distance of only a few feet, one could no longer make sense of the fluting: one could see nothing but a puzzling play of light and shade.

From the gallery carved into the cliff at the height of the head there were seen remains of frescoes on walls and ceiling. Horses and figures, sun, moon, tiaras and pearls could be made out and also the streamers of ribbon that characterise the Sassanian style. I remember an intense cobalt blue just like the sky of Bamian, in a fresco that Jean Carl reproduced exactly for the Musée Guimet.

A brand new buttress of masonry supported a cracked part of the cliff just by the side of the sculpture. Some years ago the Afghan Government issued a stamp reproducing the Buddha of Bamian but it was withdrawn, for too many Muslims were shocked at a representation of the human form. But when an appeal was made to preserve that same Buddha, so often damaged by zealous Muhammadans, a sum of sixty thousand afghanis was easily collected.

Having crossed the hamlet of Bamian, we reached the great Buddha who dominates lucerne and melon-fields from his height of a hundred and seventy-five feet. The legs have been almost entirely destroyed and part of the head (the ear alone is twice my size). From the top of the head the world looked splendid in the clear mountain air—the chequer-board of fields, the smiling vale of Foladi and beyond, the gentle Koh-i-Baba. The nearby frescoes showed darkly draped Bodhisattvas in the traditional seated posture; they are dated back to the third century.

With its spirit of smiling restfulness, the landscape was the best part of Bamian. That is probably why Buddhists came here to build monasteries at the beginning of our era. Hsuan Tsang, my guide in so many places, was here in 632, twenty years before the Islamic conquest added to the damage begun by the White Huns. He counted ten monasteries with several thousand monks. Of the people he wrote that "they are hard and fierce by nature, but they are superior to their neighbours in the candour of their faith."

We crossed the valley where people were harvesting broad beans and reached the small Buddha of Foladi in another cliff honey-combed with inhabited cells. Potters were firing their jars: the *buta* or scrub they burned gave out a thick black smoke. I saw the windowless farm where two years ago we had gone to meet a blind poet of great charm; with the help of

Ahmed Ali the interpreter, Ria Hackin had noted down verses and legends. I felt at home in the simple Bamian of to-day, but not in the Old Bamian.

Seated on a bank of gravel, we stared.

What were the urges that lived in the men who hacked such symbols of their faith in those worn-out cliffs? What were the thoughts, prayers and meditations of these thousands of monks who once upon a time were headed by a Grand Lama?

Though famous for his learning in China, Hsuan Tsang had come to the West in search of wisdom. He visited all the great men of his time. The Master Asanga taught him many aspects of Buddhism. One of the most important is compassion. When I read the teaching of Asanga, I feel we need it to-day more than ever—"for the wretched, for the wrathful, for the hot-tempered, for the heedless, for the servants of matter, for stubbornness in error!"

Compassion and ultimate knowledge are the great qualities advocated by Mahayana Buddhism. No knowledge can be gained without detachment of heart and mind, yet this detachment is slow to come. "By countless trials," Asanga wrote, "by countless accumulation of good, total knowledge is achieved. All obstacles disappear and the Buddha-state is revealed like a shrine of precious stones, great in Power." If such is the case, that state implies none of the negativeness that I thought was meant by Nirvana. "The universality of the Buddha-state in the multitude of beings is attested by the fact that it admits all of them into itself. As space is universal in the multitude of forms, so it is universal in the multitude of beings." A state that admits all beings into itself cannot be a negation!

Anyhow, here were only words; but what was the direct experience they referred to? Was there anyone to-day who knew what was actually meant by them? And then what relation can there be between such a one and that inconceivable Buddha-state? "Their personality consists in capital impersonality. This transcendent Impersonality is no other than the Absolute Nature of things."*

There we sat, reading these words in Grousset's book on Hsuan Tsang. Did Grousset know what they meant? I

* René Grousset: *In the Footsteps of the Buddha*.

remembered the day he wanted to introduce me to "Parisians one has to know". But happily his plan was forgotten as soon as we came across a table sagging under a mountain of *tarte-lettes aux fraises*. We pounced on them shamelessly, glad to feel we could still be nothing but big children, the enjoyment of the moment drowning all self-consciousness. Why had I not asked him what he knew about those sentences?

To Christina I said: "If someone knows what such words mean, it would be worth our while to go to him and live near him as long as possible."

"Yes . . . perhaps," she answered; "but if war breaks out at home, should we not go back to help?"

We walked past a great mound of dazzling white clay—Shahr-i-Golgola, a dead hill said to have been a Greek town. Here it was that the King of Bamian was besieged by Genghis Khan. That citadel would have been impregnable if the King's daughter had not fallen in love with the son of Genghis Khan: she showed him a secret passage leading from her people to their water-supply. The town was doomed. It was in 1222. Infuriated at having lost his grandson Mutugen in the battle, Genghis Khan killed all the inhabitants of the valley and rased all the houses. He was then pursuing the son of Muhammad of Khwarezm and could not afford to leave his enemies alive behind him.

The car took us back to the foot of purple Shahr-i-Zohak, the prow-shaped mountain at the head of the valley. They were a great sight, these bluish-red cliffs crowned by walls and round towers and crenellated castles (built by the Arabs, perhaps). Most of these fortifications were so worn away that in many places it was impossible to differentiate them from the gullied cliffs.

They are named after Zohak, the extraordinary character mentioned in the *Zend Avesta* and in the *Shah Nameh*. Did he ever live in this sombre place: it would well have suited him.

At the beginning of things, the serpent Azi Dahak or Zohak was the demon of storms; contamination of waters was due to his venom. In the *Shah Nameh* I read that he was the son of a desert king. Letting himself be subjugated by the evil Ahriman, he kills his father. Ahriman becomes his cook and makes him commit the sacrilege of eating meat. Pleased with this unknown dish, Zohak offers to reward the cook. The simple desire of Ahriman is to kiss his master's shoulders. No sooner is the wish granted than from each shoulder springs a black serpent. Cut, they grow again. Ahriman advises Zohak to feed them daily on human brains. Zohak is now a demon.

Having become proud and therefore vulnerable, the great king Jemshid is cut in two by Zohak who then rules unchallenged for a thousand years. Zohak has a dreadful dream which one of his sages interprets to mean that he will be defeated by young Feridun. The demon orders all male children of the kingdom to be killed. But Feridoun escapes and is safely brought up in India till he grows old enough to punish Zohak. He first liberates the daughters of Jemshid (captive all this time), then with his great club he vanquishes Zohak. An angel asks him not to kill the demon but to chain him in a cave of the Demavend.

As we climbed down from Shahr-i-Zohak, we saw brown tents being pitched near the waters we had to ford. The people were a crowd of mixed types, only two or three old men wearing the Afghan smock. Most of them accompanied us to the car. The little girls' coiffure was striking: the smallness and number of their plaits made it impossible for them to have even a weekly combing. And to keep the whole thing tidy, it was smeared with a setting lotion made of mud. (I forgot to ask if this mud perhaps has anti-parasitic properties.)

I took a great liking to the Elder. With his flowing white beard, he remained noble though lively and curious. The others were friendly, gay even, but with something of the alertness of a cat who knows her claws are ready. They all wanted *dawa*, so we opened the medicine chest. A woman needed some ointment, her palms were one layer of corn with deep red crevasses. Halima, with silver ornaments round her neck and pinned through the top of her ears, brought her baby boy Kabuli who had a cough; she had cupped him (we saw the purple circles on his back), the cupping-glass being a copper vessel with a tube through which to suck the air.

When we took leave, White-Beard offered to accompany us to Kabul: women should not travel alone! We had not done more than two miles when I noticed that my second Leica

camera was missing: it had been stolen while we were doctoring.
And this just when I was remarking to Christina how grand
the nomads were compared with town blackguards who pinch
whatever they can!

Back we went. The Malik was summoned. We were shocked,
with downcast faces. No words were spoken—our mimicry
sufficed: while we were trying to help his people one of them
was robbing us . . . Yes, there was no doubt about it . . .
an object like this. It was a shame!

Silent, dejected, we sat by the road-side. On the green
meadow the Elder was holding a council. I felt he was bound
to know the black sheep of his flock. Quite soon a laughing
man, fair-haired and dirty, came to us, pushing in front of him
a frightened boy holding the camera. The Malik played his
part with great style, simulated spitting now on the boy, now
on the Leica (to curse away so disreputable an action?), then
invited us to share bread and salt under his tent. We declined
his offer since night was falling and we had to return to our
camp at Ain Garan; moreover we were harbouring no ill
feelings towards his people.

27

BAND-I-AMIR

"Theory of true civilisation. It is not in gas or in steam or in table-tapping. But in lessening of the traces of original sin. Nomads, shepherds, hunters, farmers, even cannibals, all may be superior, by their energy, by their personal dignity, to our peoples of the West. Who perhaps will be destroyed."

BAUDELAIRE
(*Mon cœur mis à nu, XV.*)

WE now had to cover forty-eight miles of mountain tracks leading to the Band-i-Amir in the direction of Herat. To the west of Bamian we followed the pleasant ravine where we had often fished trout with the Hackins. Once out of it, there was not a rock, not a trace of cliff to remind us of what we had left behind us. We were in a splendid world where barren hills of yellow earth shadowed with mauve succeeded each other to the distant horizon. Plaques of snow covered the misty blueness of the Koh-i-Baba that barred the south.

From far away the earth looked goose-fleshed; near at hand one saw that the small asperities were thorny knobs of spare *buta*.

We rushed up the steep gradient to the Shahidan pass—much too steep for a heavily laden car. We grew anxious; we even thought we should have to give up our attempt. It was like a victory when, after many efforts, at last we crept to the top, beholding once more a sea of arid, treeless hills. The coldness of the whipping wind reminded us that we were at a height of ten thousand feet, some one thousand five hundred feet higher than Bamian.

We were in the heart of an old, a very old world. Was it not already old sixteenth centuries B.C. (young were the forests of Europe then) when Aryan tribes speaking vedic Sanskrit came from the North on their way to Kurdistan and India? In this great empty space there were now myself and the earth, a pair in good accord. Reduced to essentials, a skeleton of hills covered with the leanest flesh, for all the little it gave, the world pleased me as it was. Nothing too much. Almost nothing at all: sometimes among a succession of yellow shoulders, a small patch of lucerne in a lean armpit; ridges with their fading, fleeing lines that call us, draw us; tracks followed by our rushing ideas, rudiments of such simple landscapes that our imagination can make them resemble memories of the Issyk Kul or Kuen Lun. Attraction of an horizon we want to reach but push back with every step.

To be accepted by the earth. To understand its meaning. Then to feel how much it is one whole, to live the strength of that unity. Then only will it be time to love each part of that whole, freed at last from the blindness of partial love.

My meditation was interrupted by two successive punctures which forced us to deal with inner tubes. Just as we were beginning to worry about the possibility of a breakdown on this deserted track, a rider ambled towards us. Something in his long refined face made us think him an Arab and it was no surprise to hear him say he was a Sayid, a descendant of the Prophet. A bazaar rumour having announced the arrival of Englishmen from Kabul, we asked our Sayid to take a written message to the hotel. We gave our whereabouts, asking for a car to be sent to our rescue should we fail to reach the hotel by the evening of next day.

Greatly relieved, we bumped towards the Shibartu pass.

Dreamy camels on a slope; then a horse bolted in front of the car, its mane waving wildly. Soon afterwards we reached a little dale where two tents were caught in a web of ropes. Squatting on the earth, a woman was weaving at a tripod loom, some twenty yards of narrow warp firmly pegged down. These details were very like what I had seen in the T'ien Shan or among the shepherds of Sinkiang: I felt as if approaching old friends.

The women were reserved while we exchanged the usual questions. And how many camels did we have at home? Were we Russian? Or English? "Oh, then, please" said the chief woman smiling "you must share food with us!" Rice was brought in an enamelled basin: it might have meant that our new friends were well off, for as a rule nomads can only afford wheat-cakes. They are cooked either on an iron disk or wrapped round a cobble-stone near the embers. By counting the round stones of an abandoned camp one knows how strong the party was.

They were all very good-looking, the women in their black and red attire showing Roman features framed by tiny plaits neat and austere like metallic chains looped up to leave the forehead free; the girls with a coin dangling at the end of a short lock, in long dresses pinned up with amulets. The women moved easily and with commanding gestures, continually pulling up the great black cloth that fell loosely from the top of the head. The men were away with the herds.

They were a Mandozai tribe and would soon return, they told us, to the plains near Khanabad: the nights were beginning to be too cold.

We took leave (*Khoda hafiz!*), giving a red scarf to a boy and Russian sweets to the other children.

With the Hackins I had visited a similar camp. The tribesmen were hard hit by the new lorry-transport. Since no-one bought their camels they were trying to develop their sheep-breeding.

Without counting the few tens of thousand *powindahs* who go every autumn to India for trading purposes, there is still a part of the Afghan population, a tenth perhaps, which is almost or quite nomadic. But, following the example of Iran and Turkey, the government was planning to change their habits.

Nomadic life is doomed even in Saudi Arabia or in Mongolia, and I think the main reasons for this disappearance are the same in all these countries. Nowadays frontiers are exactly delimited and they complicate nomadic life. The central power of every country wants to become strong, needs obedient soldiers and settled tax-paying subjects; to make his country independent, the Chief of State has to enforce these conditions at all costs; that this kind of independence is not the one wanted by nomads cannot be taken into consideration. People who obey only their tribal laws cannot be allowed in modern states.

Leaving aside those pests that live by banditry (like certain Turkomans), one can say that nomads have many good qualities: besides their handsome physique they have a greatly developed sense of honour while their laws of hospitality have become second nature to them. They are good fighters because they are not afraid of death, their customs and religions having given them an understanding of what it is. They are absolutely loyal to the tribe. It is exactly these qualities which are their undoing to-day, though so far they have helped them.

Because they are fully themselves, they can only with difficulty become peasants or artisans; not having known the old life, their children may be more adaptable. In the mean-time this wonderful human material is wasted. The Kurds are in utter misery, their ways of living crushed, whether in Turkey, Iran or Iraq. Other nomads, some two hundred thousand of them, were sent away from the mountains of South Persia or fled to sun-scorched Mesopotamia where they all died within two years. In Turkestan, the Kazak-Kirghizes as well as the Turkomans have melted away by millions. The Mongols had to give away their pasture-land to innumerable Chinese settlers supported by the authorities; after a few years of hoeing, the thin soil was blown away and the land became a desert. In Arabia, King Ibn Saud knew he would obtain allegiance only from a settled people: he had to break their tribal system and their blood-feuds and turn them into peasants obeying God and King instead of their own chief.

Those who do not know the nomads may ask: Does it matter whether one or two million more disappear from the face of Asia when so many are already killed by floods, famine or epidemics? Yes, it matters indeed, it is greatly to be deplored. For the nomads are a good leaven that could regenerate the tired Syrians, exhausted Persians, decimated Chinese. In the past, the period of devastation once ended, the nomads infused their boldness of conception into the conquered people. Grafted on to old trunks, they brought forth new blossoming in China, Persia, India, Turkey. From the Aryans long ago down to the Arabs, the Seljuks, the Mongols, how much poorer our world would have been without the impulse given by those who, like King David, were wandering shepherds?

"We are content with discord, alarms, blood, but we will never be content with a master" is a saying attributed to the Ghilzai tribesman; and if he remains unruly now, he will be broken. But it seems foolish forcibly to settle nomads who used to tend their flocks, since sheep will have to be looked after anyhow, whether in Arabia, Mongolia, Iran or Afghanistan. Why not leave this work to those who love it instead of destroying their life and skill?

I stopped the car with a jerk: straight ahead in a trough between steep slopes of rose-coloured earth, a tiny jewel of an incredible blue density dazzled in the silent solitude. It was our first glimpse of the King's Dam, the Band-i-Amir. Mountain wheat grew sparsely at our feet, short, stiff, solid, its ear like a broad blade.

Further on we found an amazing scene spread at our feet— a string of lakes caught between pink cliffs, their colours passing from apple-green, turquoise, gentian and Prussian blue to dark indigo. Shallow, the two first were set in a ring of bright white limestone. The last were linked by a wide sloping threshold dotted with round bushes, the only touch of vegetation in a barren world.

"I love it . . ." said Christina, her face lit with surprise. Not a soul nor a house in sight but for the small *ziarat* across the big lake. "You haven't seen all," I said; "but let us first follow the track down that cliff."

We slid down till we were actually forty feet below the level of the lake: slowly through the ages, these waters had built a beautifully curved rim at their southern end. Down this barrage came the overflowing ripples sparkling over gluey terraces; at one point spurting among its asperities, at another building a waterfall that was caught by the wheel of a mill.

We skirted the foot of the dam, our tyres splashing through clear rivulets, and climbed up to the small platform before the *ziarat* of Hazrat Ali. Steps led down to a little shore beyond which the lake was a dark-blue fjord meandering between mauve sandstone cliffs: it was astonishing to meet the radiance of these waters. Wavelets rocked a few blades of amphibian grass while big fish that no-one is allowed to catch soared up to look at us.

A bearded man in quilted rags, the keeper of the shrine, said the lake was bottomless. He led us to one of the three rooms of the *ziarat*, vaulted, blackened by smoke. There, in the heart of the dense silence, we camped.

While the lake became a mass of fretting molten metal, the

sunset painted the hills with dahlia, lilac, hyacinth. And when we went to sleep there were two freezing Milky Ways, the one at our feet just as many millions of miles away as the one above our heads.

But the windless early morning gave the best spectacle. A crack in the steep bank led to the table-land above the shrine; from there we saw at our feet a huge surface of polished bronze, a gigantic curved mirror that reproduced every tint, slope, gully, stone and mood that existed in the upper world.

No sooner had it opened our eyes to the beauty of the earth than the enchanted mirror altered: a lively breeze changed it into an opaque arena of lapis lazuli hung half-way between a pale lowland and tall blushing cliffs. We walked through that ethereal atmosphere till we dominated the second barrage where green bushes grew between white rivulets. Every detail had the sharpness not only of something one sees for the first time but of a beauty that can be compared with nothing else.

At the shrine three witches wanted drugs. One was blind, her hand led over the car by her companion. The windscreen delayed them: I imagine it was difficult to convey the idea that a solid can be transparent. The tomb is supposed to contain the remains of Ali, son-in-law of the Prophet. Two men were worshipping in the clean, whitewashed sanctuary. Seeing once more with what devotion the shrines of Afghanistan are cared for, I realised that Islam is the main force that links together a population in which blood, language and customs differ so widely. I have seen Afghans praying not only in mosques, but in fields, in shops, on the road—till I came to understand that it means much to them. And I think he was an exception, my neighbour in the bus who when I had remarked that Europeans do sometimes pray but mostly when alone, retorted: "But what is the good of praying if you aren't seen doing it?" Reforms or plans for reconstruction will have to agree with the spirit of Islam if they are to stay for good. It is only because he had successfully reawakened the faith that Ibn Saud could draw to himself allegiances that formerly went to the tribes: thus he brought together in the army or in the fields men whose ancestors had for generations been at feud.

A legend explains the origin of the Band-i-Amir (I reproduce here the details given by Major Rupert Hay*). King Barbar, an infidel, was oppressing his subjects. A man who had been searching for Hazrat Ali and found him near Haibak, was ordered to bind that saint and bring him as a slave to the king. Ali was then asked to perform three tasks—kill the dragon of Bamian, build dams in a valley and lastly, save his own head. The dragon was killed. With mighty rage a rock was hurled down which built the Band-i-Haibat or Dam of Wrath; while with his sword he clove the Band-i-Zulfikar, the Dam of the Sword. Then Ali told Barbar to load him with chains. When he had rendered everybody senseless by reciting the Muhammadan profession of faith, he freed himself and converted King Barbar.

* Geographical Journal, April, 1936.

28

BEGRAM

INSTEAD of returning to our idyllic camp at Ain Garan, we drove to the hotel: Christina had a bad cold. One morning when we were living under the tent, I opened my eyes to find her looking at me with envy: she was shivering in her kapok sleeping-bag while my eiderdown sack looked like a balloon swollen with warmth. It was too late to scold her for not having let me buy her equipment.

The best was to reach a warmer climate as quickly as possible. We took leave of the decorative Englishman who had arrived (a tall ascetic-looking red-beard who devoted his life to chasing a rare miniature jerboa) and were soon on the great slopes of the Shibar pass.

We seemed to be in Hazara country, at least the women inhabiting the vast *kaleh* of Bullula (a square fort with round towers at the angles) as well as those we saw in a hamlet at the top of the pass had the slit eyes and high check-bones of that tribe. They are Shia Muslims who used to quarrel with the Sunni Afghans, a fact which strengthens their apartness. In Mongol, *hazara* means "a thousand"—one of the sub-divisions of Genghis Khan's army.

On these heights, round and harmless in summer, where the short mountain wheat hurries to grow, I enjoyed a sight I should have liked to paint: intense blue sky, golden straw piled on the roofs, brown mud walls and red dresses of women weaving on the ground; and running about, girls with bright skull-caps and many tiny plaits. They were friendly. We sat on the earth trying to imagine what it meant to live all the year on the Shibar. A few riders stopped and smiled, their quilted coverlets rolled up behind their saddles.

Down the Shibar we went from hairpin bend to hairpin bend—the Shibar where Hsuan Tsang had lost his way in a snowstorm, the Shibar that stands between two great water-sheds of Asia, and over which had passed every piece of machinery, every girder or sheet of roofing that went to the making of Pol-i-Khumri—after it had already, on its way from Germany, overcome the Khyber and the Lattaband pass before Kabul.

There on the road we overtook a shrouded woman who walked alone, decidedly, with heels that did not seem to be low. As we came up with her we saw that the front of her grey *chadur* was lifted: emaciated, pierced by pale blue eyes, unyielding, the face was European, a face that but for a while lived freely under the open sky. She stopped veiling herself when she saw that we were women. Her passenger bus was ahead but she preferred to walk over this steep part of the road. She was German, married to an Afghan who worked in Mazar-i-Sharif. She was returning to Kabul after having been very ill with malaria. She thought the time was ripe for the *chadur* to be given up; but it was not for the foreign women married to Afghans to show the way unless they wanted their lives to become impossible: it was for some of the ladies related to King Zaher to give the signal. More than ten years ago the wife of King Amanullah had started an unveiling campaign; but she was unpopular and had no success, partly because her mother was a Syrian Catholic. In those days, thinking that the womanhood of Kabul was being emancipated, a few French, German and English girls had married their Afghan fiancés.

We had brought her to the bus. The *chadur* was down again; she was an anonymous pyramid of cotton with an embroidered wicket let in before the eyes.

Twelve years of patient waiting to be freed from that masquerading, waiting to be herself again, waiting for the wind and the sun to play on her cheek! I was grateful to have bare arms at the mercy of the sky. We felt grateful for our freedom— so difficult to bear, but more necessary than life.

We hummed down the seventy miles of the Ghorband valley, passing little fields, bosky hamlets, gurgling water-courses lined with thickets. The torrential Ghorband flows eastward to unite with the Panjir near Sharikar and the Panjir in its turn meets the Kabul river north of the Lattaband pass; having joined the great Indus east of Peshawar, these waters then reach the Indian Ocean.

I forded the stream to film Turkoman women pitching the supple poles that support their round tent. But they did not like me. I yielded. Putting up the camera, I looked at them sheepishly, unable to tell them that I was fond of them and that a felt yurt like theirs had been for years the symbol of my most cherished desires.

As we halted at Chahardeh Ghorband, the voice of a muezzin was somewhere calling for the midday prayer. The *chaikhana* boy brought our tea to the earthen platform under the one tree that marked the centre of the village. We exchanged stares with the young bloods strolling by.

Though still shy with adolescence, a youth stood there aimlessly, quite pleased with himself. He was extremely smart under a *chapan* of indigo cotton embroidered with magenta flowers—the coat typical of the valley. It tempted me. I stopped him, spectators turned advisers and a lively talk ensued until I produced two banknotes of twenty afghanis each—approximately twelve shillings. Having never seen banknotes, the youth asked an elder if he should accept them. He walked away much lighter than he had come and with a calculating expression that could mean either: "This is just what I wanted," or "What will mother say?"

On the slope above, curious women peeped at us from behind a wall: white-skinned and golden-eyed, they handsomely nodded at us, inviting us to their courtyard. But impatient to join the Hackins, we went away.

Passing the side valley of Fondukistan incited me to talk archæology: two years ago, Jean Carl had dug there, a shepherd having seen a Buddha-head in the crack of a conical hill. The excavation revealed a four-sided sanctuary with a central stupa. One of the painted niches contained two princely figures of coloured clay, wearing Central Asian costumes with great lapels. Urns contained funerary ashes and Kushan coins. Buddhas and Bodhisattvas were worked in the opulent Sassanian style or sometimes with rich Indian curves. In the museum at Kabul I had seen a small head smiling knowingly to itself: it showed a few remaining flakes of the gold that had once entirely covered it.

Afghans working on the dig explained in their own way why Carl spent so much time and money unearthing these old things:

they were the gods of the Faranghis which had been destroyed by the Muslims of old!

In Siaghird where the corn was reaped, the busy threshing places "smoked" in the sun by the side of big *kalehs*. Slipping through a last gorge and skirting a last cliff, we suddenly caught sight of dense green vegetation, the plain of Kohistan. Eastward, a cleft in the mountains gave exit to the Panjir: near it was the site of Begram where my friends had been expecting us for the last month.

From Sharikar I telephoned to Kabul to find out where the Hackins were. Lorries, bicycles, gigs, donkeys, crowds, dust, noise and bustle seemed overwhelming. A few gaudily turbaned Sikhs sitting cross-legged in their booths, their faces black with fuzzy beards, conveyed that India was just round the corner: that huge country with its four hundred millions of men still frightened me.

Peddlars chanted, pigeons cooed, brats wailed on their father's arm, sewing machines hummed in a stall, water pipes bubbled, innumerable flies probed and sucked the world dry, oil sizzled in the warm cook-shops, cobblers hammered nails into boat-shaped shoes, people threw their melon-rinds in the gutter. We were back in civilisation.

One or two stalwarts who walked with the suppleness of panthers did not belong to the herd. Nobly draped in a dark-blue shawl with one red line across, sinewy ankles showing below the ample trousers, their detached expression seemed to say: What is the good of all this fever?

Crossing a waste-land and rolling over dried-up ditches, we covered the last lap of our journey. We reached a solitary mud hut on the desolate plateau which is the Begram of to-day. Joseph and Ria Hackin, Carl and Meunié received us as if we had been their children. We were too late: they had just finished packing all the finds of their summer campaign.

Put to bed with two aspirins, Christina was looked after by Ria with such motherly care that her heart was won at once. Meanwhile, in the next room, I was making a pig of myself by taking three helpings of *coq au vin* followed by chocolate soufflé.

Begram gave us a few beautiful days.

We did not know it then: they were to be the last days of peace, and four of us were not to walk alive through the long mad tunnel of war-time.*

Even without knowing that one stood above a ruined capital, we could feel that the site had a meaning—particularly at sunset or at sunrise when the light accentuates the relief of the earth instead of annihilating it. Nowhere else have I seen such dense ultramarine shadows by the side of such brazen masses when the first darts of the sun hit the ranges north of the Panjir. There even death could be beautiful: in the lilac mist of dawn, the silky blackness of a kid stiffened in the blood-red rivulet flowing from the severed throat. Nowhere else have I listened with more intensity to the rush of a great wind coming down from great mountains. Was it perhaps because I had at last outgrown my need of seeing "the land beyond the horizon"?

Lhassa or Papeete could have loomed ahead, I think, without my heart missing a beat. I had ceased to be proud of having, by my own efforts, turned the world into a playground. One evening I should have fallen on my knees to thank my eyes for seeing so well but for two men weaving on the ground at a distance.

Instead, I sat and drank the peace of Kohistan. Across the river, like a white gash in a rocky hillock, I could see the Khwaja-i-Reg Rawan, a slope of well-known "sonorous sands": sometimes they rumble or sing or drum during the heat of the day. The same thing has been observed in other parts of the world and there is no very good explanation for it.

Further away I looked towards the Nijrao valley where Hackin had taken us with his bold six-wheel lorry—a remote part of the world not yet spoilt by tin cans like Sharikar. There, gates of carved wood reminded me that Kafiristan began at the next valley. Of Nijrao, Emperor Babur writes that "it is quite a sequestered place, it grows grapes and fruits in abundance. Its people make much wine but they boil it. They fatten many fowls in winter, are wine-bibbers, do not pray, have no scruples and are Kafir-like". In the same chapter of his

---

* "Commander Joseph Hackin was lost at sea with Madame Hackin when the ship which was taking them back to the East on a mission for Free France, was torpedoed in the ocean."

(Extract from a lecture by C. F. A. Schaeffer, 6th October, 1942, at the Royal Central Asian Society.)

Memoirs a passage tells that he too suffered from rheumatism. As he was collecting the Nijrao tribute, "on the thirteenth of Ramzan such sciatic pain attacked me that for forty days someone had to turn me over from one side to the other."

Yes, I was looking at the sky that blazed above Kafiristan, but should I ever go there? Would I be more lucky than an American couple now confined to Kabul when they aimed at studying the Hazaras of the hills? Their initial plan had been to observe the Turkomans of Iran but then Teheran told them there were no Turkomans nowadays. Kabul would have found it difficult to deny the existence of the Hazaras. But half-seriously, Hackin maintained that with modern "politics" the Hazaras were as dangerous as dynamite: the Afghans could not afford to have them mentioned for fear that the Japanese pursuing their pro-Mongol policy and claiming the Hazaras as one of their minorities, might invade Afghanistan to protect them!

Ria joined me. We walked to the weavers where I bought the first piece of our collection for Christina's museum—a rough winder. Among the Parsivans, or Tadjiks, weaving is done only by the men. One of them had water by his side in a bowl of turquoise glaze from Istalif. We could see it in the distance, sloping Istalif, devoid of *kalehs* but built like a Provençal village sunning itself among vineyards. It was founded by Alexander's men and its name was originally Staphylia, the Greek for grapes.

Joseph Hackin was introducing Christina to the archæology of Begram. It was decided that she would work with him in the museum to familiarise herself with Græco-Buddhist art. Later, if my mountains proved out of reach, I would go with them all to Kunduz.

We stood above the dig—dreary, dusty, sun-bitten pits. We saw the many rooms that had yielded nothing. But in the tenth they had reached a layer of decomposed glass; and lower still Ria found a collection of cut vases and bowls as good as Murano's; they stood next to painted glass with figures in Greek costumes and decorative fishes of blown glass and fluted bowls of a cobalt colour. For two months Ria remained bent over these finds, clearing the earth away with a spoon and a toothbrush. Precious ivory caskets worked in the Indian style displayed women curved like peaches and bulging cherries. Many objects had been piled up in this treasure-room and then the passage had been walled in.

The quality as well as the origin of these two-thousand-year-old pieces gives them great importance. They prove that in the first century B.C. Indian and Greek art met here in the kingdom of Kapisa and not in the Gandhara of the Upper Indus. The meeting gave birth to that hybrid art which influenced the whole of Sinkiang, China and Japan.

Long before Alexander the Great founded near here Alexandria ad Caucasum, Kapisi was the capital of the land of Kapisa: Cyrus had conquered it in the sixth century B.C. At the beginning of our era, during the reign of the Kushan or Indo-Scythian kings, Buddhism was well established as far as Balkh; in the year A.D. 50 Kadphises struck coins at Begram. Kapisi was the summer residence of Kanishka, the most famous of these Kushans who, according to the historian Sir Percy Sykes, had all curved noses though they were not of Hebrew blood. This remark is related to the controversy that though the Afghans can be said to be of Semitic type, it is not sufficient to confirm their claim to be one of the ten lost tribes of Israel. This could only be classified as the *literary* origin of the Afghans.

Hsuan Tsang, the Chinese Master of the Law, spent the summer of 632 in a monastery at Kapisi, which might well be the charming one we saw in ruins at Shotorak, by the turbulent waters of the Panjir. We read in Hsuan Tsang's book that the King of Kapisa, a devout Buddhist "of a brave and impetuous disposition . . . rules over a dozen kingdoms". This king sent Afghan horses to Tai Tsung, Emperor of China. At Kapisi, Hsuan Tsang also interviewed Jain and Saivite ascetics.

At the end of the same century, the Arabs who had conquered Seistan attacked in vain Rutbil, the Kushan King of Kabul. Islam was only established in the whole country two centuries later, a Turkish King of Kabul having been defeated by the Muhammadans.

29

KABUL

THE houses and trees of Kabul were in sight.

Arriving at a bit of good road, the heavy car slid along evenly, noiselessly, advancing once more with steadiness, might and aloofness like a ship unaware of the earth under her keel. After thousands of miles of bumpy roads, my relaxing body could once more enjoy its existence.

Kabul was reached, and for a minute I felt triumphant. What a fool I was! My watchfulness slackened when it should have increased and I started brooding over my plans.

Christina was still suffering from her cold, so we called on the doctor at the British Legation. Diagnosing bronchitis, he ordered ten days in bed and smoking to be given up. The Hackins who lived in a small lodge at their Legation, had no room for us, so we were glad to be able to camp in the study of Marthe and Gabriel whom I knew from Paris.

There, though still coughing, Christina would not obey the doctor's orders. She looked tired and bored except when we called on the Hackins. No longer sustained, as she had been all these months, by the need to realise our plan, she began to show wantonness. She had no faith in the doctor's potion, she did not want to see him again and she forced me to get a syrup of codeine from the chemist in the town. I did not know then what codeine contains.

Anyhow it was imperative to stop the fits of coughing that prevented both of us from sleeping.

Then the war broke out in far-away Europe.

Uncertainty took hold of our lives. Hackin and Gabriel put themselves at the disposal of their consul. Foreigners were forbidden to leave Kabul for the interior: this sealed off "my" Kafiristan.

Though its mainspring was broken, the spirit of our journey revived when we visited the town.

Babur's tomb was a simple marble slab in a terraced garden.

A true hillman, the Emperor did not want to be buried in Hindustan, a country devoid, as he said, of good men, good horses, good dogs and good fruit. I quite understand that viewpoint, but shall I ever agree with the belief he expressed in these lines?:—

> "If a sword shook the earth from her place
> Not a vein would it cut till God wills."

The lines were written because, fighting his way to Kabul, the future Emperor was struck by the sword of Dost Sirpuli without being wounded in the least, a fact that no-one could understand. Babur means "Tiger".

Youthful voices filled the air: we came upon a swimming-pool where children with their instructor were practising high diving. We were greeted by a disciplined yell: "Gooten-tak!" which I only understood when I heard they all were pupils of the German school. Two or three years later some of these children were to weep saying good-bye to their German teachers then forced to leave Afghanistan. But their masters, sure of victory, replied "Don't cry! We shall be back within four months".

We also visited the girls' school at the back of the women's hospital: its existence was not yet official for fear of hurting the mullahs. I have never met so many hundreds of keen children tightly packed into a single building. Each form was filled to the limit, and I felt that some of the girl-teachers (Afghan of course) were burning with enthusiasm for their work. There were a few masters—as old as Methuselah so as to leave no ground for scandal should they accidentally touch a pupil as they walked between the ranks.

Showing very different kinds of faces or dresses, most of the children were pretty. Many of them had a golden sparkle in their eyes. They looked frankly at the world. They nearly all showed the same keenness, the same defiant attitude, as if to say: "It is daring of us to be here. But we are proud to be the new Afghanistan."

How I wished I could do something for them! How I wished they would be taught to think, feel and live rightly! This must be particularly difficult in a town where, till lately education has meant to learn the Quran by rote. There was an inspector of schools who came to the French college; he did not know French, but noticing that some boys hesitated before answering a question put by the master, he concluded that the lazy fellows had not learned their lessons. The feelings of the master can be guessed—he who had spent years trying to awake thought and judgment among his pupils! Also, the Afghan professors of another college were declared the best of Kabul because "all their boys had received excellent notes!"

Afghanistan was divided between Ancients and Moderns. Grouped around the mullahs, the ancients were against all innovation. At a meeting where 1,600 mullahs gathered, a programme of forty-eight points was drawn up; one demand was that the girls' school should be closed, for modern education only causes mischief in feminine heads. The government refused. Another point insisted on the closing of the cinema— where I saw men not used to chairs manage to squat on these uncomfortable pieces of furniture. This was also refused, government maintaining that films have an educative value: they bring a glimpse of the world to those not fortunate enough to travel.

The government thinks that the mullahs must be converted to new ideas so as to be sent back to their villages as supporters of the actual regime: at present they, only, could become the cadre with which to build the skeleton of the new country.

The daring moderns, who have nearly all of them been abroad, are the governing clan. Their efforts go to strengthen the country "so as not to bear a fate like the one of Abyssinia in 1935". Not only was there no money and no army ten years ago when Nadir Shah became king, but Amanullah's too hurried reforms had prejudiced everyone against any kind of change.

The best way to make Christina appreciate the results attained by this handful of courageous moderns was to make her hear something about the common man of the country. We visited the matron of the Aliabad sanatorium for consumptives.

I greatly admired that woman, who had come from Switzerland. She lived by herself a good way outside Kabul, ruling over her world of men as if she were a veteran major, teaching them all, from her assistant chemist to the cook and the laundry-man.

The matron had learned the Quran in order to have the last word with her patients. Though suffering from a high fever, some of them would insist on kneeling five times a day on the stone floor to say their prayers; but in the Book she found a passage allowing those who are laid up to make their prostrations symbolically with the eyelids. She fought a long battle to teach them not to spit all over the place and not to upset the wards by turning their beds towards Mecca.

At another period there was never enough water for washing shirts and sheets: the gardeners used it all to flood their flower-beds. The matron remarked: "Perhaps from the Afghan point of view the sight of a flower does more good than a clean shirt."

Even convalescing patients were not allowed to visit their people: the family would never understand that they should eat and sleep alone. According to them, illnesses were brought by bad jinns who were defeated by amulets or by eating a mouthful of earth from the tomb of one's family saint. What the matron found most tiresome was that they always knew everything better than herself!

For a long time she had been defeated by the fact that the men drank the tea from the kitchen but not from the samovar in their own ward. In order to find out why, she hid in the sideboard: they were emptying their medicines in the samovar, afraid it might contain alcohol, the use of which is forbidden by the Quran. She calmed them, saying that the water was not contaminated since the Sacred Book says that whatever is boiled, were it even urine, is purified.

The good matron! And not a trace of fear in her—boxing the ears of coolies and sweepers if they did not obey her orders, if the cooking pots were dirty, if they stole wood, broke glasses or hid in corners to avoid work. It was the only way of getting any work done.

I worried about Christina. She was feverish, smoked more than ever and, though she suffered from a bad digestion, would not observe her diet when we dined out. My affection for her was far from sufficient to tell me how to help her. Rather I thought that I was exasperating her, that I should leave her in peace. She was ill but would not admit it; she would not relax or submit herself to the laws of nature. She could not bear the thought of remaining inactive, for then she felt like dying. She was afraid of immobility. Always a fear worming at her heart.

I tried to talk to her once more. Whatever we decided to do, she had to be strong and healthy first. As I appealed to her sense of proportion, muttering about the misery of the Poles in burning Warsaw, she answered angrily:

"I don't want to become detached like you and Gabriel. I want to remain human. The greatest creations of men were born in suffering."

"I know," I interrupted her, "you want to cry with Musset:

> *"Les plus désespérés sont les chants les plus beaux,*
> *Et j'en sais d'immortels qui sont de purs sanglots."**

But you wallow again. It is a dreadful half-truth. When they create a masterpiece they have transcended their suffering."

Exasperated, her eyes shining with hardness, she shouted: "But *let* me suffer!"

I did.

Apart from the meaning of what she said, that "let me suffer" tore through her with such intensity, such truthfulness, that I was to ponder over it many a time. I ceased to interfere and she moved to the French Legation where she was invited as the wife of a colleague. There, I said to myself, she will sleep between sheets, in a real bed, the rich food will do her good, she will have the peace and rest she needs. And a separation is timely: we have been together day and night for months and months. Moreover just now Gabriel's cook is away in Ghazni, there to find and buy a man to do his military service for him.

I really gathered these excellent reasons to hide the fact that I felt selfish once more. Yes, I was tired of Christina, I had been centred on her for the last six months and I could not sustain the effort. I was now absorbed in my immediate future.

We sorted our belongings. From the box containing our mountain boots, to my surprise she produced a hypodermic needle which she gave me, saying:

"This journey has freed me from the drug."

I decided to believe her.

---

* The most despairing are the most beautiful songs. And I know some eternal ones that are pure crying.

The study where I lived was full of interesting books. Perhaps to forget my annoyance at finding no solution about my plans, I drugged myself for weeks with an orgy of reading. I knew Kabul already, the old citadel of Bala Hissar, the half-built (and already abandoned) buildings of King Amanullah at Dar-ul-Aman, the suburban villas of Paghman, the splendidly barren hills around the town. Nothing called me out.

Niccle and Raymond dropped in sometimes (they had long ago come down from the Hazarejat with their battered bikes) and we tried to find out what the war was really about. I had a theory that the Germans might become more civilised if they could only cease to feel themselves "have-nots"—the story of the Mongol hordes and China. Their ruthlessness was a temporary necessity as long as they must prepare themselves for war. I even wondered if they might not be the means of uniting Europe at last? But smiling and calling me a dreaming child, Christina maintained that nothing good could come from the Germans: their understanding was totally warped.

Like a shrewd lawyer, Nicole probed for the causes:

"The Nazis would not have turned their backs on the ideas of freedom and Christian love which alone can help man get along, if these ideas had not put up such a miserable show during the last centuries."

During all this time in Kabul there lived in me a pin-point of uneasiness which expressed itself months later in the feeling: I failed Christina. According to our pact I was not to leave her alone whatever she might say or do. But the intensity of my desire to help her had spoilt my intention. That intensity had brought with it a kind of effort that had tired me. Had goodness been part of me I should have helped her with detachment, quite simply and because I could not do otherwise —as the sun shines, or as one gives a hand to a tumbling child; I should not have vitiated the movement by thinking: "*I* must succeed, *I* have to succeed!"

I called on her every day, walking through the town if it was cloudy (though six thousand feet high, Kabul can be very warm sometimes), or I was trotted along in a gay gig whose imperative bell cleaved a crowd of idlers. By then Christina was suffering not only from bronchitis but also from a double carbuncle that propagated itself and was tapping her neck—

a gaping crater that immobilised her head and made her feel miserable. Sometimes we extracted a core which looked like a candle-wick. Even then she never complained.

She was still going about, seeing a German refugee doctor or a Swiss who was a commercial representative. But she was often sick and still losing weight. Dr. Moody took me apart: she was absolutely exhausted and needed two months of convalescence before she could travel; otherwise her daily fever might develop into consumption.

Happily Christina had grown fond of Ria who lived next door and was a companion more human than I could ever be.

One day Christina lay prostrate. It looked as if at last she had ceased to revolt, had abdicated. But no. It was an attitude adopted because it best hid the lack of frankness that had crept between us: I, keeping my worn-out thoughts to myself, she . . .

At last she spoke. A confession of her total wretchedness. She had lied all the time. As soon as the war had shaken our plans, her old demon had raised its head. Her craving for codeine had marked the start. And then once more the old story: with mad recklessness, with fierce cunning, her second self had found the great number of ampoules she needed.

But now she was so sick, so far gone, that something drastic must be done. She could not bring herself to follow the declining doses ordered by the German doctor. Once more she had no choice but to adopt the most radical remedy—run away from the town! Not yet recalled to France, Hackin and Ria had left for Kunduz (they could travel since they worked for the Afghans), Christina had decided to join them: she wanted me to help her. With an expressionless face she asked me to forgive her for her lack of confidence in me.

But I was responsible for it. After the Sofia incident I chose to appear hard and determined not to forgive another relapse. So, when the hour of trial came, Christina was naturally afraid of me. I had singled out that line of action imagining that it might be more successful than the tenderness of her former friends.

I tried to soothe her shame, her despair. But I could find no new words, only those I had already used too often. Many years of a certain habit cannot be wiped away in a few months;

o

ups and downs are normal, the "old man" must be re-educated till years of new habit have erased the past. "You are bound to meet again silly doctors (like the one at Therapia) who will tempt you, thinking they are kind-hearted. You are bound to have illnesses or depressions that will weaken your resolve. But you know for certain that you are not an addict, since you can *perfectly well* live without 'it' for months. As surely as I speak, I know you will recover!"

I seemed to talk to a wall. The role and the tone of the school-teacher are irritating unless he knows a very great deal: in that case his personality is forgotten by the pupil whose whole attention gets focused on the truth which is taught.

But her sullen eyes annoyed me so much that before I knew what I was doing, I was hammering at her—not in dream this time as at Istanbul: "Can't you be thoroughly sick of yourself for once? When will you be able to flatten yourself on the floor, even lower than the floor? When will you admit your lowness, admit you are at the end of your cleverness? And there, humble at last, beg for help . . . addressing yourself to that miraculous part of yourself which you have seen at work before, when it rescued you from your previous hells? Not only the drug has to be vomited as it was, but the whole of your false self. . . ."

No, she couldn't do it. Not in that way. Not yet. She was still in love with the torment of the fallen angel.

Did she feel my distress, did she know I cried because she was strangling her radiant selfhood?

I kissed her damp forehead. I left her.

I went to the German doctor, to the English one, to the Swiss, to old residents in Kabul. The first admitted he had tried everything without success; the second said that Christina could never travel and camp now that winter ruled in the mountains, the third helped me to piece together her strange actions; the latter told me that no-one could obtain a permit for the interior and I felt depressed.

But luck came to the rescue. Driven by Meunié, a light car came from Kunduz to fetch material for Hackin. I explained everything to him without hiding how mad it was to send Christina to their Kunduz camp. But I could think of no other way out: she showed no interest in the studies we might

start in India. Would Meunié bear the responsibility of taking
Christina back with him?

He said he would.

I too was "handing her over" . . .

More ghost-like than ever, Christina was to dine out. She
was starting next morning for her two days' drive to Turkestan.
Sheepskins, rugs, leather jerkins had been prepared: her
underclothing was not thick enough, but try as I might she
would not believe that Asiatic winters have little in common
with those of the Engadine.

I had driven with her to the gate of the house she was
visiting. I stepped out of the car and stood on the wooden
culvert above the ditch. The stagnant water mirrored clean,
sharp stars. She was late already. My throat was tight. I tried
to utter a cheerful good-bye. The silence of an indifferent
Kabul night embraced me as I turned away.

She called me back.

She had dropped her stiffening mask. She was herself
again, her shining honesty alive once more. She said:

"I used to think that you did not suffer from our months of
suspense as much as I did. I thought you were distant and
hard. But I know I was wrong. It's because I was too pre-
occupied with myself! Kini, I wanted to say this: you puzzle
me . . . I don't understand how you love me."

"Christina, I don't know myself. How can I answer? But
I think I now see very clearly something great in you. Is it
perhaps what people mean when they say they love someone
'in God'?"

30

MANDU

We met once more.

The last tirade I had discharged at Christina was based on a deep experience I had just gone through; ever after, my circumstances appeared somewhat easier. Events seemed to take shape of themselves: I only had to use discrimination.

I was invited to India. Thinking it would probably be impossible for me to travel after the war, I decided to stay there for some years. In order to have the necessary means I began to write *Gypsy Afloat*, hoping a sufficient number of people would buy it.

At New Year 1940, I was in Central India. On her way to Bombay where a ship was taking her home, Christina came to see me. We spent two days among the ruins of Mandu, the "City of Joy," once upon a time the residence of the Afghan kings of the Khilji and Ghori dynasties. Among dead palaces mirrored in silent lakes, among dusty mosques adapted out of Hindu temples, near the austere mausoleums or fortifications that crown the rocky plateau of Malwa, in an atmosphere rich in past history, we spoke of to-day's history, of to-day's war.

Having caught influenza during her northward journey, Christina had nearly died of weakness at Kunduz. And I believed her when she said I could not imagine what she went through. But somehow it had done her all the good in the world: her eye was once more filled with light, her body poised, the past not weighing on her. She was thinner than ever but healthy and not unlike the young Bhils we played with on these reedy shores where they fish with bow and arrow, their nakedness showing long slim thighs, ribbed chests and a mop of hair falling over the brow.

The past had lost its bitterness. She smiled when she mentioned a remark I had made in Kabul to rouse her from her lethargy: "Kini, you remember the day you showed me a photo of myself saying that I want everybody to love me but how can I be loved when my poison gives me the eyes of a dead fish? How right you were! Though I want to speak with caution, this time I feel that I am rid of 'it' for good."

Her resurrection filled me with joy, but it was hardly two weeks old and I was worried. It would have been wise to postpone her return for a while.

"Listen, Christina, you are going back to Switzerland, the cockpit of Europe where all the hair-raising stories of tortured countries are gathered. You will breakfast on the horrors brought by your newspaper and dine on hatred in the black-out of a continent. You will be deadly ashamed of belonging to the human species long before you can be cheered by its deeds of greatness. That atmosphere is destructive, it will undo you and then you will hardly be able to help others. It would upset me less than you: I wish I could wish to go back in your stead!" Very gently I then concluded: "But if you stayed one year with me you would grow strong, you would be a great asset to whatever you might tackle."

"No, I haven't the courage to stay, I have to go home. And I think you have seen enough of me. But I shall come back. I know much about Nazism and my articles can show why we are fighting. I can't remain here while they are suffering there. I belong there."

"Whereas I belong nowhere—unless it is everywhere. I am sorry I can't keep you. But you will discover for yourself whether you should have stayed or not. As for me, I have no doubt about it: you are a poet, not a journalist, and it is in yourself that you must look, not at a war."

"Kini, don't you think you could be useful in Geneva?"

"I am sure they can do without me. One more, one less, it makes no difference. Let those go back who feel compelled to help. I don't want others to do what I am doing, you excepted . . . But to tell you the truth: I had thought this war would sweep me off my feet, force me to rush where I could do my bit and in the meantime make me forget my own dissatisfaction. It did not happen. Nothing of what Europe has lately under-taken seems able to fire my enthusiasm: the main point is always missing. And since it is my luck that no duty is imposed on me, I shall pursue what to me seems absolutely imperative, what I set out to do when I left home. If I went back now, I should be as despairing as before, always listening for a step approaching—unbearably waiting for something to come to me *from outside!*"

"Don't you think we have to postpone our individual pursuits till peace is restored?"

"With intensity I feel that peace is not our greatest need, victory is not our greatest need. Look how dearly we paid for them twenty years ago! When they were ours at last, we did not know what to do with them. We had lost the foundations of our living. I know: I could feed refugees, clothe orphans or mend broken bodies, all are good work. But when the wounded man is normal again, he does not know what to live for. Unless he imagines that a revolution solves everything! Enough of this circle that swings from 'die in order to live' to 'live in order to die'. Something more is needed. The joke is that I am looking for it, though I don't know what it is! But I must see first if what Indian sages know can be of use to us."

"Don't you think you simply want to remain away from the war?"

"I have asked myself that. If I find that such is my motive I shall join you. Logically it would be easier for me to return with you, to live among our people, to do what the others will do, being thus supported by the common spirit. Here in a country which is the opposite of what I like, I shall be quite alone, forced to live on a bare minimum."

Among these ruins mellowed by centuries of burning sun, in an atmosphere befitting some Sleeping Beauty, war seemed an impossible nightmare. I mentioned it again. I tried to explain: "You see, Christina, I am a few years older than you and it makes a great difference. Though too young to be directly hit by the last war—like Gerbault, whose three best companions died by his side—I think I suffered by proxy what my friends went through. It has deeply influenced me. The last war sent me down to the clean life of the seas, for ever rid of illusions about our civilisation. This war compels me to search for 'the meaning of all this', for the common denominator in all of us, the basis on which to live anew."

The moment had come to part.

We were fortified to feel that something solid and lasting had been built between us.

"Christina, you have not explained to me how you recovered,

how you decided to leave Ria and how you travelled so far;
but it took place. Once more you saw at work in you an
immense reserve of positive forces. They are there all the
time: they are you. Remember this, always."

There was a radiant smile on Christina's face: "I shall come
back to you and then you will be proud of me." On the
switchboard she turned the flat key we had lost and found in
the Trieste shop; and started for Silvaplana.

Later, too late for the discovery to be useful, I became
convinced that Christina's "Let me suffer!" had a profound
meaning. That cry was the symbol of the unusual path she
had chosen, unconsciously perhaps, to free herself. Her
unceasing preoccupation with herself might have appeared
sickly. But by caring for grief she was accomplishing much:
she was uninterruptedly lessening the small ego which by
clamouring for enjoyment prevents in us all the ripening of
our consciousness. Desire for pain is against all the dictates of
the egoism that generally rules us.

To me it seems certain that through suffering she succeeded
in transcending suffering. I used to be sorry for her, but there
was no need: she did live the deepest in her, the most precious,
the unalterable truth. Its transcendence at last illumined her,
though I do not know if it had time to change her daily life.

In 1942 Christina was forced to remain for many months
in the Belgian Congo, unable to reach the Free French Forces
to whom she had been appointed journalist. There, flooded by
a current of rich inspiration at which she marvelled, she
wrote many pages based on her new understanding of life—
an understanding most dearly acquired in New York through
the worst crisis she had ever experienced. All her energy went
into her book. When too tired to work, she sometimes wrote
to me desultorily about the discoveries she made in the unknown
valleys of her heart.

Though she cannot answer me, I think she would have
allowed me to quote some of her sentences: without them her
life fails of its full significance. They are surprising when one
knows that throughout her last book she was obsessed by the
loss of childhood innocence, by the necessity of doing penance.
They need no commentary:—

"I know now, smoke or dope are useless. Without them I turn towards another concentration much nearer to what I need in order to write, nearer still to the concentration and inner liberation you teach me . . . For the drug had meant an escape from my excessive sensitiveness; it was the fatal desire to kill life, to wipe out pain and joy, the tension-source of human activity."

Another day:—

"My problem of illness, unhappiness, catastrophe, wasted life has haunted you while it has nearly killed me. It is queer that I needed that double experience of detainment in New York and psychological revolt because I felt victim of a love without solution and was putting all my hope in joining the war (sacrifice which I thought noble and just and my contribution to this reality outside ourselves) for me to understand that our relationship with the world has to take place in a realm infinitely more true and invulnerable—which is that of the soul . . . In spite of all its external good or bad fortune, our soul remains untouched—and therefore our better wills and beliefs.

. . . the kind of struggle, loving or hateful, this fierce desire to reach the world outside oneself and to be accepted by it at all cost, is wrong, because its basis is warped.

My African experience has taught me, better than any of my other 'downs', the futility of the external world, its false reality. For to explain my former downs, illnesses, etc., there were grave faults on my part. Thus the wrong belief grew that if I stopped such mistakes I should be saved, all would be well, I should make a career and so forth. But here where on the contrary, I came full of good will . . . I met a wall fiercer than a prison, than lack of money. Every word in vain for people answered me 'Why should we believe you?' Quite. Perhaps my name is not Christina. But in spite of all, my identity, my integral human essence remains. Only, it is wrong to count on men. We are brothers, yes, but only through our common origin as children of God.

What was left for me to do was to find the means not to be wounded by this random power of the external world. For, if I can be killed by men as by hunger or stones—it does not touch what is eternal in me. And we are nevertheless born free outside all the world's laws."

In the spring of 1943, uneasy about Christina's prolonged silence, I sent her this telegram: "Remember truth prevails."

From Switzerland I received the following answer: "Christina died peacefully 15th November, 1942, suite bicycle accident Engadine "

     *   *   *   *   *

ENVOI

CHRISTINA, I miss the depth that shone in your eyes, your all-claiming demand, your unquenchable need that could only be satisfied by something absolute.

As the news of your death struck me like a lie, my thoughts began once more to dwell with you. And slowly, diffidently, the number of these sheets has grown. If you are not very often mentioned in them, you are nevertheless present in each of them; for each is a witness of the pain and the remorse that tied me to your steps. Can you forgive my clumsiness, my misinterpretations as I try to recall some of your gestures? You know my heart, its admiration, its respect for your integrity, and you know how impossible it is to describe you. May these pages help me to remember that only by demanding all can we hope to obtain That without which, we said, our life is not worth living.

TRIVANDRUM. *May*, 1945.

DATES

Aryans arrive in Persia	about 1400	B.C.
Achæmenian period	550–330	,,
Xenophon's Ten Thousand	402	,,
Alexander's conquests	330	,,
Seleucids	330–200	,,
Parthian period	200 B.C.–222	A.D.
Sassanian period	222–650	,,
Hsuan Tsang in Afghanistan	630	,,
Islamic conquests begin	637	,,
Abbasid Caliphate	750–949	,,
Harun al Rashid dies	809	,,
Imam Reza dies	819	,,
King Kabus (Ziyarid dynasty, 928–1042) dies	1012	,,
Mahmud of Ghazni rules	998–1030	,,
Seljuk period	1037–1197	,,
Mongol Il-Khans	1221–1387	,,
Sultan Oljaitu dies at Sultanieh	1316	,,
Timurids	1369–1500	,,
Gohar Shad, daughter-in-law of Timur dies at Herat	1556	,,
Safavids in Persia	1501–1736	,,
Uzbeks conquer Herat	1506	,,
Babur conquers Kabul	1504	,,
Kajars	1798–1925	,,
Riza Shah Pahlevi	1925–1944	,,

BIBLIOGRAPHY

ARMSTRONG: *Lord of Arabia*, 1934, Barker.
AUROBINDO GHOSE: *Thoughts and Glimpses*, Arya Pub. House, Calcutta, 1932.
BABUR: Memoirs, trans., John Leyden, 1827.
BOVERI, M.: *Minaret and Pipe-line*, 1939, Oxford Un. Press.
BRETSCHNEIDER: *Medieval Researches*, 1910, Kegan Paul.
BROWN, J. P. and ROSE, H. A.: *The Darvishes*, 1927, Oxford Un. Press.
BROWNE, E. G.: *Year Amongst the Fersians*, 1926, Camb. Un. Press.
    Literary History of Persia, 1920, Camb. Un. Press.
BYRON, ROBERT: *Road to Oxiana*, 1937, Macmillan.
DARMESTETER, J.: *Zend Avesta*, 1895, Oxford.
DONALDSON, B. A.: *The Wild Rue*, 1938, Luzac.
FILMER, HENRY: *Pageant of Persia*, 1937, Kegan Paul.
FIRDAUSI: *Shah Nameh, Jules Mohl*, 1838–78, Paris, Bibliothèque Nationale.
GROTE: *History of Greece*, vol. ix, Murray, 1856.
GROUSSET, RENE: *In the Footsteps of the Buddha*, 1932, Routledge.
HAMILTON, ANGUS: *Afghanistan*, 1906, Heinemann.
HERRLICH, A.: *Land des Lichtes*, 1938, München, Hirth and Knorr.
IBN, BATUTA: *Travels*, 1929, Routledge.
KOMROFF: *Contemporaries of Marco Polo*, Cape, 1928.
MAILLART, E. K.: *Turkestan Solo*, Heinemann.
MANN, THOMAS: *Der Zauberberg*, Fisher Verlag, Stockholm.
MALCOLM, SIR JOHN: *History of Persia*, 1815, Murray.
MACGREGOR, C. M.: *Central Asia*, part iv, Calcutta, 1871, Gov. Print.
NICHOLSON, R. A.: *The Mystics of Islam*, 1914, London.
PALLIS, MARCO: *Peaks and Lama*, 1939, Cassell.
POLO, MARCO: *Travels, Dent's Everyman's Library*, 1914.
POPE, A. U.: *Introduction to Persian Art*, 1930, Peter Davies.
REITLINGER, G.: *A Tower of Skulls*, 1932, Duckworth.
STRATIL-SAUER: *From Leipzig to Kabul*, 1929, Hutchinson.
SYKES, SIR PERCY: *History of Persia*, 1915, Macmillan.
TARIK-I-RASHIDI: *Sir Denison Ross*, 1895, Low. *History of Afghanistan*,
    1940, Macmillan.
TOLSTOY, L.: *War and Peace*, 1925, Heinemann.
TRINKLER: *Through the Heart of Afghanistan*, 1928, Faber and Gwyer.
XENOPHON: *Anabasis, Brownson*, trans., vol. iv, Loeb Class. Library, 1921,
    Heinemann.

HEIGHTS AND DISTANCES

Simplon pass	..	..	..	..	6,592 feet.
Kop pass (Pontic Range)		..	..	9,100	,,
Ararat	..	..	..	..	17,000 ,,
Kandevan pass (Elburz Range)			..	9,800	,,
Firuzkuh	..	..	..	..	6,800 ,,
Demavend	..	..	..	..	18,600 ,,
Bamian	..	..	..	..	8,496 ,,
Shibar	..	..	..	..	9,800 ,,
Kabul	..	..	..	..	6,000 ,,

Geneva–Istanbul	..		..	..	1,750 miles.
Trebizond–Iran border		..	..	401	,,
Border–Tabriz (via Khoi)		..	..	177	,,
Tabriz–Teheran	..		..	..	390 ,,
Teheran–Gumbad-i-Kabus		..	..	305	,,
Gurgan–Shahrud	..		..	..	121 ,,
Shahrud–Meshed	..		..	..	316 ,,
Meshed–Afghan border		..	..	155	,,
Islam Kaleh–Herat	..		..	..	76 ,,
Herat–Mazar-i-Sharif	..		..	..	510 ,,

–Kala-i-Nao	..	99	miles.
–Bala Murghau	..	71	,,
–Maimeneh	..	107	,,
–Andkhoi	..	85	,,
–Balkh	..	133	,,
–Mazar	..	15	,,
		510	,,

Mazar-i-Sharif–Kabul (direct)	..		390 ,,
–Haibak	90	miles.	
–Do-au	..	136	,,
–Bamian (about)	50		,,
–Band-i-Amir	48		,,
–Bamian-Kabul	147		,,
Kabul–Peshawar (India)	..	..	250 ,,
			4,641 ,,

Distances on the Southern road:

Herat–Kandahar	..	..	..	335 miles.
Kandahar–Kabul	..	..	..	320 ,,

INDEX

213

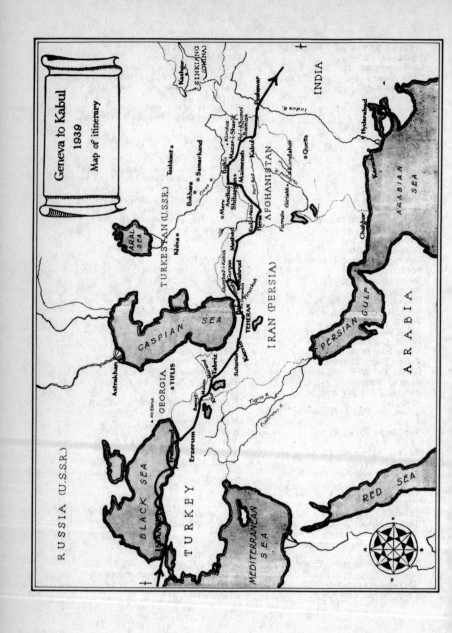

Geneva to Kabul
1939
Map of itinerary

Afghanistan

ELLA MAILLART was born in Geneva in 1903, the daughter of a Swiss father and Danish mother. As a child she suffered from ill health, but found a cure in sport; very early on she discovered the joys of sailing and represented Switzerland in the 1924 Paris Olympic Games in the single-handed sailing competition and, later, in 1931, captained the Swiss Ladies Hockey team and skied for Switzerland in the FIS races from 1931 to 1934. In the early 1930s she travelled widely throughout Europe and Russia where she spent six months studying film production and wrote a book entitled *Parmi la Jeunesse Russe* which appeared at Fasquelle, Paris, in 1931. A year later, in 1932, she travelled for six months in Russian Turkestan and wrote about this dangerous trip through inhospitable deserts and mountain ranges in *Des Monts Celestes aux Sables Rouges*, published in English under the title *Turkestan Solo* (1938, reprinted 1985). As a journalist, Ella Maillart travelled to Manchoukuo for the *Petit Parisien* in 1934 and returned through Asia accompanied by Peter Fleming via Peking and Kashmir, crossing the uninhabited plains of Northern Tibet, and arriving in Delhi in October 1935, at the time of the Ethiopian war. *Forbidden Journey*, the account of her journey across the Gobi desert, was published in 1937 in English and in French and was reprinted in 1984. She continued to travel widely and went to work for the *Petit Parisien* in Iran and Afghanistan in 1937. In *The Cruel Way*, out of print since 1947, she describes the journey she made to this region again in 1939 with her friend Christina. Ella Maillart spent the war years from 1940–45 in South India, living off the royalties of *Gypsy Afloat* (1942) and *Cruises and Caravans* (1942), and writing *Ti-Puss* (1952) which tells of her life among the Hindus in South India. *The Land of the Sherpas* (1955) describes her first stay in Nepal, the last independent kingdom of India which opened its frontiers in 1949.

Ella Maillart is an honorary member of the Ski Club of Great Britain and Ski Club de Dames Suisse and was awarded the Sir Percy Sykes Medal in 1955. Since 1957 she has been organising trips for groups visiting Asia and spent two months camping at the base of Everest in 1965; as energetic as ever, she continues to travel widely, staying three weeks in Tibet in 1986, but spends six months of every year in Switzerland.